Full Stack Development with Spring Boot 3 and React

Fourth Edition

Build modern web applications using the power of Java, React, and TypeScript

Juha Hinkula

BIRMINGHAM—MUMBAI

Full Stack Development with Spring Boot 3 and React
Fourth Edition

Publishing Product Manager: Lucy Wan

Acquisition Editor – Peer Reviews: Tejas Mhasvekar

Project Editor: Amisha Vathare

Content Development Editors: Lucy Wan and Shazeen Iqbal

Copy Editor: Safis Editing

Technical Editor: Anjitha Murali

Proofreader: Safis Editing

Indexer: Subalakshmi Govindhan

Presentation Designer: Ganesh Bhadwalkar

Developer Relations Marketing Executive: Priyadarshini Sharma

First published: June 2018

Second edition: May 2019

Third edition: April 2022

Fourth edition: October 2023

Production reference: 1261023

Published by Packt Publishing Ltd.

Grosvenor House

11 St Paul's Square

Birmingham

B3 1RB, UK.

ISBN 978-1-80512-246-3

www.packt.com

Contributors

About the author

Juha Hinkula is a software development lecturer at Haaga-Helia University of Applied Sciences in Finland. He received an MSc degree in Computer Science from the University of Helsinki and has over 17 years of industry experience in software development. Over the past few years, he has focused on modern full stack development. He is also a passionate mobile developer with Android-native technology, and he uses React Native.

I am really proud of the Packt editorial team for their outstanding work. Your constructive feedback and dedication have made this journey truly exceptional.

I would also like to give special thanks to my editor, Lucy Wan. Your ability to provide constructive feedback and offer suggestions for improvement has been invaluable.

I want to extend my gratitude to our technical reviewers, Dirk and Jose, for helping me grow as a writer and author. Your deep knowledge, attention to detail, and commitment to excellence have elevated my work beyond my expectations.

Finally, I want to thank my wife and daughter for the time and space you've given me for writing.

About the reviewers

Dirk Wichmann is a software architect who has been working in IT for more than 20 years. Professionally, he deals mainly with topics relating to security and architecture. He has worked for various companies across the fields of energy supply, water, logistics, healthcare, and security. As a senior IT specialist, Dirk's knowledge naturally includes the modern technology stack (for instance, Docker, Keycloak, and Jenkins). He loves agile approaches and clean code, as well as domain-driven design.

Since the very beginning, Dirk has used Java and Spring in the development and design of software, but he is interested in all areas of the development process – backend, frontend, testing, operations, and so on. In recent years, he has focused increasingly on microservices with Spring/Spring Boot in the backend and React in the frontend.

Jose Galdamez has worked on full stack web app projects since the year 2000, across a variety of organizations in the public sector, private sector, and academia. While he has spent most of that time working with loosely typed languages like JavaScript, PHP, and Perl, he has come around more to utilizing strongly typed systems like TypeScript and Java. The bulk of his expertise lies in updating legacy systems to be more reliable, maintainable, scalable, and user-friendly. Jose currently works as a software engineer for Clarity Innovations.

This publication is the first on which Jose has had the chance to collaborate, and it is also one that he read and benefited from as a consumer, for his previous work.

I'd like to thank my wife and two children for being loving and patient with me while I spent evenings and weekends ensuring every last detail for this book was perfect. I would also like to recognize my employer, Clarity Innovations, for pushing me to exceed what I thought was possible as an engineer while being surrounded and cheered on by the best minds in the business.

Learn more on Discord

To join the Discord community for this book – where you can share feedback, ask the author questions, and learn about new releases – follow the QR code below:

https://packt.link/FullStackSpringBootReact4e

Table of Contents

Preface

If you're an existing Java developer who wants to go full stack or pick up another frontend framework, this book is your concise introduction to React. In this three-part build-along, you'll create a robust Spring Boot backend, a React frontend, and then deploy them together.

This new edition is updated to Spring Boot 3 and includes expanded content on security and testing. For the first time ever, it also covers React development with the in-demand TypeScript.

You'll explore the elements that go into creating a REST API and testing, securing, and deploying your applications. You'll learn about custom Hooks, third-party components, and MUI.

By the end of this book, you'll be able to build a full stack application using the latest tools and modern best practices.

Who this book is for

This book is for Java developers who have basic familiarity with Spring Boot but don't know where to start when it comes to building full stack applications. Basic knowledge of JavaScript and HTML will help you to follow along.

You'll also find this book useful if you're a frontend developer with knowledge of JavaScript basics and looking to learn full stack development, or a full stack developer experienced in other technology stacks looking to learn a new one.

What this book covers

Part 1: Backend Programming with Spring Boot

Chapter 1, Setting Up the Environment and Tools – Backend, explains how to install the software needed in this book for backend development and how to create your first Spring Boot application.

Chapter 2, Understanding Dependency Injection, explains the basics of dependency injection and how it is achieved in Spring Boot.

Chapter 3, Using JPA to Create and Access a Database, introduces JPA and explains how to create and access databases with Spring Boot.

Chapter 4, Creating a RESTful Web Service with Spring Boot, explains how to create RESTful web services using Spring Data REST.

Chapter 5, Securing Your Backend, explains how to secure your backend using Spring Security and JWTs.

Chapter 6, Testing Your Backend, covers testing in Spring Boot. We will create a few unit and integration tests for our backend and learn about test-driven development.

Part 2: Frontend Programming with React

Chapter 7, Setting Up the Environment and Tools – Frontend, explains how to install the software needed in this book for frontend development.

Chapter 8, Getting Started with React, introduces the basics of the React library.

Chapter 9, Introduction to TypeScript, covers the basics of TypeScript and how to use it to create React apps.

Chapter 10, Consuming the REST API with React, shows how to use REST APIs with React using the Fetch API.

Chapter 11, Useful Third-Party Components for React, demonstrates some useful components that we'll use in our frontend development.

Part 3: Full Stack Development

Chapter 12, Setting Up the Frontend for Our Spring Boot RESTful Web Service, explains how to set up the React app and Spring Boot backend for frontend development.

Chapter 13, Adding CRUD Functionalities, shows how to implement CRUD functionalities to the React frontend.

Chapter 14, Styling the Frontend with MUI, shows how to polish the user interface using the React MUI component library.

Chapter 15, Testing Your Frontend, explains the basics of React frontend testing.

Chapter 16, Securing Your Application, explains how to secure the frontend using JWTs.

Chapter 17, Deploying Your Application, demonstrates how to deploy an application with AWS and Netlify, and how to use Docker containers.

To get the most out of this book

You will need Spring Boot version 3.x in this book. All code examples are tested using Spring Boot 3.1 and React 18 on Windows. When installing any React libraries, you should check the latest installation command from their documentation and see whether there are any major changes related to the version used in this book.

The technical requirements for each chapter are stated at the start of the chapter.

 If you are using the digital version of this book, we advise you to type the code yourself or access the code from the book's GitHub repository at `https://github.com/PacktPublishing/Full-Stack-Development-with-Spring-Boot-3-and-React-Fourth-Edition`. Doing so will help you avoid any potential errors related to the copying and pasting of code.

Download the example code files

You can download the example code files for this book from GitHub at `https://github.com/PacktPublishing/Full-Stack-Development-with-Spring-Boot-3-and-React-Fourth-Edition`. If there's an update to the code, it will be updated in the GitHub repository.

We also have other code bundles from our rich catalog of books and videos available at `https://github.com/PacktPublishing/`. Check them out!

Download the color images

We also provide a PDF file that has color images of the screenshots and diagrams used in this book. You can download it here: `https://packt.link/gbp/9781805122463`

Conventions used

There are a number of text conventions used throughout this book.

`Code in text`: Indicates code words in text, database table names, folder names, filenames, file extensions, pathnames, dummy URLs, user input, and Twitter handles. Here is an example: "Import `Button` into the `AddCar.js` file."

A block of code is set as follows:

```
<dependency>
    <groupId>org.springframework.boot</groupId>
    <artifactId>spring-boot-starter-web</artifactId>
</dependency>
```

When we wish to draw your attention to a particular part of a code block, the relevant lines or items are set in bold:

```
public class Car {
    @Id
    @GeneratedValue(strategy=GenerationType.AUTO)
    private long id;
    private String brand, model, color, registerNumber;
    private int year, price;
}
```

Any command-line input or output is written as follows:

```
npm install component_name
```

Bold: Indicates a new term, an important word, or words that you see onscreen. For instance, words in menus or dialog boxes appear in **bold**. Here is an example: "You can select the **Run** menu and press **Run as | Java Application**."

IMPORTANT NOTES

Appear like this.

TIPS

Appear like this.

Get in touch

Feedback from our readers is always welcome.

General feedback: If you have questions about any aspect of this book, email us at customercare@ packtpub.com and mention the book title in the subject of your message.

Errata: Although we have taken every care to ensure the accuracy of our content, mistakes do happen. If you have found a mistake in this book, we would be grateful if you would report this to us. Please visit www.packtpub.com/support/errata and fill in the form.

Piracy: If you come across any illegal copies of our works in any form on the internet, we would be grateful if you would provide us with the location address or website name. Please contact us at copyright@packt.com with a link to the material.

If you are interested in becoming an author: If there is a topic that you have expertise in and you are interested in either writing or contributing to a book, please visit authors.packtpub.com.

Share your thoughts

Once you've read *Full Stack Development with Spring Boot 3 and React, Fourth Edition*, we'd love to hear your thoughts! Scan the QR code below to go straight to the Amazon review page for this book and share your feedback.

https://packt.link/r/1805122460

Your review is important to us and the tech community and will help us make sure we're delivering excellent quality content.

Download a free PDF copy of this book

Thanks for purchasing this book!

Do you like to read on the go but are unable to carry your print books everywhere?

Is your eBook purchase not compatible with the device of your choice?

Don't worry, now with every Packt book you get a DRM-free PDF version of that book at no cost.

Read anywhere, any place, on any device. Search, copy, and paste code from your favorite technical books directly into your application.

The perks don't stop there, you can get exclusive access to discounts, newsletters, and great free content in your inbox daily

Follow these simple steps to get the benefits:

1. Scan the QR code or visit the link below

https://packt.link/free-ebook/9781805122463

2. Submit your proof of purchase

3. That's it! We'll send your free PDF and other benefits to your email directly

Part I

Backend Programming with Spring Boot

1

Setting Up the Environment and Tools — Backend

In this book, we will learn about full stack development using Spring Boot in the backend and React in the frontend. The first part of this book focuses on backend development. The second part of this book focuses on frontend programming with React. In the third part, we will *implement* the frontend.

In this chapter, we will set up the environment and tools needed for backend programming with Spring Boot. Spring Boot is a modern Java-based backend framework that makes development faster than traditional Java-based frameworks. With Spring Boot, you can make a standalone web application that has an embedded application server.

There are a lot of different **integrated development environment** (IDE) tools that you can use to develop Spring Boot applications. In this chapter, we will install **Eclipse**, which is an open-source IDE for multiple programming languages. We will create our first Spring Boot project by using the **Spring Initializr** project starter page. Reading the console logs is a crucial skill when developing Spring Boot applications, which we will also cover.

In this chapter, we will look into the following topics:

- Installing Eclipse
- Understanding Gradle
- Using Spring Initializr
- Installing MariaDB

Technical requirements

The **Java software development kit (JDK)**, version 17 or higher, is necessary to use with Eclipse and Spring Boot 3. In this book, we are using the Windows operating system, but all tools are available for Linux and macOS as well. You can get the JDK installation package from Oracle (`https://www.oracle.com/java/technologies/downloads/`) or you can use OpenJDK versions as well. You can check the version of the installed Java SDK by typing the `java -version` command in your terminal.

Download the code for this chapter from GitHub at `https://github.com/PacktPublishing/Full-Stack-Development-with-Spring-Boot-3-and-React-Fourth-Edition/tree/main/Chapter01`.

Installing Eclipse

Eclipse is an open-source programming IDE developed by the Eclipse Foundation. An installation package or installer can be downloaded from `https://www.eclipse.org/downloads`. Eclipse is available for Windows, Linux, and macOS. You can also use other IDE tools like IntelliJ or VS Code if you are familiar with them.

You can either download a ZIP package of Eclipse or an installer package that executes the installation wizard. In the installer, you should select **Eclipse IDE for Enterprise Java and Web Developers**, as shown in the following screenshot:

Figure 1.1: Eclipse installer

If using the ZIP package, you have to extract the package to your local disk, and it will contain an executable `eclipse.exe` file, which you can run by double-clicking on the file. You should download the **Eclipse IDE for Enterprise Java and Web Developers** package.

Eclipse is an IDE for multiple programming languages, such as Java, C++, and Python. Eclipse contains different **perspectives** for your needs, which are a set of views and editors in the Eclipse workbench. The following screenshot shows common perspectives for Java development:

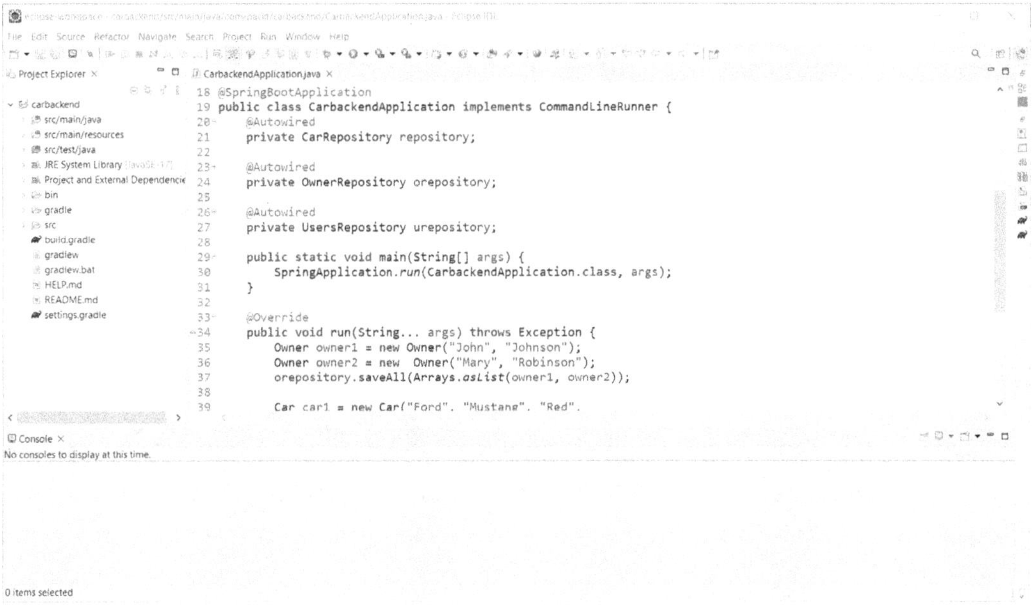

Figure 1.2: Eclipse workbench

On the left-hand side, we have the **Project Explorer**, where we can see our project structure and resources. The **Project Explorer** is also used to open files by double-clicking on them. The files will be opened in the editor, which is in the middle of the workbench. The **Console** view can be found in the lower section of the workbench. This view is really important because it shows application logging messages.

IMPORTANT NOTE

You can get **Spring Tool Suite** (**STS**) for Eclipse if you want, but we are not going to use it in this book because the plain Eclipse installation is enough for our purposes. STS is a set of plugins that makes Spring application development simple, and you can find more information about it here: `https://spring.io/tools`.

Now that we have installed Eclipse, let's take a quick look at what Gradle is and how it helps us.

Understanding Gradle

Gradle is a build automation tool that makes the software development process simpler and also unifies the development process. It manages our project dependencies and handles the build process.

> **IMPORTANT NOTE**
>
> You can also use another project management tool called **Maven** with Spring Boot, but we will focus on using Gradle in this book because it's faster and more flexible than Maven.

We don't need to perform any installations to use Gradle in our Spring Boot project since we are utilizing the Gradle wrapper within our project.

The Gradle configuration is done in the project's build.gradle file. The file can be customized to fit the specific needs of the project and can be used to automate tasks such as building, testing, and deploying the software. The build.gradle file is an important part of the Gradle build system and is used to configure and manage the build process for a software project. The build.gradle file typically includes information about the project's dependencies, like external libraries and frameworks that are needed for the project to compile. You can use either the Kotlin or Groovy programming languages to write build.gradle files. In this book, we are using **Groovy**. The following is one example of a Spring Boot project's build.gradle file:

```
plugins {
    id 'java'
    id 'org.springframework.boot' version '3.1.0'
    id 'io.spring.dependency-management' version '1.1.0'
}

group = 'com.packt'
version = '0.0.1-SNAPSHOT'
sourceCompatibility = '17'

repositories {
    mavenCentral()
}
```

```
dependencies {
    implementation 'org.springframework.boot:spring-boot-starter-web'
    developmentOnly 'org.springframework.boot:spring-boot-devtools'
    testImplementation 'org.springframework.boot:spring-boot-starter-
    test'
}

tasks.named('test') {
    useJUnitPlatform()
}
```

The build.gradle file typically contains the following parts:

- **Plugins**: The plugins block defines the Gradle plugins that are used in the project. In this block, we can define the version of Spring Boot.

- **Repositories**: The repositories block defines the dependency repositories that are used to resolve dependencies. We are using the Maven Central repository, from which Gradle pulls the dependencies.

- **Dependencies:** The dependencies block specifies the dependencies that are used in the project.

- **Tasks:** The tasks block defines the tasks that are part of the build process, such as testing.

Gradle is often used from the command line, but we are using the Gradle wrapper and Eclipse, which handles all the Gradle operations we need. The wrapper is a script that invokes a declared version of Gradle, and it standardizes your project to a given Gradle version. Therefore, we are not focusing on Gradle command-line usage here. The most important thing is to understand the structure of the build.gradle file and how to add new dependencies to it. We will learn how to add dependencies using Spring Initializr in the next section. Later in this book, we will also add new dependencies manually to the build.gradle file.

In the next section, we will create our first Spring Boot project and see how we can run it using the Eclipse IDE.

Using Spring Initializr

We will create our backend project using **Spring Initializr**, a web-based tool that's used to create Spring Boot projects. Then, we will learn how to run our Spring Boot project using the Eclipse IDE. At the end of this section, we will also look at how you can use Spring Boot logging.

Creating a project

To create our project using Spring Initalizr, complete the following steps:

1. Open Spring Initializr by navigating to `https://start.spring.io` using your web browser. You should see the following page:

Figure 1.3: Spring Initializr

2. We will generate a **Gradle - Groovy** project with **Java** and the latest stable **Spring Boot 3.1.x** version. If you are using a newer major or minor version, you should check the release notes about what's changed. In the **Group** field, we will define our group ID (**com.packt**), which will also become a base package in our Java project. In the **Artifact** field, we will define an artifact ID (**cardatabase**), which will also be the name of our project in Eclipse.

IMPORTANT NOTE

Select the correct Java version in Spring Initializr. In this book, we are using Java version 17. In Spring Boot 3, the Java baseline is Java 17.

3. By clicking the **ADD DEPENDENCIES...** button, we will select the starters and dependencies that are needed in our project. Spring Boot provides starter packages that simplify your Gradle configuration. Spring Boot starters are actually a set of dependencies that you can include in your project. We will start our project by selecting two dependencies: **Spring Web** and **Spring Boot DevTools**. You can type the dependencies into the search field or select from a list that appears, as illustrated in the following screenshot:

Figure 1.4: Adding dependencies

The **Spring Boot DevTools** dependency gives us the Spring Boot developer tools, which provide an automatic restart functionality. This makes development much faster because the application is automatically restarted when changes have been saved.

The **Spring Web** starter pack is a base for full stack development and provides an embedded Tomcat server. After you have added dependencies, your **Dependencies** section in Spring Initializr should look like this:

Figure 1.5: Spring Initializr dependencies

4. Finally, click on the **GENERATE** button, which generates a project starter ZIP package for us.

Next, we will learn how to run our project using the Eclipse IDE.

Running the project

Perform the following steps to run the Gradle project in the Eclipse IDE:

1. Extract the project ZIP package that we created in the previous section and open **Eclipse**.

2. We are going to import our project into the Eclipse IDE. To start the import process, select the **File | Import** menu and the import wizard will be opened. The following screenshot shows the first page of the wizard:

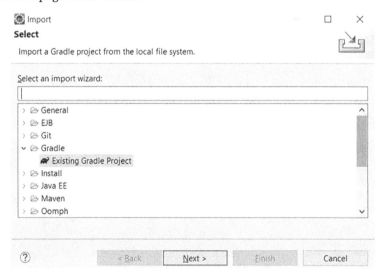

Figure 1.6: Import wizard (step 1)

3. In the first phase, you should select **Existing Gradle Project** from the list under the **Gradle** folder, and then click the **Next >** button. The following screenshot shows the second step of the import wizard:

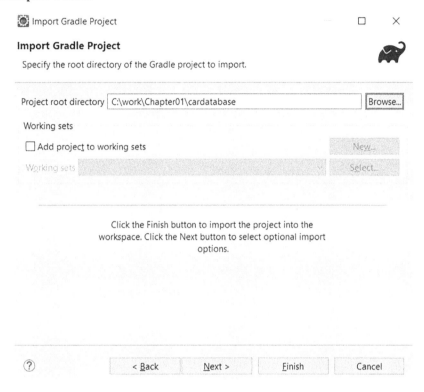

Figure 1.7: Import wizard (step 2)

4. In this phase, click the **Browse...** button and select the extracted project folder.

5. Click the **Finish** button to finalize the import. If everything ran correctly, you should see the cardatabase project in the Eclipse IDE **Project Explorer**. It takes a while before the project is ready because all the dependencies will be downloaded by Gradle after importing them. You can see the progress of the dependency download in the bottom-right corner of Eclipse. The following screenshot shows the Eclipse IDE **Project Explorer** after a successful import:

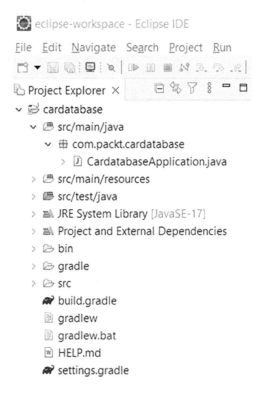

Figure 1.8: Project Explorer

6. The **Project Explorer** also shows the package structure of our project. In the beginning, there is only one package called com.packt.cardatabase. Under that package is our main application class, called CardatabaseApplication.java.

7. Now, we don't have any functionality in our application, but we can run it and see whether everything has started successfully. To run the project, open the main class by double-clicking on it, as shown in the following screenshot, and then click the **Run** button (the play icon) in the Eclipse toolbar. Alternatively, you can select the **Run** menu and click **Run as | Java Application**:

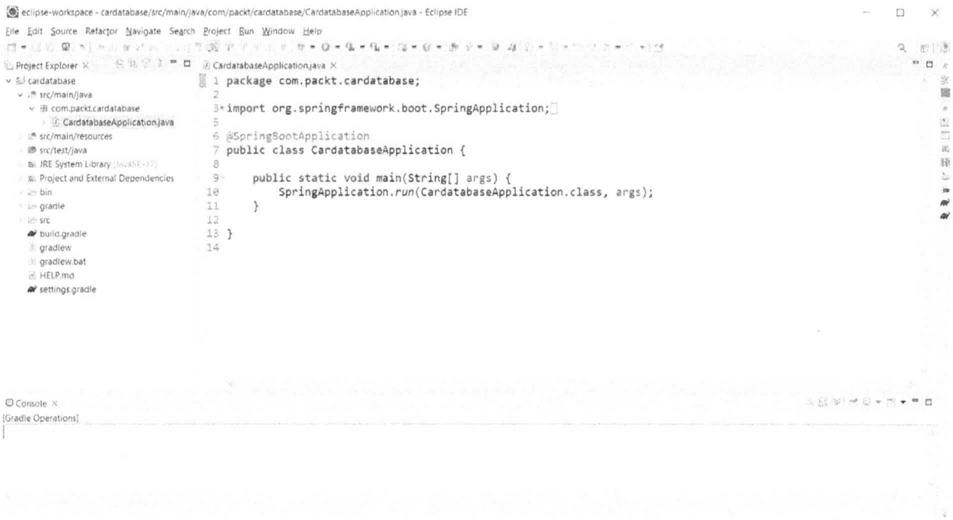

Figure 1.9: The Cardatabase project

You can see the **Console** view open in Eclipse, which contains important information about the execution of the project. As we discussed before, this is the view where all log text and error messages appear, so it is really important to check the content of the view when something goes wrong.

If the project was executed correctly, you should see the started `CardatabaseApplication` class in the text at the end of the console. The following screenshot shows the content of the Eclipse console after our Spring Boot project has been started:

Figure 1.10: Eclipse console

You can also run your **Spring Boot Gradle** project from the command prompt or terminal using the following command (in your project folder):

```
gradlew bootRun
```

In the root of our project, there is the build.gradle file, which is the Gradle configuration file for our project. If you look at the dependencies inside the file, you can see that there are now dependencies that we selected on the Spring Initializr page. There is also a test dependency included automatically, as illustrated in the following code snippet:

```
dependencies {
    implementation 'org.springframework.boot:spring-boot-starter-
    web'
    developmentOnly 'org.springframework.boot:spring-boot-
    devtools'
    testImplementation 'org.springframework.boot:spring-boot-
    starter-test'
}
```

In the following chapters, we are going to add more functionality to our application, and then we will add more dependencies manually to the build.gradle file.

Let's look at the Spring Boot main class more carefully:

```
package com.packt.cardatabase;

import org.springframework.boot.SpringApplication;
import org.springframework.boot.autoconfigure.SpringBootApplication;

@SpringBootApplication
public class CardatabaseApplication {
    public static void main(String[] args) {
        SpringApplication.run(CardatabaseApplication.class, args);
    }
}
```

At the beginning of the class, there is the `@SpringBootApplication` annotation, which is actually a combination of multiple annotations:

Annotation	Description
`@EnableAutoConfiguration`	This enables Spring Boot's automatic configuration, so your project will automatically be configured based on dependencies. For example, if you have the `spring-boot-starter-web` dependency, Spring Boot assumes that you are developing a web application and configures your application accordingly.
`@ComponentScan`	This enables the Spring Boot component scan to find all the components of your application.
`@Configuration`	This defines a class that can be used as a source of bean definitions.

Table 1.1: SpringBootApplication annotations

The execution of the application starts from the `main()` method, as in standard Java applications.

IMPORTANT NOTE

It is recommended that you locate the main application class in the root package above other classes. All packages under the package containing the application class will be covered by Spring Boot's component scan. A common reason for an application not working correctly is due to Spring Boot being unable to find critical classes.

Spring Boot development tools

Spring Boot development tools make the application development process simpler. The most important feature of the development tools is automatic restart whenever files on the `classpath` are modified. Projects will include the developer tools if the following dependency is added to the Gradle `build.gradle` file:

```
developmentOnly 'org.springframework.boot:spring-boot-devtools'
```

Development tools are disabled when you create a fully packaged production version of your application. You can test automatic restart by adding one comment line to your main class, as follows:

```
package com.packt.cardatabase;

import org.springframework.boot.SpringApplication;
import org.springframework.boot.autoconfigure.SpringBootApplication;

@SpringBootApplication
public class CardatabaseApplication {
    public static void main(String[] args) {
        // After adding this comment the application is restarted
        SpringApplication.run(CardatabaseApplication.class, args);
    }
}
```

After saving the file, you can see in the console that the application has restarted.

Logs and problem-solving

Logging can be used to monitor your application flow, and it is a good way to capture unexpected errors in your program code. The Spring Boot starter package provides the **Logback**, which we can use for logging without any configuration. The following sample code shows how you can use logging. The Logback uses **Simple Logging Façade for Java (SLF4J)** as its native interface:

```
package com.packt.cardatabase;

import org.slf4j.Logger;
import org.slf4j.LoggerFactory;
import org.springframework.boot.SpringApplication;
import org.springframework.boot.autoconfigure.SpringBootApplication;

@SpringBootApplication
public class CardatabaseApplication {
    private static final Logger logger = LoggerFactory.getLogger(
        CardatabaseApplication.class
    );

    public static void main(String[] args) {
        SpringApplication.run(CardatabaseApplication.class, args);
        logger.info("Application started");
    }
}
```

The `logger.info` method prints a log message to the console. Log messages can be seen in the console after you run a project, as shown in the following screenshot:

```
Console ×
CardatabaseApplication [Java Application] C:\Program Files\Java\jdk-17.0.2\bin\javaw.exe  (31.3.2023 klo 10.00.09) [pid: 15288]
2023-03-31T10:00:11.747+03:00  INFO 15288 --- [  restartedMain] w.s.c.ServletWebServerApplicationContext : Root WebApplication
2023-03-31T10:00:12.159+03:00  INFO 15288 --- [  restartedMain] o.s.b.d.a.OptionalLiveReloadServer       : LiveReload server
2023-03-31T10:00:12.198+03:00  INFO 15288 --- [  restartedMain] o.s.b.w.embedded.tomcat.TomcatWebServer  : Tomcat started on
2023-03-31T10:00:12.210+03:00  INFO 15288 --- [  restartedMain] c.p.cardatabase.CardatabaseApplication   : Started Cardatabase
2023-03-31T10:00:12.214+03:00  INFO 15288 --- [  restartedMain] c.p.cardatabase.CardatabaseApplication   : Application started
```

Figure 1.11: Log message

There are seven different levels of logging: TRACE, DEBUG, INFO, WARN, ERROR, FATAL, and OFF. You can configure the level of logging in your Spring Boot `application.properties` file. The file can be found in the `/resources` folder inside your project, as illustrated in the following screenshot:

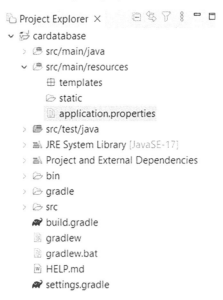

Figure 1.12: Application properties file

If we set the logging level to DEBUG, we can see log messages from levels that are log level DEBUG or higher (that is DEBUG, INFO, WARN, and ERROR). In the following example, we set the log level for the root, but you can also set it at the package level:

```
logging.level.root=DEBUG
```

Now, when you run the project, you can no longer see TRACE messages. The TRACE level contains all application behavior details, which is not needed unless you need full visibility of what is happening in your application. It might be a good setting for a development version of your application. The default logging level is INFO if you don't define anything else.

There is one common failure that you might encounter when running a Spring Boot application. Spring Boot uses Apache Tomcat (`http://tomcat.apache.org/`) as an application server by default, which runs on port 8080 by default. You can change the port in the `application.properties` file. The following setting will start Tomcat on port 8081:

```
server.port=8081
```

If the port is occupied, the application won't start, and you will see the following **APPLICATION FAILED TO START** message in the console:

```
🖥 Console ✕                                                                                 ■ ✖ ❄ | ☷ ⌄
<terminated> CardatabaseApplication [Java Application] C:\Program Files\Java\jdk-17.0.2\bin\javaw.exe  (31.3.2023 klo 10.32.49 – 10.32.51) [pid: 17928]

***************************
APPLICATION FAILED TO START
***************************

Description:

Web server failed to start. Port 8080 was already in use.

Action:

Identify and stop the process that's listening on port 8080 or configure this application to listen on another port.
```

Figure 1.13: Port already in use

If this happens, you will have to stop the process that is listening on port 8080 or use another port in your Spring Boot application. You can avoid this by clicking the **Terminate** button (red square) in the Eclipse console before running the application.

In the next section, we will install a **MariaDB** database to use as a database in our backend.

Installing MariaDB

In *Chapter 3, Using JPA to Create and Access a Database*, we are going to use MariaDB, so you will need to install it locally on your computer. MariaDB is a widely used open-source relational database. MariaDB is available for Windows, Linux, and macOS, and you can download the latest stable community server at `https://mariadb.com/downloads/community/`. MariaDB is developed under a *GNU General Public License, version 2 (GPLv2)* license.

The following steps guide you to install MariaDB:

1. For Windows, there is the **Microsoft Installer** (**MSI**), which we will use here. Download the installer and execute it. Install all features from the installation wizard, as illustrated in the following screenshot:

Figure 1.14: MariaDB installation (step 1)

2. In the next step, you should give a password for the root user. This password is needed in the next chapter when we connect our application to the database. The process is illustrated in the following screenshot:

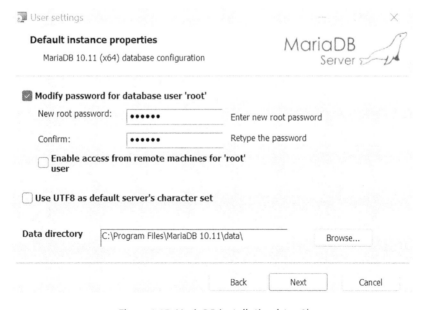

Figure 1.15: MariaDB installation (step 2)

3. In the next phase, we can use the default settings, as illustrated in the following screenshot:

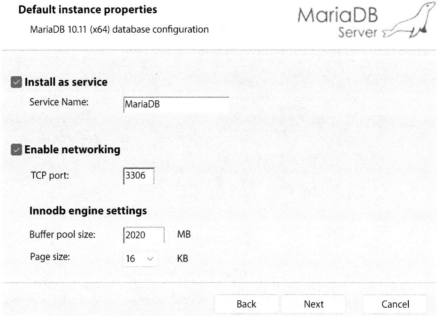

Figure 1.16: MariaDB installation (step 3)

4. Now, the installation will start, and MariaDB will be installed on your local computer. The installation wizard will install **HeidiSQL** for us. This is an easy-to-use, graphical database client. We will use this to add a new database and make queries to our database. You can also use the Command Prompt included in the installation package.

5. Open **HeidiSQL** and log in using the password that you gave in the installation phase. You should then see the following screen:

Figure 1.17: HeidiSQL

IMPORTANT NOTE

HeidiSQL is only available for Windows. If you are using Linux or macOS, you can use DBeaver (`https://dbeaver.io/`) instead.

We now have everything needed to start the implementation of the backend.

Summary

In this chapter, we installed the tools that are needed for backend development with Spring Boot. For Java development, we set up Eclipse, a widely used programming IDE. We created a new Spring Boot project using the Spring Initializr page. After creating the project, it was imported to Eclipse and executed. We also covered how to solve common problems with Spring Boot and how to find important error and log messages. Finally, we installed a MariaDB database, which we are going to use in the following chapters.

In the next chapter, we will understand what **dependency injection** (**DI**) is and how it can be used with the Spring Boot framework.

Questions

1. What is Spring Boot?

2. What is the Eclipse IDE?

3. What is Gradle?

4. How do we create a Spring Boot project?

5. How do we run a Spring Boot project?

6. How do we use logging with Spring Boot?

7. How do we find error and log messages in Eclipse?

Further reading

Packt has other resources for learning about Spring Boot, as listed here:

- *Learning Spring Boot 3.0, Third Edition*, by Greg L. Turnquist (`https://www.packtpub.com/product/learning-spring-boot-30-third-edition/9781803233307`)

- *Microservices with Spring Boot 3 and Spring Cloud, Third Edition*, by Magnus Larsson (`https://www.packtpub.com/product/microservices-with-spring-boot-3-and-spring-cloud-third-edition/9781805128694`)

Learn more on Discord

To join the Discord community for this book – where you can share feedback, ask the author questions, and learn about new releases – follow the QR code below:

`https://packt.link/FullStackSpringBootReact4e`

2

Understanding Dependency Injection

In this chapter, we will learn what **dependency injection** (**DI**) is and how we can use it with the Spring Boot framework. The Spring Boot framework provides DI; therefore, it is good to understand the basics. DI allows for loose coupling between components, making your code more flexible, maintainable, and testable.

In this chapter, we will look into the following:

- Introducing dependency injection
- Using dependency injection in Spring Boot

Technical requirements

All of the code for this chapter can be found at the following GitHub link: `https://github.com/PacktPublishing/Full-Stack-Development-with-Spring-Boot-3-and-React-Fourth-Edition/tree/main/Chapter02`.

Introducing dependency injection

Dependency injection is a software development technique whereby we can create objects that depend on other objects. DI helps with interaction between classes, but at the same time keeps the classes independent.

There are three types of classes in DI:

- A **service** is a class that can be used (this is the dependency).

- The **client** is a class that uses the dependency.

- The **injector** passes the dependency (the service) to the dependent class (the client).

The three types of classes in DI are shown in the following diagram:

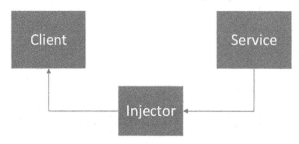

Figure 2.1: DI classes

DI makes classes loosely coupled. This means that the creation of client dependencies is separated from the client's behavior, which makes unit testing easier.

Let's take a look at a simplified example of DI using Java code. In the following code, we don't have DI, because the Car client class is creating an object of the service class:

```
public class Car {
    private Owner owner;

    public Car() {
        owner = new Owner();
    }
}
```

In the following code, the service object is not directly created in the client class. It is passed as a parameter in the class constructor:

```
public class Car {
    private Owner owner;

    public Car(Owner owner) {
        this.owner = owner;
    }
}
```

The service class can also be an abstract class; we can then use any implementation of that in our client class and use mocks when testing.

There are different types of dependency injection; let's take a look at two of them here:

- **Constructor injection**: Dependencies are passed to a client class constructor. An example of constructor injection was already shown in the preceding Car code. Constructor injection is recommended to use for mandatory dependencies. All dependencies are provided using the class constructor and an object cannot be created without its required dependencies.

- **Setter injection**: Dependencies are provided through setters. The following code shows an example of setter injection:

```
public class Car {
    private Owner owner;

    public void setOwner(Owner owner) {
        this.owner = owner;
    }
}
```

Here, the dependency is now passed in the setter as an argument. Setter injection is more flexible because objects can be created without all their dependencies. This approach allows for optional dependencies.

The DI reduces dependencies in your code and makes your code more reusable. It also improves the testability of your code. We have now learned the basics of DI. Next, we will look at how DI is used in Spring Boot.

Using dependency injection in Spring Boot

In the Spring Framework, dependency injection is achieved through the Spring ApplicationContext. ApplicationContext is responsible for creating and managing objects – **beans** – and their dependencies.

Spring Boot scans your application classes and registers classes with certain annotations (@Service, @Repository, @Controller, and so on) as Spring beans. These beans can then be injected using dependency injection.

Spring Boot supports several dependency injection mechanisms, and the most common ones are:

- **Constructor injection**: Dependencies are injected through a constructor. This is the most recommended way because it ensures that all required dependencies are available when the object is created. A fairly common situation is when we need database access for some operations. In Spring Boot, we use repository classes for that. In this situation, we can inject the repository class using constructor injection and start using its methods, as shown in the code example below:

```
// Constructor injection
public class Car {
    private final CarRepository carRepository;

    public Car(CarRepository carRepository) {
        this.carRepository = carRepository;
    }

    // Fetch all cars from db
    carRepository.findAll();
}
```

If you have multiple constructors in your class, you have to use the @Autowired annotation to define which constructor is used for dependency injection:

```
// Constructor to used for dependency injection
@Autowired
public Car(CarRepository carRepository) {
    this.carRepository = carRepository;
}
```

- **Setter injection**: Dependencies are injected through setter methods. Setter injection is useful if you have optional dependencies or if you want to modify dependencies at runtime. Below is an example of setter injection:

```
// Setter injection
@Service
public class AppUserService {
    private AppUserRepository userRepository;

    @Autowired
```

```
public void setAppUserRepository(
    AppUserRepository userRepository) {
        this.userRepository = userRepository;
    }

// Other methods that use userRepository
}
```

- **Field injection**: Dependencies are injected directly into fields. The benefit of field injection is its simplicity, but it has some drawbacks. It can cause runtime errors if the dependency is not available. It is also harder to test your class because you can't mock the dependencies for testing. Here is an example:

```
// Field injection
@Service
public class CarDatabaseService implements CarService {
// Car database services
}

public class CarController {
    @Autowired
    private CarDatabaseService carDatabaseService;
//...
}
```

 You can read more about Spring Boot injection in the Spring documentation: https://spring.io/guides.

Summary

In this chapter, we learned what dependency injection is and how to use it in the Spring Boot framework, which we are using in our backend.

In the next chapter, we will look at how we can use the **Java Persistent API (JPA)** with Spring Boot and how to set up a MariaDB database. We will also learn about the creation of CRUD repositories and the one-to-many connection between database tables.

Questions

1. What is dependency injection?
2. How does the @Autowired annotation work in Spring Boot?
3. How do you inject resources in Spring Boot?

Further reading

Packt has some video resources for learning about Spring Boot:

- *Learn Spring Core Framework the Easy Way*, by Karthikeya T. (`https://www.packtpub.com/product/learn-spring-core-framework-the-easy-way-video/9781801071680`)
- *Mastering Spring Framework Fundamentals*, by Matthew Speake (`https://www.packtpub.com/product/mastering-spring-framework-fundamentals-video/9781801079525`)

Learn more on Discord

To join the Discord community for this book – where you can share feedback, ask the author questions, and learn about new releases – follow the QR code below:

`https://packt.link/FullStackSpringBootReact4e`

3

Using JPA to Create and Access a Database

This chapter covers how to use **Jakarta Persistence API (JPA)** with Spring Boot and how to define a database by using entity classes. In the first phase, we will be using the **H2** database. H2 is an in-memory SQL database that is good for fast development or demonstration purposes. In the second phase, we will move from H2 to **MariaDB**. This chapter also describes the creation of CRUD repositories and a one-to-many connection between database tables.

In this chapter, we will cover the following topics:

- Basics of ORM, JPA, and Hibernate
- Creating the entity classes
- Creating CRUD repositories
- Adding relationships between tables
- Setting up the MariaDB database

Technical requirements

The Spring Boot application we created in previous chapters is required.

A MariaDB installation is necessary to create the database application: `https://downloads.mariadb.org/`. We went through the installation steps in *Chapter 1*.

The code for this chapter can be found at the following GitHub link: `https://github.com/PacktPublishing/Full-Stack-Development-with-Spring-Boot-3-and-React-Fourth-Edition/tree/main/Chapter03`.

Basics of ORM, JPA, and Hibernate

ORM and JPA are widely used techniques in software development for handling relational databases. You don't have to write complex SQL queries; instead, you can work with objects, which is more natural for Java developers. In this way, ORM and JPA can speed up your development process by reducing the time you spend writing and debugging SQL code. Many JPA implementations can also generate a database schema automatically based on your Java entity classes. In brief:

- **Object-Relational Mapping (ORM)** is a technique that allows you to fetch from and manipulate a database by using an object-oriented programming paradigm. ORM is really good for programmers because it relies on object-oriented concepts rather than database structures. It also makes development much faster and reduces the amount of source code. ORM is mostly independent of databases, and developers don't have to worry about vendor-specific SQL statements.

- **Jakarta Persistence API (JPA,** formerly **Java Persistence API)** provides object-relational mapping for Java developers. The JPA entity is a Java class that represents the structure of a database table. The fields of an entity class represent the columns of the database tables.

- **Hibernate** is the most popular Java-based JPA implementation and is used in Spring Boot by default. Hibernate is a mature product and is widely used in large-scale applications.

Next, we will start to implement our first entity class using the H2 database.

Creating the entity classes

An **entity class** is a simple Java class that is annotated with JPA's `@Entity` annotation. Entity classes use the standard JavaBean naming convention and have proper getter and setter methods. The class fields have private visibility.

JPA creates a database table with the same name as the class when the application is initialized. If you want to use some other name for the database table, you can use the `@Table` annotation in your entity class.

At the beginning of this chapter, we will use the H2 database (`https://www.h2database.com/`), which is an embedded in-memory database. To be able to use JPA and the H2 database, we have to add the following dependencies to the `build.gradle` file:

```
dependencies {
    implementation 'org.springframework.boot:spring-boot-starter-web'
    implementation 'org.springframework.boot:spring-boot-starter-data-jpa'
```

```
    developmentOnly 'org.springframework.bout:spring-boot-devtools'
    runtimeOnly 'com.h2database:h2'
    testImplementation 'org.springframework.boot:spring-boot-starter-test'
}
```

After you have updated the build.gradle file, you should update your dependencies by selecting the project in Eclipse's **Project Explorer** and right-clicking to open the context menu. Then, select **Gradle | Refresh Gradle Project**, as shown in the next screenshot:

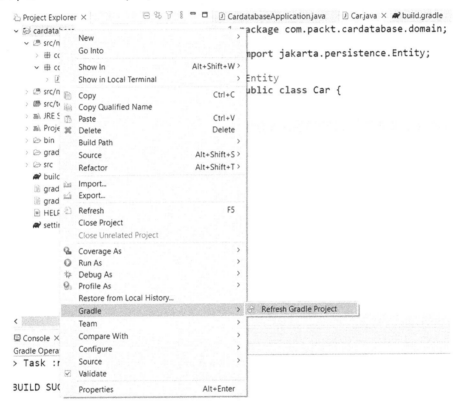

Figure 3.1: Refresh Gradle Project

You can also enable automatic project refresh by opening the **Window | Preferences** menu. Go to the **Gradle** settings and there is an **Automatic Project Synchronization** checkbox that you can check. Then, your project will be synchronized automatically if you make changes to your build script file. This is recommended and means you don't have to manually refresh the project when you update your build script:

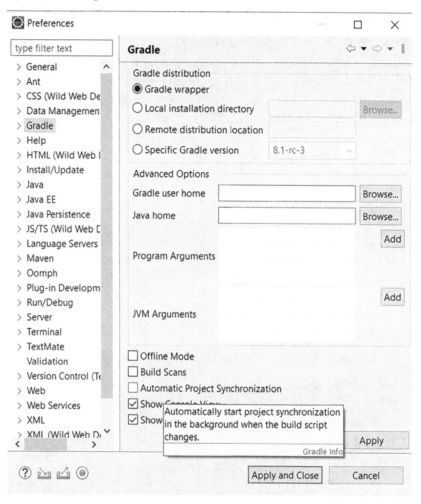

Figure 3.2: Gradle wrapper settings

You can find the project dependencies from the **Project and External Dependencies** folder in the Eclipse **Project Explorer**. Now, you should find spring-boot-starter-data-jpa and h2 dependencies there:

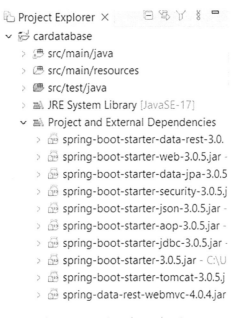

Figure 3.3: Project dependencies

Let's look at the following steps to create entity classes:

1. To create an entity class in Spring Boot, we must create a package for entities. The package should be created under the root package. To begin this process, activate the root package in Eclipse's **Project Explorer** and right-click to make a context menu appear.

2. From this menu, select **New | Package**. The following screenshot shows how to create a package for entity classes:

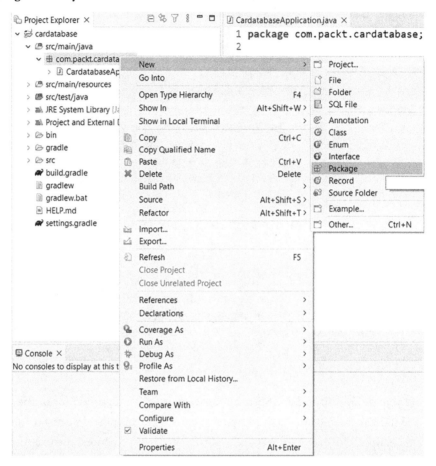

Figure 3.4: New package

3. We will name our package com.packt.cardatabase.domain:

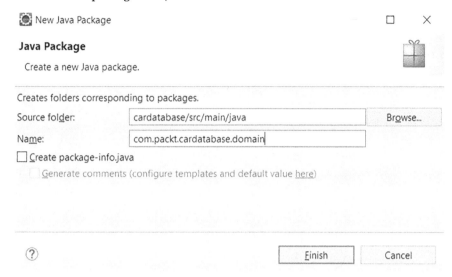

Figure 3.5: New Java package

4. Next, we will create our entity class. Activate the new com.packt.cardatabase.domain package, right-click it, and select **New | Class** from the menu.

5. Because we are going to create a car database, the name of the entity class will be Car. Type Car into the **Name** field and then press the **Finish** button, as shown in the following screenshot:

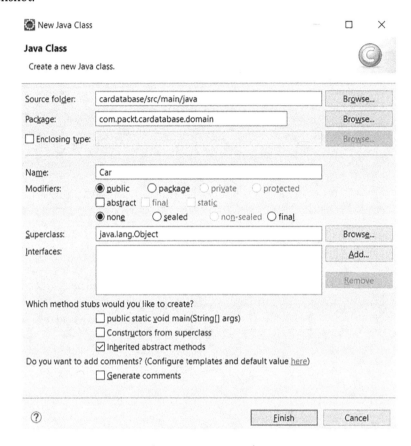

Figure 3.6: New Java class

6. Open the Car class file in the editor by double-clicking it in the **Project Explorer**. First, we must annotate the class with the @Entity annotation. The @Entity annotation is imported from the jakarta.persistence package:

```
package com.packt.cardatabase.domain;

import jakarta.persistence.Entity;

@Entity
public class Car {
}
```

You can use the *Ctrl* + *Shift* + *O* shortcut in the Eclipse IDE to import missing packages automatically. In some cases, there might be multiple packages that contain the same identifier, so you have to be careful to select the correct import. For example, in the next step, Id can be found in multiple packages, but you should select jakarta.persistence.Id.

7. Next, we must add some fields to our class. The entity class fields are mapped to database table columns. The entity class must also contain a unique ID that is used as a primary key in the database:

```
package com.packt.cardatabase.domain;

import jakarta.persistence.Entity;
import jakarta.persistence.GeneratedValue;
import jakarta.persistence.GenerationType;
import jakarta.persistence.Id;

@Entity
public class Car {
    @Id
    @GeneratedValue(strategy=GenerationType.AUTO)
    private Long id;

    private String brand, model, color, registrationNumber;

    private int modelYear, price;
}
```

The primary key is defined by using the @Id annotation. The @GeneratedValue annotation defines that the ID is automatically generated by the database. We can also define our key generation strategy; the AUTO type means that the JPA provider selects the best strategy for a particular database and it is also the default generation type. You can create a composite primary key by annotating multiple attributes with the @Id annotation.

The database columns are named according to class field naming conventions by default. If you want to use some other naming convention, you can use the @Column annotation. With the @Column annotation, you can define the column's length and whether the column is nullable. The following code shows an example of using the @Column annotation. With this definition, the column's name in the database is explanation, the length of the column is 512, and it is not nullable:

```
@Column(name="explanation", nullable=false, length=512)
private String description
```

8. Finally, we must add getters, setters, a default constructor, and constructors with attributes to the entity class. We don't need an ID field in our constructor due to automatic ID generation. The source code of the Car entity class constructors is as follows:

 Eclipse provides the automatic addition of getters, setters, and constructors. Activate your cursor in the place where you want to add the code and right-click. From the menu, select **Source | Generate Getters and Setters...** or **Source | Generate Constructor using Fields....**

```
// Car.java constructors
public Car() {
}

public Car(String brand, String model, String color,
    String registrationNumber, int modelYear, int price) {
        super();
        this.brand = brand;
        this.model = model;
        this.color = color;
        this.registrationNumber = registrationNumber;
        this.modelYear = modelYear;
        this.price = price;
    }
```

The following is the source code for the Car entity class's getters and setters:

```
    public Long getId() {
            return id;
    }
```

```
public String getBrand() {
        return brand;
}

public void setBrand(String brand) {
        this.brand = brand;
}

public String getModel() {
        return model;
}

public void setModel(String model) {
        this.model = model;
}
// Rest of the setters and getters. See the whole source code from
GitHub
```

9. We also have to add new properties to the application.properties file. This allows us to log the SQL statements to the console. We also have to define the data source URL. Open the application.properties file and add the following two lines to the file:

```
spring.datasource.url=jdbc:h2:mem:testdb
spring.jpa.show-sql=true
```

 When you are editing the application.properties file, you have to make sure that there are no extra spaces at the end of the lines. Otherwise, the settings won't work. This might happen when you copy/paste settings.

10. Now, the car table will be created in the database when we run the application. At this point, we can see the table creation statements in the console:

```
Console ×                                                                                    ■ × ■ | ⅗ ▄ ⌄
CardatabaseApplication [Java Application] C:\Program Files\Java\jdk-17.0.2\bin\javaw.exe  (31.3.2023 klo 14.30.53) [pid: 9964]
2023-03-31T14:30:56.873+03:00  INFO 9964 --- [  restartedMain] SQL dialect                              : HHH000400: Using dia
Hibernate: drop table if exists car cascade
Hibernate: drop sequence if exists car_seq
Hibernate: create sequence car_seq start with 1 increment by 50
Hibernate: create table car (id bigint not null, brand varchar(255), color varchar(255), model varchar(255), model_year intege
2023-03-31T14:30:57.493+03:00  INFO 9964 --- [  restartedMain] o.h.e.t.j.p.i.JtaPlatformInitiator       : HHH000490: Using Jta
2023-03-31T14:30:57.502+03:00  INFO 9964 --- [  restartedMain] j.LocalContainerEntityManagerFactoryBean : Initialized JPA Enti
2023-03-31T14:30:57.545+03:00  WARN 9964 --- [  restartedMain] JpaBaseConfiguration$JpaWebConfiguration : spring.jpa.open-in-v
2023-03-31T14:30:57.844+03:00  INFO 9964 --- [  restartedMain] o.s.b.d.a.OptionalLiveReloadServer       : LiveReload server is
2023-03-31T14:30:57.870+03:00  INFO 9964 --- [  restartedMain] o.s.b.w.embedded.tomcat.TomcatWebServer  : Tomcat started on po
```

Figure 3.7: Car table SQL statements

If `spring.datasource.url` is not defined in the application.
properties file, Spring Boot creates a random data source URL that
can be seen in the console when you run the application; for example,
`H2 console available at '/h2-console'. Database available at`
`'jdbc:h2:mem:b92ad05e-8af4-4c33-b22d-ccbf9ffe491e'`.

11. The H2 database provides a web-based console that can be used to explore a database
     and execute SQL statements. To enable the console, we have to add the following lines
     to the `application.properties` file. The first setting enables the H2 console, while the
     second defines its path:

```
spring.h2.console.enabled=true
spring.h2.console.path=/h2-console
```

12. You can access the H2 console by starting your application and navigating to
     `localhost:8080/h2-console` using your web browser. Use `jdbc:h2:mem:testdb` as the
     JDBC URL and leave the **Password** field empty in the **Login** window. Press the **Connect**
     button to log in to the console, as shown in the following screenshot:

Figure 3.8: H2 console login

You can also change the H2 database username and password by using the following settings in the `application.properties` file: `spring.datasource.username` and `spring.datasource.password`.

Now, you can see our CAR table in the database. You may notice that the registration number and model year have an underscore between the words. The reason for the underscore is the camel case naming of the attribute (`registrationNumber`):

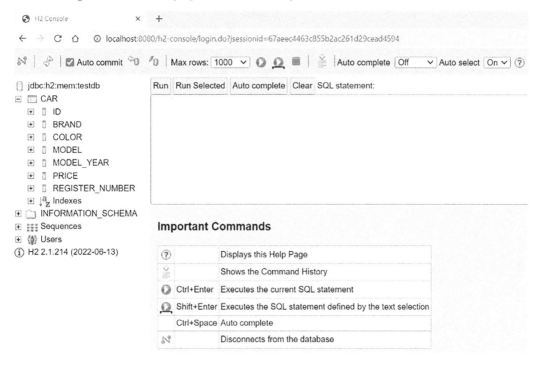

Figure 3.9: H2 console

Now, we have created our first entity class and learned how JPA generates a database table from the entity class. Next, we will create a repository class that provides CRUD operations.

Creating CRUD repositories

The Spring Boot Data JPA provides a `CrudRepository` interface for **Create**, **Read**, **Update**, and **Delete (CRUD)** operations. It provides CRUD functionalities to our entity class.

Let's create our repository in the domain package, as follows:

1. Create a new interface called CarRepository in the com.packt.cardatabase.domain package and modify the file according to the following code snippet:

```
package com.packt.cardatabase.domain;

import org.springframework.data.repository.CrudRepository;

public interface CarRepository extends CrudRepository<Car,Long> {
}
```

CarRepository now extends the Spring Boot JPA CrudRepository interface. The <Car, Long> type arguments define that this is the repository for the Car entity class and that the type of the ID field is Long.

The CrudRepository interface provides multiple CRUD methods that we can now start to use. The following table lists the most commonly used methods:

Method	Description
long count()	Returns the number of entities
Iterable<T> findAll()	Returns all items of a given type
Optional<T> findById(ID Id)	Returns one item by ID
void delete(T entity)	Deletes an entity
void deleteAll()	Deletes all the entities in the repository
<S extends T> save(S entity)	Saves an entity
List<S> saveAll(Iterable<S> entities)	Saves multiple entities

Table 3.1: CRUD methods

If the method returns only one item, Optional<T> is returned instead of T. The Optional class was introduced in Java 8 SE and is a type of single-value container that either contains a value or doesn't. If there is a value, the isPresent() method returns true and you can get it by using the get() method; otherwise, it returns false. By using Optional, we can prevent **null pointer exceptions**. Null pointers can lead to unexpected and often undesirable behavior in Java programs.

After adding the `CarRepository` class, your project structure should look as follows:

Figure 3.10: Project structure

2. Now, we are ready to add some demonstration data to our H2 database. For that, we will use the Spring Boot `CommandLineRunner` interface. The `CommandLineRunner` interface allows us to execute additional code before the application has fully started. Therefore, it is a good point to add demo data to your database. Your Spring Boot application's main class implements the `CommandLineRunner` interface. Therefore, we should implement the run method, as shown in the following `CardatabaseApplication.java` code:

```
package com.packt.cardatabase;

import org.springframework.boot.CommandLineRunner;
import org.springframework.boot.SpringApplication;
import org.springframework.boot.autoconfigure.SpringBootApplication;
```

```
@SpringBootApplication
public class CardatabaseApplication implements CommandLineRunner {
    public static void main(String[] args) {
        SpringApplication.run
            (CardatabaseApplication.class, args);
    }


    @Override
    public void run(String... args) throws Exception {
        // Place your code here
    }
}
```

3.   Next, we have to inject our car repository into the main class to be able to save new car objects to the database. We use constructor injection to inject CarRepository. We will also add a logger to our main class (the code for which we saw in *Chapter 1*):

```
package com.packt.cardatabase;

import org.slf4j.Logger;
import org.slf4j.LoggerFactory;
import org.springframework.boot.CommandLineRunner;
import org.springframework.boot.SpringApplication;
import org.springframework.boot.autoconfigure.SpringBootApplication;
import com.packt.cardatabase.domain.Car;
import com.packt.cardatabase.domain.CarRepository;

@SpringBootApplication
public class CardatabaseApplication implements CommandLineRunner {
    private static final Logger logger =
        LoggerFactory.getLogger(
            CardatabaseApplication.class
        );

    private final CarRepository repository;

    public CardatabaseApplication(CarRepository repository) {
        this.repository = repository;
```

```
        }

        public static void main(String[] args) {
            SpringApplication.run
                (CardatabaseApplication.class, args);
        }

        @Override
        public void run(String... args) throws Exception {
          // Place your code here
        }
    }
```

4. Once we have injected the repository class, we can use the CRUD methods it provides in the run method. The following sample code shows how to insert a few cars into the database using the save method. We will also use the repository's findAll() method to fetch all the cars from the database and print them to the console using the logger:

```
// CardataseApplication.java run method
@Override
public void run(String... args) throws Exception {
    repository.save(new Car("Ford", "Mustang", "Red",
            "ADF-1121", 2023, 59000));
    repository.save(new Car("Nissan", "Leaf", "White",
            "SSJ-3002", 2020, 29000));
    repository.save(new Car("Toyota", "Prius",
            "Silver", "KKO-0212", 2022, 39000));

    // Fetch all cars and log to console
    for (Car car : repository.findAll()) {
        logger.info("brand: {}, model: {}",
            car.getBrand(), car.getModel());
    }
}
```

The `insert` statements and cars we logged can be seen in the Eclipse console once the application has been executed:

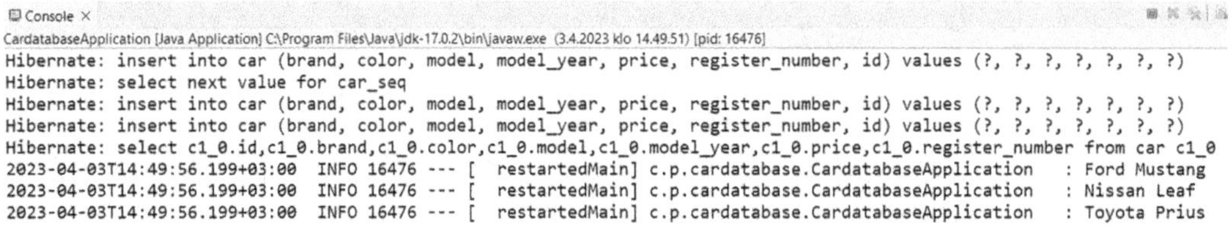

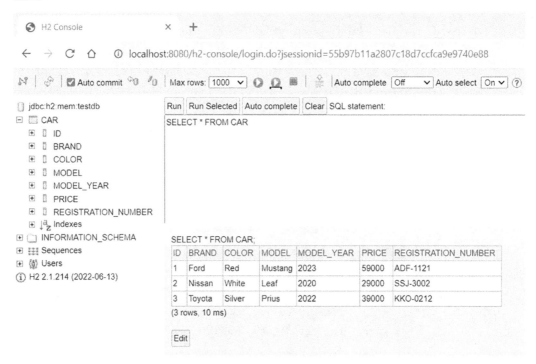

Figure 3.11: Insert statements

You can now use the H2 console to fetch cars from the database, as shown in the following screenshot:

Figure 3.12: H2 console: Select cars

You can define queries in the Spring Data repositories. A query must start with a prefix, for example, findBy. After the prefix, you must define the entity class fields that are used in the query. The following is some sample code for three simple queries:

```
package com.packt.cardatabase.domain;

import java.util.List;
import org.springframework.data.repository.CrudRepository;

public interface CarRepository extends CrudRepository <Car, Long> {
    // Fetch cars by brand
    List<Car> findByBrand(String brand);

    // Fetch cars by color
    List<Car> findByColor(String color);

    // Fetch cars by model year
    List<Car> findByModelYear(int modelYear);
}
```

There can be multiple fields after the By keyword, concatenated with the And and Or keywords:

```
package com.packt.cardatabase.domain;

import java.util.List;
import org.springframework.data.repository.CrudRepository;

public interface CarRepository extends CrudRepository <Car, Long> {
    // Fetch cars by brand and model
    List<Car> findByBrandAndModel(String brand, String model);

    // Fetch cars by brand or color
    List<Car> findByBrandOrColor(String brand, String color);
}
```

Queries can be sorted by using the OrderBy keyword in the query method:

```
package com.packt.cardatabase.domain;

import java.util.List;
```

```
import org.springframework.data.repository.CrudRepository;

public interface CarRepository extends CrudRepository <Car, Long> {
    // Fetch cars by brand and sort by year
    List<Car> findByBrandOrderByModelYearAsc(String brand);
}
```

You can also create queries by using SQL statements via the @Query annotation. The following example shows the usage of a SQL query in CrudRepository:

```
package com.packt.cardatabase.domain;

import java.util.List;
import org.springframework.data.jpa.repository.Query;
import org.springframework.data.repository.CrudRepository;

public interface CarRepository extends CrudRepository <Car, Long> {
    // Fetch cars by brand using SQL
    @Query("select c from Car c where c.brand = ?1")
    List<Car> findByBrand(String brand);
}
```

With the @Query annotation, you can use more advanced expressions, such as like. The following example shows the usage of the like query in CrudRepository:

```
package com.packt.cardatabase.domain;

import java.util.List;
import org.springframework.data.jpa.repository.Query;
import org.springframework.data.repository.CrudRepository;

public interface CarRepository extends CrudRepository <Car, Long> {
    // Fetch cars by brand using SQL
    @Query("select c from Car c where c.brand like %?1")
    List<Car> findByBrandEndsWith(String brand);
}
```

If you use the @Query annotation and write SQL queries in your code, your application might be less portable across different database systems.

Spring Data JPA also provides PagingAndSortingRepository, which extends CrudRepository. This offers methods to fetch entities using pagination and sorting. This is a good option if you are dealing with larger amounts of data because you don't have to return everything from a large result set. You can also sort your data into some meaningful order. PagingAndSortingRepository can be created in a similar way to how we created CrudRepository:

```
package com.packt.cardatabase.domain;

import org.springframework.data.repository.PagingAndSortingRepository;

public interface CarRepository extends
    PagingAndSortingRepository <Car, Long> {
    }
```

In this case, you now have the two new additional methods that the repository provides:

Method	Description
Iterable<T> findAll(Sort sort)	Returns all entities sorted by the given options
Page<T> findAll(Pageable pageable)	Returns all entities according to the given paging options

Table 3.2: PagingAndSortingRepository methods

At this point, we have completed our first database table and we are ready to add relationships between the database tables.

Adding relationships between tables

We will create a new table called owner that has a one-to-many relationship with the car table. In this case, a one-to-many relationship means that the owner can own multiple cars, but a car can only have one owner.

The following **Unified Modeling Language (UML)** diagram shows the relationship between the tables:

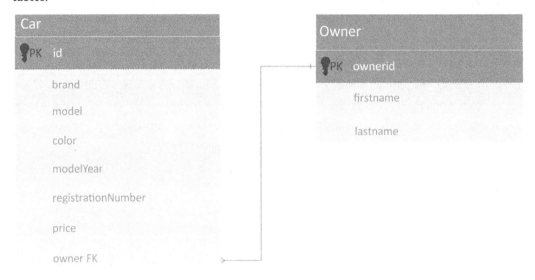

Figure 3.13: One-to-many relationship

The following are the steps to create a new table:

1. First, we must create the Owner entity and repository classes in the com.packt.cardatabase. domain package. The Owner entity and repository are created in a similar way to the Car class.

    The following is the source code for the Owner entity class:

    ```java
    // Owner.java
    package com.packt.cardatabase.domain;

    import jakarta.persistence.Entity;
    import jakarta.persistence.GeneratedValue;
    import jakarta.persistence.GenerationType;
    import jakarta.persistence.Id;

    @Entity
    public class Owner {
        @Id
        @GeneratedValue(strategy = GenerationType.AUTO)
        private Long ownerid;
    ```

```
        private String firstname, lastname;

        public Owner() {
        }

        public Owner(String firstname, String lastname) {
            super();
            this.firstname = firstname;
            this.lastname = lastname;
        }

        public Long getOwnerid() {
            return ownerid;
        }

        public String getFirstname() {
            return firstname;
        }

        public void setFirstname(String firstname) {
            this.firstname = firstname;
        }

        public String getLastname() {
            return lastname;
        }

        public void setLastname(String lastname) {
            this.lastname = lastname;
        }
    }
```

The following is the source code for `OwnerRepository`:

```
// OwnerRepository.java
package com.packt.cardatabase.domain;
import org.springframework.data.repository.CrudRepository;
```

```
public interface OwnerRepository extends
    CrudRepository<Owner, Long> {
    }
```

2. Now, we should check that everything is working. Run the project and check that both database tables have been created and that there are no errors in the console. The following screenshot shows the console messages when the tables are created:

Figure 3.14: The car and owner tables

Now, our domain package contains two entity classes and repositories:

Figure 3.15: The Project Explorer

3. The one-to-many relationship can be added by using the @ManyToOne and @OneToMany annotations (jakarta.persistence). In the car entity class, which contains a foreign key, you must define the relationship with the @ManyToOne annotation. You should also add the getter and setter for the owner field. It is recommended that you use FetchType.LAZY for all associations. For the toMany relationships, that is the default value, but for the toOne relationships, you should define it. FetchType defines the strategy for fetching data from the database. The value can be either EAGER or LAZY. In our case, the LAZY strategy means that when the owner is fetched from the database, the cars associated with the owner will be fetched *when needed*. EAGER means that the cars will be fetched immediately by the owner. The following source code shows how to define a one-to-many relationship in the Car class:

```
// Car.java
@ManyToOne(fetch=FetchType.LAZY)
@JoinColumn(name="owner")
private Owner owner;

// Getter and setter
public Owner getOwner() {
    return owner;
}

public void setOwner(Owner owner) {
    this.owner = owner;
}
```

4. On the owner entity site, the relationship is defined with the @OneToMany annotation. The type of field is List<Car> because an owner may have multiple cars. Add the getter and setter for this, as follows:

```
// Owner.java
@OneToMany(cascade=CascadeType.ALL, mappedBy="owner")
private List<Car> cars;

public List<Car> getCars() {
    return cars;
}
```

```java
public void setCars(List<Car> cars) {
    this.cars = cars;
}
```

The @OneToMany annotation has two attributes that we are using. The cascade attribute defines how cascading affects the entities in the case of deletions or updates. The ALL attribute setting means that all operations are cascaded. For example, if the owner is deleted, the cars that are linked to that owner are deleted as well. The mappedBy="owner" attribute setting tells us that the Car class has the owner field, which is the foreign key for this relationship.

When you run the project, by looking in the console, you will see that the relationship has been created:

```
Console  ×  Ju JUnit
CardatabaseApplication [Java Application] C:\Program Files\Java\jdk-17.0.2\bin\javaw.exe  (18.9.2023 klo 14.17.05) [pid: 1080]
Hibernate: insert into app_user (password,role,username,id) values (?,?,?,?)
Hibernate: select next value for app_user_seq
Hibernate: insert into app_user (password,role,username,id) values (?,?,?,?)
Hibernate: select c1_0.id,c1_0.brand,c1_0.color,c1_0.model,c1_0.model_year,c1_0.owner,c1_0.price,c1_0
2023-09-18T14:17:51.179+03:00  INFO 1080 --- [  restartedMain] c.p.cardatabase.CardatabaseApplication
2023-09-18T14:17:51.179+03:00  INFO 1080 --- [  restartedMain] c.p.cardatabase.CardatabaseApplication
2023-09-18T14:17:51.179+03:00  INFO 1080 --- [  restartedMain] c.p.cardatabase.CardatabaseApplication
```

Figure 3.16: Console

5. Now, we can add some owners to the database with CommandLineRunner. Let's also modify the Car entity class constructor and add an owner object there:

```java
// Car.java constructor
public Car(String brand, String model, String color,
           String registrationNumber, int modelYear, int price,
           Owner owner)
{
    super();
    this.brand = brand;
    this.model = model;
    this.color = color;
    this.registrationNumber = registrationNumber;
    this.modelYear = modelYear;
    this.price = price;
    this.owner = owner;
}
```

6. First, we will create two owner objects and save these to the database using the repository's saveAll method, which we can use to save multiple entities at once. To save the owners, we have to inject OwnerRepository into the main class. Then, we must connect the owners to the cars by using the Car constructor. First, let's modify the CardatabaseApplication class by adding the following imports:

    ```java
    // CardatabaseApplication.java
    import com.packt.cardatabase.domain.Owner;
    import com.packt.cardatabase.domain.OwnerRepository;
    ```

7. Now, let's also inject OwnerRepository into the CardatabaseApplication class using constructor injection:

    ```java
    private final CarRepository repository;
    private final OwnerRepository orepository;

    public CardatabaseApplication(CarRepository repository,
                                  OwnerRepository orepository)
    {
        this.repository = repository;
        this.orepository = orepository;
    }
    ```

8. At this point, we must modify the run method to save owners and link owners and cars:

    ```java
    @Override
    public void run(String... args) throws Exception {
        // Add owner objects and save these to db
        Owner owner1 = new Owner("John" , "Johnson");
        Owner owner2 = new Owner("Mary" , "Robinson");
        orepository.saveAll(Arrays.asList(owner1, owner2));

        repository.save(new Car("Ford", "Mustang", "Red",
                        "ADF-1121", 2023, 59000, owner1));
        repository.save(new Car("Nissan", "Leaf", "White",
                        "SSJ-3002", 2020, 29000, owner2));
        repository.save(new Car("Toyota", "Prius", "Silver",
                        "KKO-0212", 2022, 39000, owner2));
        // Fetch all cars and log to console
        for (Car car : repository.findAll())
    ```

```
    {
        logger.info("brand: {}, model: {}", car.getBrand(),
        car.getModel());
    }
}
```

9. Now, if you run the application and fetch cars from the database, you will see that the owners are now linked to the cars:

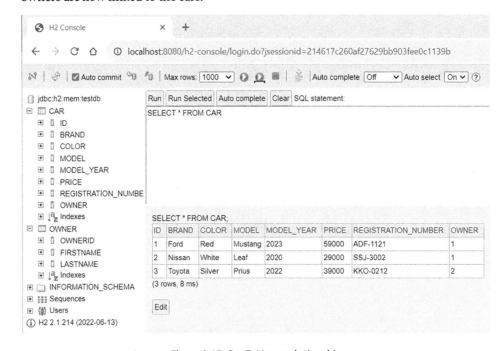

Figure 3.17: OneToMany relationship

If you want to create a many-to-many relationship instead, which means, in practice, that an owner can have multiple cars and a car can have multiple owners, you should use the @ManyToMany annotation. In our example application, we will use a one-to-many relationship. The code that you have completed here will be needed in the next chapter.

Next, you will learn how to change the relationship to many-to-many. In a many-to-many relationship, it is recommended that you use Set instead of List with Hibernate:

1. In the Car entity class's many-to-many relationship, define the getters and setters in the following way:

    ```java
    // Car.java
    @ManyToMany(mappedBy="cars")
    private Set<Owner> owners = new HashSet<Owner>();

    public Set<Owner> getOwners() {
        return owners;
    }

    public void setOwners(Set<Owner> owners) {
        this.owners = owners;
    }
    ```

2. In the Owner entity class, the many-to-many relationship is defined as follows:

    ```java
    // Owner.java
    @ManyToMany(cascade=CascadeType.PERSIST)
    @JoinTable(name="car_owner",joinColumns =
            {
            @JoinColumn(name="ownerid") },
            inverseJoinColumns =
            {
            @JoinColumn(name="id") }
    )
    private Set<Car> cars = new HashSet<Car>();

    public Set<Car> getCars() {
        return cars;
    }

    public void setCars(Set<Car> cars) {
        this.cars = cars;
    }
    ```

3. Now, if you run the application, there will be a new **join table** called car_owner that is created between the car and owner tables. The join table is a special kind of table that manages the many-to-many relationship between two tables.

The join table is defined by using the @JoinTable annotation. With this annotation, we can set the name of the join table and join columns. The following screenshot shows the database structure when using a many-to-many relationship:

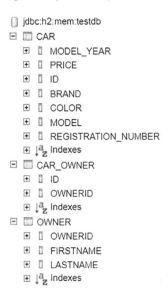

Figure 3.18: Many-to-many relationship

Now, the database UML diagram looks as follows:

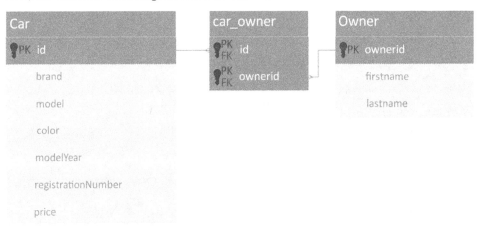

Figure 3.19: Many-to-many relationship

We have used an in-memory H2 database in the chapter so far. In the next section, we will be using a one-to-many relationship, so *change your code back if you followed the previous many-to-many example.*

Next, we are going to look at how to use a MariaDB database instead.

Setting up a MariaDB database

Now, we will switch the database we are using from H2 to MariaDB. H2 is a good database for test and demonstration purposes, but MariaDB is a better option for a proper production database when applications require performance, reliability, and scalability.

In this book, we are using MariaDB version 10. The database tables are still created automatically by JPA. However, before we run our application, we have to create a database for it.

 In this section, we will be using the one-to-many relationship from the previous section.

The database can be created using HeidiSQL (or DBeaver, if you are using Linux or macOS). Open HeidiSQL and follow these steps:

1. Activate the top database connection name (**Unnamed**) and right-click it.

2. Then, select **Create new | Database**:

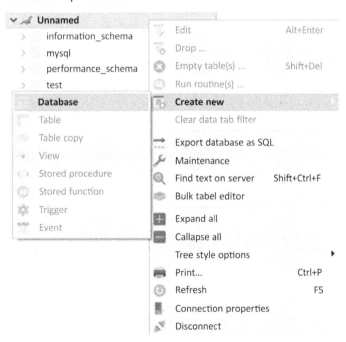

Figure 3.20: Create new database

3. Let's name our database `cardb`. After clicking **OK**, you should see the new `cardb` database in the database list:

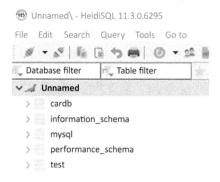

Figure 3.21: The cardb database

4. In Spring Boot, add a MariaDB Java client dependency to the `build.gradle` file and remove the H2 dependency since we don't need it anymore. Remember to refresh your Gradle project after you have modified your `build.gradle` file:

```
dependencies {
    implementation 'org.springframework.boot:spring-boot-starter-web'
    implementation 'org.springframework.boot:spring-boot-starter-
data-jpa'
    developmentOnly 'org.springframework.boot:spring-boot-devtools'
    runtimeOnly 'org.mariadb.jdbc:mariadb-java-client'
    testImplementation 'org.springframework.boot:spring-boot-
starter-test'
}
```

5. In the `application.properties` file, you must define the database connection for MariaDB. In this phase, you should remove the old H2 database settings. First, you must define the database's URL, username, password (defined in *Chapter 1*), and database driver class:

```
spring.datasource.url=jdbc:mariadb://localhost:3306/cardb
spring.datasource.username=root
spring.datasource.password=YOUR_PASSWORD
spring.datasource.driver-class-name=org.mariadb.jdbc.Driver
```

 In this example, we are using the database root user, but in production, you should create a user for your database that doesn't have all root database rights.

6. Add the `spring.jpa.generate-ddl` setting, which defines whether JPA should initialize the database (`true`/`false`). Also add the `spring.jpa.hibernate.ddl-auto` setting, which defines the behavior of the database initialization:

```
spring.datasource.url=jdbc:mariadb://localhost:3306/cardb
spring.datasource.username=root
spring.datasource.password=YOUR_PASSWORD
spring.datasource.driver-class-name=org.mariadb.jdbc.Driver
spring.jpa.generate-ddl=true
spring.jpa.hibernate.ddl-auto=create-drop
```

The possible values for `spring.jpa.hibernate.ddl-auto` are `none`, `validate`, `update`, `create`, and `create-drop`. The default value depends on your database. If you are using an embedded database such as H2, the default value is `create-drop`; otherwise, the default value is `none`. `create-drop` means that the database is created when an application starts, and it is dropped when the application is stopped. The `create` value only creates the database when the application is started. The `update` value creates the database and updates the schema if it has changed.

7. Check that the MariaDB database server is running and restart your Spring Boot application. After running the application, you should see the tables in MariaDB. You might have to refresh the database tree in HeidiSQL first by pressing the *F5* key. The following screenshot shows the HeidiSQL user interface once the database has been created:

Figure 3.22: MariaDB cardb
You can also run SQL queries in HeidiSQL.

Now, your application is ready to use with MariaDB.

Summary

In this chapter, we used JPA to create our Spring Boot application database. First, we created entity classes, which are mapped to database tables.

Then, we created a `CrudRepository` for our entity class, which provides CRUD operations for the entity. After that, we managed to add some demo data to our database by using `CommandLineRunner`. We also created one-to-many relationships between two entities. At the beginning of this chapter, we used the H2 in-memory database, and we switched the database to MariaDB at the end.

In the next chapter, we will create a RESTful web service for our backend. We will also look at testing the RESTful web service with the cURL command-line tool and the Postman GUI.

Questions

1. What are ORM, JPA, and Hibernate?
2. How can you create an entity class?
3. How can you create a `CrudRepository`?
4. What does a `CrudRepository` provide for your application?
5. How can you create a one-to-many relationship between tables?
6. How can you add demo data to a database with Spring Boot?
7. How can you access the H2 console?
8. How can you connect your Spring Boot application to MariaDB?

Further reading

Packt has other resources for learning more about MariaDB, Hibernate, and JPA:

*   *Getting Started with MariaDB*, by Daniel Bartholomew (`https://www.packtpub.com/product/getting-started-with-mariadb/9781785284120`)
*   *Master Hibernate and JPA with Spring Boot in 100 Steps [Video]*, by In28Minutes Official (`https://www.packtpub.com/product/master-hibernate-and-jpa-with-spring-boot-in-100-steps-video/9781788995320`)

Learn more on Discord

To join the Discord community for this book – where you can share feedback, ask the author questions, and learn about new releases – follow the QR code below:

`https://packt.link/FullStackSpringBootReact4e`

4

Creating a RESTful Web Service with Spring Boot

Web services are applications that communicate over the internet using the HTTP protocol. There are many different types of web service architectures, but the principal idea across all designs is the same. In this book, we will create a RESTful web service: nowadays, a really popular design.

In this chapter, we will first create a **RESTful web service** using a controller class. Then, we will use **Spring Data REST** to create a RESTful web service that also provides all CRUD functionalities automatically, and document it with **OpenAPI 3**. After you have created a RESTful API for your application, you can implement the frontend using a JavaScript library such as React. We will be using the database application that we created in the previous chapter as a starting point.

In this chapter, we will cover the following topics:

- Basics of REST
- Creating a RESTful web service with Spring Boot
- Using Spring Data REST
- Documenting a RESTful API

Technical requirements

The Spring Boot application created in the previous chapters is required.

You will also need Postman, cURL, or another suitable tool for transferring data using various HTTP methods.

The following GitHub link will be required: `https://github.com/PacktPublishing/Full-Stack-Development-with-Spring-Boot-3-and-React-Fourth-Edition/tree/main/Chapter04`.

Basics of REST

Representational State Transfer (REST) is an architectural style for creating web services. REST is neither language- nor platform-dependent; different clients like mobile apps, browsers, and other services can communicate with each other. RESTful services can be scaled easily to fulfill increased demand.

REST is not a standard but a set of constraints, defined by Roy Fielding. The constraints are as follows:

- **Stateless**: The server shouldn't hold any information about the client state.
- **Client-server independence**: The client and server should act independently. The server should not send any information without a request from the client.
- **Cacheable**: Many clients often request the same resources; therefore, caching should be applied to resources in order to improve performance.
- **Uniform interface**: Requests from different clients should look the same. Clients may include, for example, a browser, a Java application, and a mobile application.
- **Layered system**: Components can be added or modified without affecting the entire service. This constraint affects scalability.
- **Code on demand**: This is an optional constraint. Most of the time, the server sends static content in the form of JSON or XML. This constraint allows the server to send executable code if needed.

The uniform interface constraint is important, and it means that every REST architecture should have the following elements:

- **Identification of resources**: Resources should be identified by unique identifiers, for example, URIs in web-based REST services. REST resources should expose easily understood directory structure URIs. Therefore, a good resource-naming strategy is very important.

- **Resource manipulation through representation**: When making a request to a resource, the server should respond with a representation of the resource. Typically, the format of the representation is JSON or XML.

- **Self-descriptive messages**: Messages should contain enough information that the server knows how to process them.

- **Hypermedia as the Engine of Application State (HATEOAS)**: Responses should contain links to other areas of the service.

The RESTful web service that we are going to develop in the next sections follows the REST architectural principles above.

Creating a RESTful web service with Spring Boot

In Spring Boot, all HTTP requests are handled by **controller classes**. To be able to create a RESTful web service, first, we have to create a controller class. We will create our own Java package for the controller:

1. Activate the root package in the Eclipse **Project Explorer** and right-click. Select **New | Package** from the menu. We will name our new package com.packt.cardatabase.web:

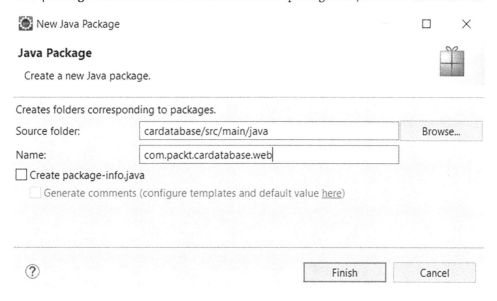

Figure 4.1: New Java package

2. Next, we will create a new `controller` class in a new web package. Activate the `com.packt.cardatabase.web` package in the Eclipse **Project Explorer**. Right-click and select **New | Class** from the menu; we will name our class `CarController`:

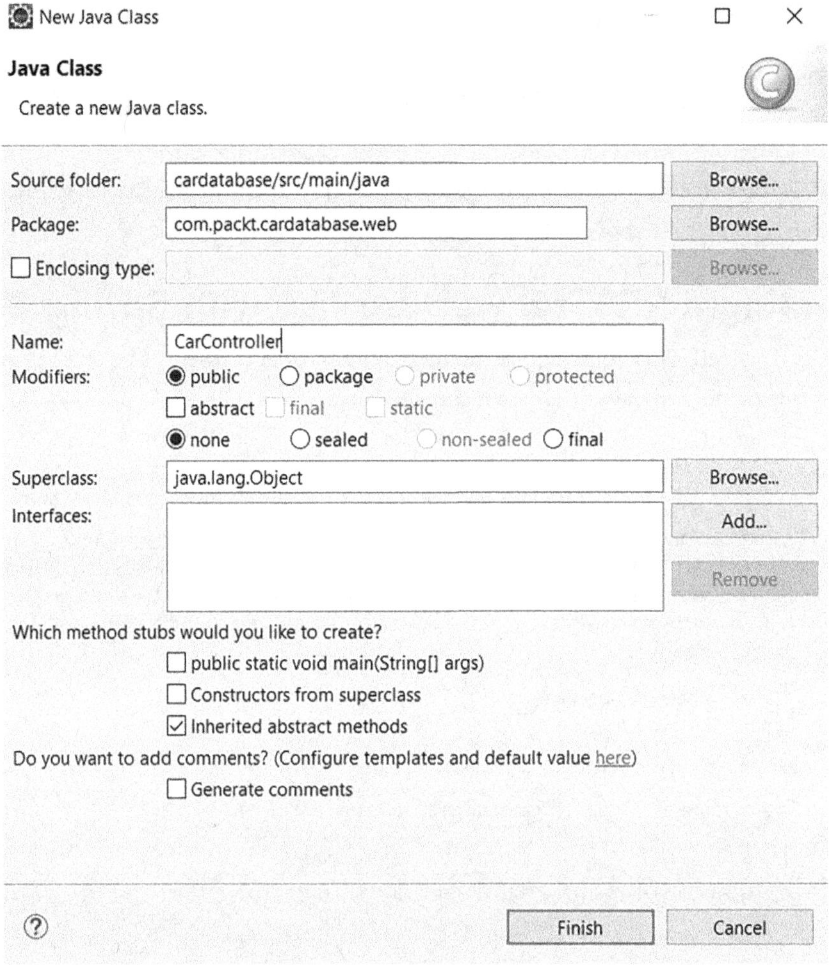

Figure 4.2: New Java class

3. Now, your project structure should look like the following screenshot:

Figure 4.3: Project structure

 If you create classes in the wrong package accidentally, you can drag and drop the files between packages in the Project Explorer. Sometimes, the Project Explorer view might not be rendered correctly when you make some changes. Refreshing the Project Explorer helps (activate the Project Explorer and press *F5*).

4. Open your controller class in the editor window and add the @RestController annotation before the class definition. Refer to the following source code. The @RestController annotation identifies that this class will be the controller for the RESTful web service:

```
package com.packt.cardatabase.web;

import org.springframework.web.bind.annotation.RestController;

@RestController
public class CarController {

}
```

5. Next, we add a new method inside our controller class. The method is annotated with the @GetMapping annotation, which defines the endpoint that the method is mapped to. In the following code snippet, you can see the sample source code. In this example, when a user makes a GET request to the /cars endpoint, the getCars() method is executed:

```
package com.packt.cardatabase.web;

import org.springframework.web.bind.annotation.GetMapping;
import org.springframework.web.bind.annotation.RestController;
import com.packt.cardatabase.domain.Car;

@RestController
public class CarController {
    @GetMapping("/cars")
    public Iterable<Car> getCars() {
//Fetch and return cars
    }
}
```

The getCars() method returns all the car objects, which are then marshaled to JSON objects automatically by the **Jackson** library (https://github.com/FasterXML/jackson).

Now, the getCars() method handles only GET requests from the /cars endpoint because we are using the @GetMapping annotation. There are other annotations for the different HTTP methods, such as @GetMapping, @PostMapping, @DeleteMapping, and so on.

6. To be able to return cars from the database, we have to inject CarRepository into the controller. Then, we can use the findAll() method that the repository provides to fetch all cars. Due to the @RestController annotation, the data is now serialized to JSON format in the response. The following source code shows the controller code:

```
package com.packt.cardatabase.web;

import org.springframework.web.bind.annotation.GetMapping;
import org.springframework.web.bind.annotation.RestController;
import com.packt.cardatabase.domain.Car;
import com.packt.cardatabase.domain.CarRepository;

@RestController
public class CarController {
    private final CarRepository repository;

    public CarController(CarRepository repository) {
        this.repository = repository;
    }

    @GetMapping("/cars")
    public Iterable<Car> getCars() {
        return repository.findAll();
    }
}
```

7. Now, we are ready to run our application and navigate to localhost:8080/cars. We can see that there is something wrong, and the application seems to be in an infinite loop. This happens on account of our one-to-many relationship between the car and owner tables. So, what happens in practice? First, the car is serialized, and it contains an owner who is then serialized, and that, in turn, contains cars that are then serialized, and so on. There are different solutions for avoiding this. One way is to use the @JsonIgnore annotation on the cars field in the Owner class, which ignores the cars field in the serialization process. You can also solve this by avoiding bidirectional mapping if it is not needed. We will also use the @JsonIgnoreProperties annotation to ignore fields that are generated by Hibernate:

```java
// Owner.java
import com.fasterxml.jackson.annotation.JsonIgnore;
import com.fasterxml.jackson.annotation.JsonIgnoreProperties;

@Entity
@JsonIgnoreProperties({"hibernateLazyInitializer","handler"})
public class Owner {
    @Id
    @GeneratedValue(strategy=GenerationType.AUTO)
    private long ownerid;
    private String firstname, lastname;

    public Owner() {}

    public Owner(String firstname, String lastname) {
        super();
        this.firstname = firstname;
        this.lastname = lastname;
    }

    @JsonIgnore
    @OneToMany(cascade=CascadeType.ALL, mappedBy="owner")
    private List<Car> cars;
```

8. Now, when you run the application and navigate to `localhost:8080/cars`, everything should go as expected and you will get all the cars from the database in JSON format, as shown in the following screenshot:

```
1    // 20230404130326
2    // http://localhost:8080/cars
3
4  ▼ [
5  ▼   {
6          "id": 1,
7          "brand": "Ford",
8          "model": "Mustang",
9          "color": "Red",
10         "registerNumber": "ADF-1121",
11         "modelYear": 2023,
12         "price": 59000,
13 ▼       "owner": {
14            "ownerid": 1,
15            "firstname": "John",
16            "lastname": "Johnson"
17          }
18       },
19 ▼     {
20         "id": 2,
21         "brand": "Nissan",
22         "model": "Leaf",
23         "color": "White",
24         "registerNumber": "SSJ-3002",
25         "modelYear": 2020,
26         "price": 29000,
27 ▼       "owner": {
```

Figure 4.4: GET request to http://localhost:8080/cars

Your output might differ from the screenshot due to browser differences. In this book, we are using the Chrome browser and the **JSON Viewer** extension, which makes JSON output more readable. JSON Viewer can be downloaded from the Chrome Web Store for free.

We have written our first RESTful web service. By leveraging the capabilities of Spring Boot, we were able to quickly implement a service that returns all the cars in our database. However, this is just the beginning of what Spring Boot has to offer for creating robust and efficient RESTful web services, and we will continue to explore its capabilities in the next section.

Using Spring Data REST

Spring Data REST (https://spring.io/projects/spring-data-rest) is part of the Spring Data project. It offers an easy and fast way to implement RESTful web services with Spring. Spring Data REST provides **HATEOAS (Hypermedia as the Engine of Application State)** support, an architectural principle that allows clients to navigate the REST API dynamically using hypermedia links. Spring Data REST also provides events that you can use to customize the business logic of your REST API endpoints.

You can read more about events in the Spring Data REST documentation: https://docs.spring.io/spring-data/rest/docs/current/reference/html/#events.

To start using Spring Data REST, you have to add the following dependency to the build.gradle file:

```
dependencies {
    implementation 'org.springframework.boot:spring-boot-starter-web'
    implementation 'org.springframework.boot:spring-boot-starter-data-jpa'
    implementation 'org.springframework.boot:spring-boot-starter-data-rest'
    developmentOnly 'org.springframework.boot:spring-boot-devtools'
    runtimeOnly 'org.mariadb.jdbc:mariadb-java-client'
    testImplementation 'org.springframework.boot:spring-boot-starter-test'
}
```

Refresh your Gradle project from Eclipse after you have modified the build.gradle file. Select the project in Eclipse's Project Explorer and right-click to open the context menu. Then, select **Gradle | Refresh Gradle Project**.

By default, Spring Data REST finds all public repositories from the application and creates RESTful web services for your entities automatically. In our case, we have two repositories: CarRepository and OwnerRepository; therefore, Spring Data REST creates RESTful web services automatically for those repositories.

You can define the endpoint of the service in your `application.properties` file as follows. You might need to restart your application for the changes to take effect:

```
spring.data.rest.basePath=/api
```

Now, you can access the RESTful web service from the `localhost:8080/api` endpoint. By calling the root endpoint of the service, it returns the resources that are available. Spring Data REST returns JSON data in the **Hypertext Application Language (HAL)** format. The HAL format provides a set of conventions for expressing hyperlinks in JSON and it makes your RESTful web service easier to use for frontend developers:

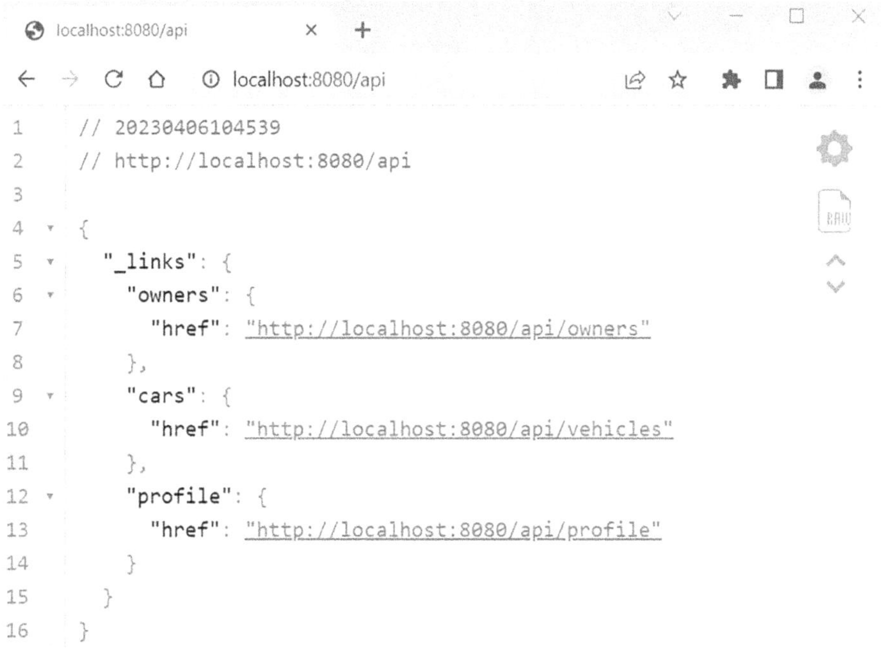

Figure 4.5: Spring Boot Data REST resources

We can see that there are links to the car and owner entity services. The Spring Data REST service path name is derived from the entity class name. The name will then be pluralized and uncapitalized. For example, the entity `Car` service path name will become `cars`. The `profile` link is generated by Spring Data REST and contains application-specific metadata. If you want to use different path naming, you can use the `@RepositoryRestResource` annotation in your repository class, as shown in the next example:

```
package com.packt.cardatabase.domain;
import org.springframework.data.repository.CrudRepository;
```

```
import org.springframework.data.rest.core.annotation.RepositoryRestResource;

@RepositoryRestResource(path="vehicles")
public interface CarRepository extends CrudRepository<Car, Long> {
}
```

Now, if you call the endpoint `localhost:8080/api`, you can see that the endpoint has been changed from `/cars` to `/vehicles`.

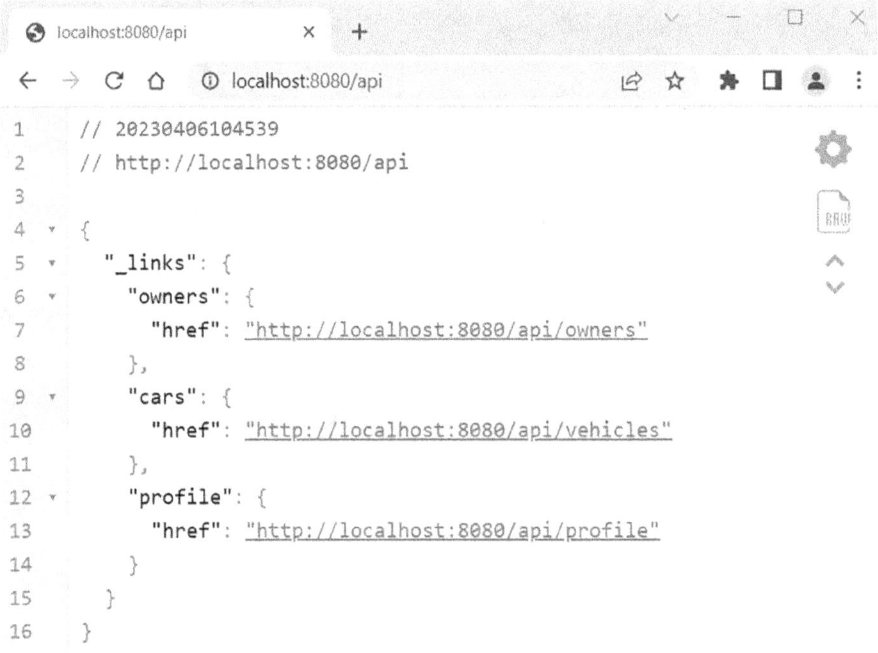

Figure 4.6: Spring Boot Data REST resources

You can remove the different naming, and we will continue with the default endpoint name, `/cars`.

Now, we'll start to examine different services more carefully. There are multiple tools available for testing and consuming RESTful web services. In this book, we are using the **Postman** (`https://www.postman.com/downloads/`) desktop app, but you can use tools that you are familiar with, such as **cURL**. Postman can be acquired as a desktop application or as a browser plugin. cURL is also available for Windows by using Windows Ubuntu Bash (**Windows Subsystem for Linux, WSL**).

If you make a request to the /cars endpoint (http://localhost:8080/api/cars) using the GET method (note: you can use a web browser for GET requests), you will get a list of all the cars, as shown in the following screenshot:

```
                 ←  →  C  ⌂   ⓘ localhost:8080/api/cars
1       // 20230830132818
2       // http://localhost:8080/api/cars
3
4    ▾  {
5    ▾    "_embedded": {
6    ▾      "cars": [
7    ▾        {
8              "brand": "Ford",
9              "model": "Mustang",
10             "color": "Red",
11             "registrationNumber": "ADF-1121",
12             "modelYear": 2023,
13             "price": 59000,
14   ▾         "_links": {
15   ▾           "self": {
16                 "href": "http://localhost:8080/api/cars/1"
17               },
18   ▾           "car": {
19                 "href": "http://localhost:8080/api/cars/1"
20               },
21   ▾           "owner": {
22                 "href": "http://localhost:8080/api/cars/1/owner"
23               }
24             }
25           },
26   ▾        {
27             "brand": "Nissan",
28             "model": "Leaf",
29             "color": "White",
30             "registrationNumber": "SSJ-3002",
31             "modelYear": 2020,
32             "price": 29000,
```

Figure 4.7: Fetch cars

In the JSON response, you can see that there is an array of cars, and each car contains car-specific data. All the cars also have the `_links` attribute, which is a collection of links, and with these links, you can access the car itself or get the owner of the car. To access one specific car, the path will be `http://localhost:8080/api/cars/{id}`.

The `GET` request to `http://localhost:8080/api/cars/3/owner` returns the owner of the car with id 3. The response now contains owner data, a link to the owner, and links to the owner's other cars.

The Spring Data REST service provides all CRUD operations. The following table shows which HTTP methods you can use for different CRUD operations:

HTTP method	CRUD
GET	Read
POST	Create
PUT/PATCH	Update
DELETE	Delete

Table 4.1: Spring Data REST operations

Next, we will look at how to delete a car from the database by using our RESTful web service. In a delete operation, you have to use the `DELETE` method and the link to the car that will be deleted (`http://localhost:8080/api/cars/{id}`).

The following screenshot shows how you can delete one car with id 3 by using the Postman desktop app. In Postman, you have to select the correct HTTP method from the drop-down list, enter the request URL, and then click the **Send** button:

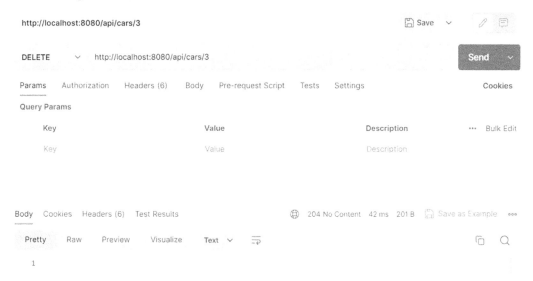

Figure 4.8: DELETE request to delete car

If everything goes correctly, you will see the response status **200 OK** in Postman. After the successful DELETE request, you will also see that there are now two cars left in the database if you make a GET request to the http://localhost:8080/api/cars/ endpoint. If you got the **404 Not Found** status in the DELETE response, check that you are using a car ID that exists in the database.

When we want to add a new car to the database, we have to use the POST method, and the request URL is `http://localhost:8080/api/cars`. The header must contain the `Content-Type` field with the value `application/json`, and the new car object will be embedded in the request body in JSON format.

Here is one car example:

```
{
    "brand":"Toyota",
    "model":"Corolla",
    "color":"silver",
    "registrationNumber":"BBA-3122",
    "modelYear":2023,
    "price":38000
}
```

If you click the **Body** tab and select **raw** in Postman, you can type a new car JSON string under the **Body** tab. Also select JSON from the drop-down list, as shown in the following screenshot:

Figure 4.9: POST request to add a new car

You also have to set a header by clicking the **Headers** tab in Postman, as shown in the following screenshot. Postman adds some headers automatically based on your request selections. Check that the Content-Type header is in the list and the value is correct (`application/json`). If it doesn't exist, you should add it manually. Automatically added headers might be hidden by default, but you can see these by clicking the **hidden** button. Finally, you can press the **Send** button:

Figure 4.10: POST request headers

The response will send a newly created car object back and the status of the response will be **201 Created** if everything went correctly. Now, if you make a GET request again to the http://localhost:8080/api/cars path, you will see that the new car exists in the database.

To update entities, we can use the PATCH method and the link to the car that we want to update (http://localhost:8080/api/cars/{id}). The header must contain the Content-Type field with the value application/json, and the car object with edited data will be given inside the request body.

 If you are using PATCH, you have to send only fields that are updated. If you are using PUT, you have to include all fields in the request body.

Let's edit the car that we created in the previous example, changing the color to white. We are using PATCH, so the payload contains only the color property:

```
{
  "color": "white"
}
```

The Postman request is shown in the following screenshot (note: we set the header as in the POST example and use the car id in the URL):

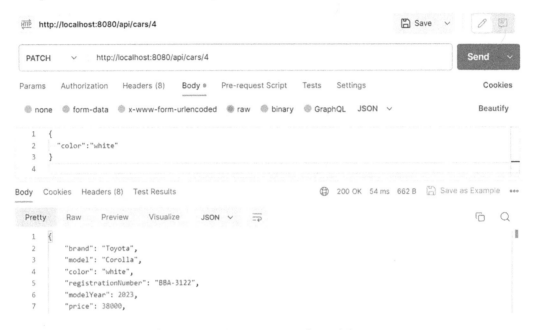

Figure 4.11: PATCH request to update existing car

If the update succeeded, the response status is **200 OK**. If you now fetch the updated car using a GET request, you will see that the color has been updated.

Next, we will add an owner to the new car that we just created. We can use the PUT method and the http://localhost:8080/api/cars/{id}/owner path. In this example, the ID of the new car is 4, so the link is http://localhost:8080/api/cars/4/owner. The content of the body is now linked to an owner, for example, http://localhost:8080/api/owners/1.

Figure 4.12: PUT request to update owner

The Content-Type value of the headers should be text/uri-list in this case. If you can't modify the automatically added header, you can disable it by unchecking it. Then, add a new one, like shown in the next image, and press the **Send** button:

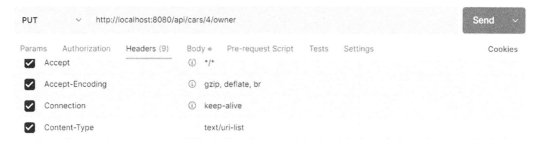

Figure 4.13: PUT request headers

Finally, you can make a GET request for the car's owner, and you should now see that the owner is linked to the car.

In the previous chapter, we created queries for our repository. These queries can also be included in our service. To include queries, you have to add the @RepositoryRestResource annotation to the repository class. Query parameters are annotated with the @Param annotation. The following source code shows CarRepository with these annotations:

```
package com.packt.cardatabase.domain;
import java.util.List;
import org.springframework.data.repository.CrudRepository;
import org.springframework.data.repository.query.Param;
import org.springframework.data.rest.core.annotation
RepositoryRestResource;

@RepositoryRestResource
public interface CarRepository extends CrudRepository<Car, Long> {
    // Fetch cars by brand
    List<Car> findByBrand(@Param("brand") String brand);
    // Fetch cars by color
    List<Car> findByColor(@Param("color") String color);
}
```

Now, when you make a GET request to the http://localhost:8080/api/cars path, you can see that there is a new endpoint called /search. Calling the http://localhost:8080/api/cars/ search path returns the following response:

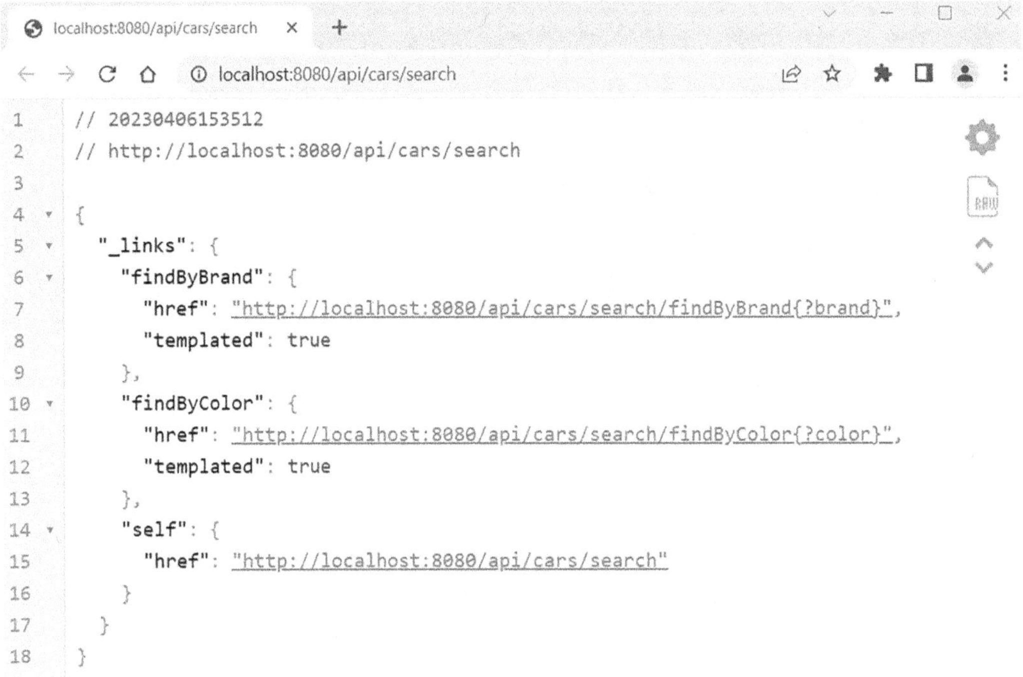

Figure 4.14: REST queries

From the response, you can see that both queries are now available in our service. The following URL demonstrates how to fetch cars by brand: http://localhost:8080/api/cars/search/ findByBrand?brand=Ford. The output will only contain cars with the brand Ford.

At the beginning of this chapter, we introduced the REST principles, and we can see that our RESTful API fulfills several aspects of the REST specification. It is stateless and requests from different clients look the same (uniform interface). The response contains links that can be used to navigate between related resources. Our RESTful API provides a URI structure that reflects the data model and relationship between resources.

We have now created the RESTful API for our backend, and we will consume it later with our React frontend.

Documenting a RESTful API

A RESTful API should be properly documented so that developers who are consuming it understand its functionality and behavior. The documentation should include what endpoints are available, what data formats are accepted, and how to interact with the API.

In this book, we will use the **OpenAPI 3** library for Spring Boot (https://springdoc.org) to generate documentation automatically. The **OpenAPI Specification** (formerly Swagger Specification) is an API description format for RESTful APIs. There are other alternatives, such as RAML (https://raml.org/), that can be used as well. You can also document your REST API using some other documentation tools, which provide flexibility but require more manual work. The use of the OpenAPI library automates this work, allowing you to focus on development.

The following steps demonstrate how you can generate documentation for your RESTful API:

1. First, we have to add the OpenAPI library to our Spring Boot application. Add the following dependency to your `build.gradle` file:

   ```
   implementation group: 'org.springdoc', name: 'springdoc-openapi-
   starter-webmvc-ui', version: '2.0.2'
   ```

2. Next, we create a configuration class for our documentation. Create a new class called `OpenApiConfig` in the `com.packt.cardatabase` package of your application. Below is the code for the configuration class where we can configure, for example, the REST API title, description, and version. We can use the `info()` method to define these values:

   ```
   package com.packt.cardatabase;

   import org.springframework.context.annotation.Bean;
   import org.springframework.context.annotation.Configuration;
   import io.swagger.v3.oas.models.OpenAPI;
   import io.swagger.v3.oas.models.info.Info;

   @Configuration
   public class OpenApiConfig {

       @Bean
       public OpenAPI carDatabaseOpenAPI() {
           return new OpenAPI()
               .info(new Info()
   ```

```
                    .title("Car REST API")
                    .description("My car stock")
                    .version("1.0"));
    }
}
```

3. In the `application.properties` file, we can define the path for our documentation. We can also enable **Swagger UI,** a user-friendly tool for visualizing RESTful APIs that are documented using the OpenAPI Specification (`https://swagger.io/tools/swagger-ui/`). Add the following settings to your `application.properties` file:

    ```
    springdoc.api-docs.path=/api-docs
    springdoc.swagger-ui.path=/swagger-ui.html
    springdoc.swagger-ui.enabled=true
    ```

4. Now, we are ready to run our project. When your application is running, navigate to `http://localhost:8080/swagger-ui.html` and you will see the documentation in Swagger UI, as shown in the following screenshot:

Figure 4.15: Car RESTful API documentation

You can see all the endpoints that are available in your RESTful API. If you open any of the endpoints, you can even try them out by pressing the **Try it out** button. The documentation is also available in JSON format at `http://localhost:8080/api-docs`.

Now that you have provided documentation for your RESTful API, it is much easier for developers to consume it.

 In the next chapter, we will secure our RESTful API, which will break access to Swagger UI. You can allow access again by modifying your security configuration (allow the "/api-docs/**" and "/swagger-ui/**" paths). You can also use Spring Profiles, but that is out of scope for this book.

Summary

In this chapter, we created a RESTful web service with Spring Boot. First, we created a controller and one method that returns all cars in JSON format. Next, we used Spring Data REST to get a fully functional web service with all CRUD functionalities. We covered different types of requests that are needed to use the CRUD functionalities of the service that we created. We also included our queries in the RESTful web service. Finally, we learned how to document our API properly with OpenAPI 3.

We will use this RESTful web service with our frontend later in this book, and now you can also easily implement a REST API for your own needs.

In the next chapter, we will secure our backend using Spring Security. We will learn how to secure our data by implementing authentication. Then, only authenticated users will be able to access the RESTful API's resources.

Questions

1. What is REST?
2. How can you create a RESTful web service with Spring Boot?
3. How can you fetch items using our RESTful web service?
4. How can you delete items using our RESTful web service?
5. How can you add items using our RESTful web service?
6. How can you update items using our RESTful web service?
7. How can you use queries with our RESTful web service?
8. What is the OpenAPI Specification?
9. What is Swagger UI?

Further reading

Packt has other resources available for learning about Spring Boot RESTful web services:

- *Postman Tutorial: Getting Started with API Testing [Video]* by Praveenkumar Bouna (https://www.packtpub.com/product/postman-tutorial-getting-started-with-api-testing-video/9781803243351)

- *Hands-On RESTful API Design Patterns and Best Practices* by Harihara Subramanian J and Pethuru Raj (https://www.packtpub.com/product/hands-on-restful-api-design-patterns-and-best-practices/9781788992664)

Learn more on Discord

To join the Discord community for this book – where you can share feedback, ask the author questions, and learn about new releases – follow the QR code below:

https://packt.link/FullStackSpringBootReact4e

5

Securing Your Backend

This chapter explains how to secure your Spring Boot backend. Securing your backend is a crucial part of code development. It is essential for protecting sensitive data, complying with regulations, and preventing unauthorized access. The backend often handles the user authentication and authorization process. Securing these aspects properly ensures that only authorized users can access the application and perform specific actions. We will use the database application that we created in the previous chapter as a starting point.

In this chapter, we will cover the following topics:

- Understanding Spring Security
- Securing your backend with a JSON Web Token
- Role-based security
- Using OAuth2 with Spring Boot

Technical requirements

The Spring Boot application that we created in the previous chapters is required.

The following GitHub link will also be required: `https://github.com/PacktPublishing/Full-Stack-Development-with-Spring-Boot-3-and-React-Fourth-Edition/tree/main/Chapter05`.

Understanding Spring Security

Spring Security (`https://spring.io/projects/spring-security`) provides security services for Java-based web applications. The Spring Security project was started in 2003 and was previously named *Acegi Security System for Spring*.

By default, Spring Security enables the following features:

- An `AuthenticationManager` bean with an in-memory single user. The username is `user` and the password is printed to the console output.

- Ignored paths for common static resource locations, such as `/css` and `/images`. HTTP basic authentication for all other endpoints.

- Security events published to Spring's `ApplicationEventPublisher` interface.

- Common low-level features turned on by default, including **HTTP Strict Transport Security (HSTS), cross-site scripting (XSS)**, and **cross-site request forgery (CSRF)**.

- A default autogenerated login page.

You can include Spring Security in your application by adding the following highlighted dependencies to the `build.gradle` file. The first dependency is for the application and the second is for testing:

```
dependencies {
    implementation 'org.springframework.boot:spring-boot-starter-web'
    implementation 'org.springframework.boot:spring-boot-starter-data-jpa'
    implementation 'org.springframework.boot:spring-boot-starter-data-rest'
    implementation 'org.springframework.boot:spring-boot-starter-security'
    developmentOnly 'org.springframework.boot:spring-boot-devtools'
    runtimeOnly 'org.mariadb.jdbc:mariadb-java-client'
    testImplementation 'org.springframework.boot:spring-boot-starter-test'
    testImplementation 'org.springframework.security:spring-security-test'
}
```

 If you haven't enabled automatic refresh, remember to refresh the Gradle project from Eclipse after you have modified your `build.gradle` file.

When you start your application, you can see from the console that Spring Security has created an in-memory user with a username of `user`. The user's password can be seen in the console output, as illustrated here:

```
Console ×
CardatabaseApplication [Java Application] C:\Program Files\Java\jdk-17.0.2\bin\javaw.exe  (7.4.2023 klo 10.33.36) [pid: 3612]
2023-04-07T10:33:41.379+03:00  WARN 3612 --- [  restartedMain] JpaBaseConfigurat:
2023-04-07T10:33:42.039+03:00  WARN 3612 --- [  restartedMain] .s.s.UserDetailsS

Using generated security password: 693a8aed-69bc-4ee5-8273-6ee7c27f940e

This generated password is for development use only. Your security configuration

2023-04-07T10:33:42.167+03:00  INFO 3612 --- [  restartedMain] o.s.s.web.Default:
2023-04-07T10:33:42.214+03:00  INFO 3612 --- [  restartedMain] o.s.b.d.a.Optiona:
2023-04-07T10:33:42.260+03:00  INFO 3612 --- [  restartedMain] o.s.b.w.embedded.·
```

Figure 5.1: Spring Security enabled

If there is no password in the console, try to restart your project by pressing the red **Terminate** button in the console and re-running it.

> The Eclipse console has limited output, and the default buffer size is 80,000 characters, so the output might be truncated before the password statement can appear. You can change this setting from the **Window | Preferences | Run/Debug | Console** menu.

Now, if you make a GET request to your REST API root endpoint, you will see that it has been secured. Open your web browser and navigate to http://localhost:8080/api. You will be redirected to the Spring Security default login page, as illustrated in the following screenshot:

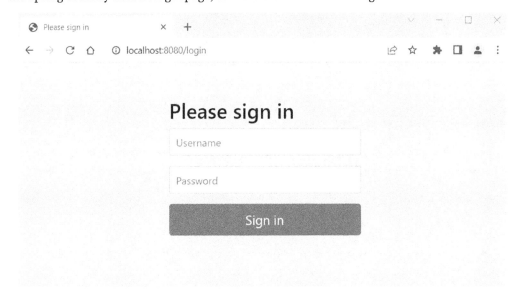

Figure 5.2: Secured REST API

To be able to make a successful GET request, we have to authenticate to our RESTful API. Type user into the **Username** field and copy the generated password from the console to the **Password** field. With authentication, we can see that the response contains our API resources, as illustrated in the following screenshot:

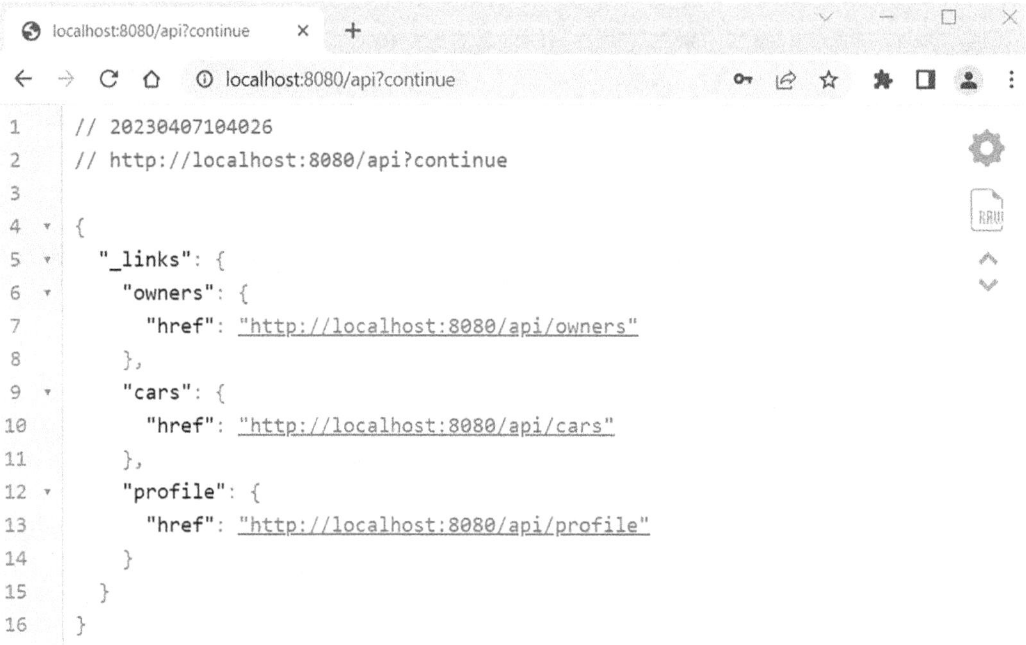

Figure 5.3: Basic authentication

To configure how Spring Security behaves, we have to add a new configuration class for Spring Security. The security configuration file can be used to define which URLs or URL patterns are accessible to which roles or users. You can also define the authentication mechanism, the login process, session management, and so on.

Create a new class called SecurityConfig in your application root package (com.packt.cardatabase). The following source code shows the structure of the security configuration class:

```
package com.packt.cardatabase;

import org.springframework.context.annotation.Configuration;
import org.springframework.security.config.annotation.web.configuration.
  EnableWebSecurity;

@Configuration
@EnableWebSecurity
```

```
public class SecurityConfig {
}
```

The @Configuration and @EnableWebSecurity annotations switch off the default web security configuration, and we can define our own configuration in this class. Inside the
filterChain(HttpSecurity http) method that we will see in action later, we can define which
endpoints in our application are secure and which are not. We don't actually need this method
yet because we can use the default settings where all the endpoints are secured.

We can also add in-memory users to our application by using Spring Security's
InMemoryUserDetailsManager, which implements UserDetailsService. Then we can implement user/password authentication that is stored in memory. We can also use PasswordEncoder
to encode passwords using the bcrypt algorithm.

The following highlighted source code will create an in-memory user with a username of user,
a password of password, and a role of USER:

```
// SecurityConfig.java
package com.packt.cardatabase;

import org.springframework.context.annotation.Bean;
import org.springframework.context.annotation.Configuration;
import org.springframework.security.config.annotation.web.configuration.
    EnableWebSecurity;
import org.springframework.security.core.userdetails.User;
import org.springframework.security.core.userdetails.UserDetails;
import org.springframework.security.crypto.bcrypt.BCryptPasswordEncoder;
import org.springframework.security.crypto.password.PasswordEncoder;
import org.springframework.security.provisioning.
    InMemoryUserDetailsManager;

@Configuration
@EnableWebSecurity
public class SecurityConfig {
    @Bean
    public InMemoryUserDetailsManager userDetailsService() {
        UserDetails user = User.builder().username("user").
            password(passwordEncoder().encode("password"))
            .roles("USER").build();

        return new InMemoryUserDetailsManager(user);
    }
```

```
@Bean
public PasswordEncoder passwordEncoder() {
    return new BCryptPasswordEncoder();
}
}
```

Now, restart the application, and you will be able to test authentication using the in-memory user. The use of in-memory users is fine in the development phase, but a proper application should save users in the database.

To save users to the database, you have to create a user entity class and repository. Passwords shouldn't be saved to the database in plaintext format. If a database containing user passwords is hacked, attackers will be able to get the passwords directly in plaintext. Spring Security provides multiple hashing algorithms, such as bcrypt, that you can use to hash passwords. The following steps show you how to implement this:

1. Create a new class called AppUser in the com.packt.cardatabase.domain package. Activate the domain package and right-click it. Select **New** | **Class** from the menu and name the new class User. After that, your project structure should look like this:

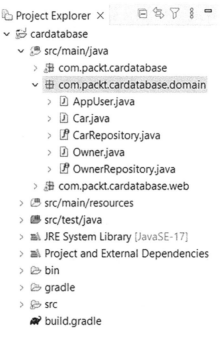

Figure 5.4: Project structure

2. Annotate the AppUser class with the @Entity annotation. Add the ID, username, password, and role class fields. Finally, add the constructors, getters, and setters. We will set all the fields to be not nullable. This means that database columns cannot hold null values. We will also specify that the username must be unique by using unique=true in the username's @Column annotation. Refer to the following AppUser.java source code for the fields:

```
package com.packt.cardatabase.domain;

import jakarta.persistence.Column;
import jakarta.persistence.Entity;
import jakarta.persistence.GeneratedValue;
import jakarta.persistence.GenerationType;
import jakarta.persistence.Id;

@Entity
public class AppUser {
    @Id
    @GeneratedValue(strategy=GenerationType.AUTO)
    @Column(nullable=false, updatable=false)
    private Long id;

    @Column(nullable=false, unique=true)
    private String username;

    @Column(nullable=false)
    private String password;

    @Column(nullable=false)
    private String role;

// Constructors, getters and setters
}
```

Here is the AppUser.java constructors source code:

```
public AppUser() {}

public AppUser(String username, String password, String role) {
    super();
```

```
        this.username = username;
        this.password = password;
        this.role = role;
    }
```

Here is the AppUser.java source code with the getters and setters:

```
    public Long getId() {
        return id;
    }

    public void setId(Long id) {
        this.id = id;
    }

    public String getUsername() {
        return username;
    }

    public void setUsername(String username) {
        this.username = username;
    }

    public String getPassword() {
        return password;
    }

    public void setPassword(String password) {
        this.password = password;
    }

    public String getRole() {
        return role;
    }

    public void setRole(String role) {
        this.role = role;
    }
```

3. Create a new interface called AppUserRepository in the domain package. To do this, activate the domain package and right-click it. Select **New** | **Interface** from the menu and name it AppUserRepository.

   The source code for the repository class is similar to what we saw in the previous chapter, but there is one query method, findByUsername, that we need for the steps that follow. This method is used to find a user from the database in the authentication process. The method returns Optional to prevent a null exception. Refer to the following AppUserRepository source code:

   ```
   package com.packt.cardatabase.domain;

   import java.util.Optional;
   import org.springframework.data.repository.CrudRepository;

   public interface AppUserRepository extends CrudRepository
     <AppUser, Long> {
       Optional<AppUser> findByUsername(String username);
   }
   ```

4. Next, we will create a class that implements the UserDetailsService interface that's provided by Spring Security. Spring Security uses this for user authentication and authorization. Create a new service package in the root package. To do this, activate the root package and right-click it. Select **New** | **Package** from the menu and name the new package service, as illustrated in the following screenshot:

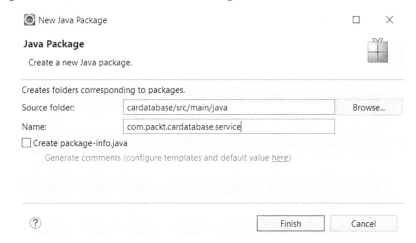

Figure 5.5: The service package

5. Create a new class called `UserDetailsServiceImpl` in the `service` package we just created. Now, your project structure should look like this (in Eclipse, refresh the Project Explorer by pressing *F5*):

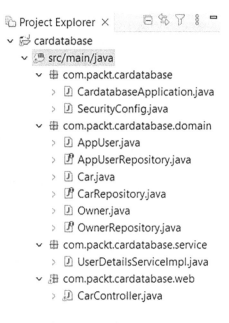

Figure 5.6: Project structure

6. We have to inject the `AppUserRepository` class into the `UserDetailsServiceImpl` class because it is needed to fetch the user from the database when Spring Security handles authentication. The `findByUsername` method that we implemented earlier returns `Optional`, therefore we can use the `isPresent()` method to check if the user exists. If the user doesn't exist, we throw a `UsernameNotFoundException` exception. The `loadUserByUsername` method returns the `UserDetails` object, which is required for authentication. We are using the Spring Security `UserBuilder` class to build the user for the authentication. Here is the source code for `UserDetailsServiceImpl.java`:

```
package com.packt.cardatabase.service;

import java.util.Optional;
import org.springframework.security.core.userdetails.User.
  UserBuilder;
import org.springframework.security.core.userdetails.UserDetails;
import org.springframework.security.core.userdetails.
  UserDetailsService;
```

```
import org.springframework.security.core.userdetails.
  UsernameNotFoundException;
import org.springframework.stereotype.Service;
import com.packt.cardatabase.domain.AppUser;
import com.packt.cardatabase.domain.AppUserRepository;

@Service
public class UserDetailsServiceImpl implements UserDetailsService {
  private final AppUserRepository repository;

public UserDetailsServiceImpl(AppUserRepository repository) {
    this.repository = repository;
}

    @Override
    public UserDetails loadUserByUsername(String username) throws
    UsernameNotFoundException {
        Optional<AppUser> user = repository.findByUsername(username);

        UserBuilder builder = null;
        if (user.isPresent()) {
            AppUser currentUser = user.get();
            builder = org.springframework.security.core.userdetails.
                    User.withUsername(username);
            builder.password(currentUser.getPassword());
            builder.roles(currentUser.getRole());
        } else {
            throw new UsernameNotFoundException("User not found.");
        }

        return builder.build();
    }
}
```

In our security configuration class, we have to specify that Spring Security should use users from the database instead of in-memory users. Delete the userDetailsService() method from the SecurityConfig class to disable in-memory users. Add a new configureGlobal method to enable users from the database.

We should never save the password as plaintext to the database. Therefore, we will define a password hashing algorithm in the `configureGlobal` method. In this example, we are using the `bcrypt` algorithm. This can be easily implemented with the Spring Security `BCryptPasswordEncoder` class, which encodes a hashed password during the authentication process. Here is the `SecurityConfig.java` source code:

```java
package com.packt.cardatabase;

import org.springframework.context.annotation.Configuration;
import org.springframework.context.annotation.Bean;
import org.springframework.security.config.annotation.
  authentication.builders.AuthenticationManagerBuilder;
import org.springframework.security.config.annotation.
  web.configuration.EnableWebSecurity;
import org.springframework.security.crypto.bcrypt.
  BCryptPasswordEncoder;
import com.packt.cardatabase.service.UserDetailsServiceImpl;
import org.springframework.security.crypto.password.PasswordEncoder;

@Configuration
@EnableWebSecurity
public class SecurityConfig {
    private final UserDetailsServiceImpl userDetailsService;

    public SecurityConfig(UserDetailsServiceImpl userDetailsService) {
        this.userDetailsService = userDetailsService;
    }

  public void configureGlobal (AuthenticationManagerBuilder auth)
    throws Exception {
      auth.userDetailsService(userDetailsService)
      .passwordEncoder(new BCryptPasswordEncoder());
    }

    @Bean
    public PasswordEncoder passwordEncoder() {
        return new BCryptPasswordEncoder();
    }
}
```

Now, the password must be hashed using bcrypt before it's saved to the database.

7. Finally, we can save a couple of test users to the database using the CommandLineRunner interface. Open the CardatabaseApplication.java file and inject AppUserRepository into the main class:

```
private final CarRepository repository;
private final OwnerRepository orepository;
private final AppUserRepository urepository;

public CardatabaseApplication(CarRepository repository,
OwnerRepository orepository, AppUserRepository urepository) {
    this.repository = repository;
    this.orepository = orepository;
    this.urepository = urepository;
}
```

8. Let's save two users to the database with bcrypt hashed passwords. You can find bcrypt calculators or generators on the internet. These generators allow you to input a plaintext password, and they will produce the corresponding bcrypt hash:

```
@Override
public void run(String... args) throws Exception {
    // Add owner objects and save these to db
    Owner owner1 = new Owner("John", "Johnson");
    Owner owner2 = new Owner("Mary", "Robinson");
    orepository.saveAll(Arrays.asList(owner1, owner2));

    repository.save(new Car(
                    "Ford", "Mustang", "Red", "ADF-1121",
                     2023, 59000, owner1));
    repository.save(new Car(
                    "Nissan", "Leaf", "White", "SSJ-3002",
                    2020, 29000, owner2));
    repository.save(new Car(
                    "Toyota", "Prius", "Silver", "KKO-0212",
                    2022, 39000, owner2));
    // Fetch all cars and log to console
    for (Car car : repository.findAll()) {
        logger.info(car.getBrand() + " " + car.getModel());
    }
```

```
// Username: user, password: user
urepository.save(new AppUser("user",
    "$2a$10$NVM0n8ElaRgg7zWO1CxUdei7vWoPg91Lz2aYavh9.
    f9q0e4bRadue","USER"));

// Username: admin, password: admin
urepository.save(new AppUser("admin",
    "$2a$10$8cjz47bjbR4Mn8GMg9IZx.vyjhLXR/SKKMSZ9.
    mP9vpMu0ssKi8GW", "ADMIN"));
}
```

 bcrypt is a strong hashing function that was designed by Niels Provos and David Mazières. Here is an example of a bcrypt hash that is generated from the admin string:

$2a$10$8cjz47bjbR4Mn8GMg9IZx.vyjhLXR/SKKMSZ9.mP9vpMu0ssKi8GW

$2a represents the algorithm version, and $10 represents the strength of the algorithm. The default strength of Spring Security's BcryptPasswordEncoder class is 10. bcrypt generates a random **salt** in hashing, so the hashed result is always different.

9. After running your application, you will see that there is now an app_user table in the database and that two user records are saved with hashed passwords, as illustrated in the following screenshot:

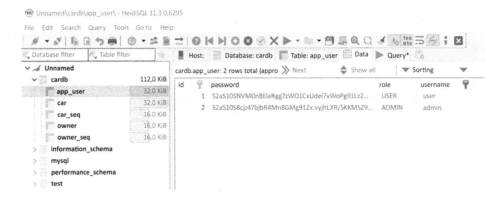

Figure 5.7: Users

10. Now, you should restart the application and you will get a `401 Unauthorized` error if you try to send a `GET` request to the `http://localhost:8080/api` path without authentication. You must authenticate to be able to send a successful request. The difference, when compared with the previous example, is that we are using the users from the database to authenticate.

Now, you can log in by sending a `GET` request to the `/api` endpoint using the browser, or we can use Postman and basic authentication, as shown in the following screenshot:

Figure 5.8: GET request authentication

11. You can see that we currently get users by calling the `api/appUsers` endpoint in our RESTful web service, which is something we want to avoid. As mentioned in *Chapter 4*, Spring Data REST generates a RESTful web service from all public repositories by default. We can use the exported flag of the `@RepositoryRestResource` annotation and set it to `false`, which means the following repository is not exposed as a REST resource:

```
package com.packt.cardatabase.domain;

import java.util.Optional;
import org.springframework.data.repository.CrudRepository;
import org.springframework.data.rest.core.annotation.
```

```
  RepositoryRestResource;

@RepositoryRestResource(exported = false)
public interface AppUserRepository extends CrudRepository
  <AppUser, Long> {
    Optional<AppUser> findByUsername(String username);
  }
```

12. Now, if you restart the application and send a GET request to the /api endpoint, you will
    see that the /appUsers endpoint is not visible anymore.

Next, we will start to implement authentication using a JSON Web Token.

Securing your backend with a JSON Web Token

In the previous section, we covered how to use basic authentication with a RESTful web service.
Basic authentication doesn't provide a way to handle tokens or manage sessions. When a user logs
in, the credentials are sent with each request, which can cause session management challenges
and potential security risks. This method is not usable when we develop our own frontend with
React, so we are going to use **JSON Web Token (JWT)** authentication instead (https://jwt.io/).
This will also give you an idea of how you can configure Spring Security in more detail.

 The other option for securing your RESTful web service is **OAuth 2**. OAuth2 (https://
oauth.net/2/) is the industry standard for authorization and it can be used quite
easily in Spring Boot applications. There is a section later on in the chapter that will
give you a basic idea about how to use it in your applications.

JWTs are commonly used in RESTful APIs for authentication and authorization purposes. They
are a compact way to implement authentication in modern web applications. A JWT is really
small in size and can therefore be sent in the URL, in the POST parameter, or inside the header.
It also contains all the necessary information about the user, such as their username and role.

A JWT contains three different parts, separated by dots: xxxxx.yyyyy.zzzzz. These parts are
broken up as follows:

- The first part (xxxxx) is the **header,** which defines the type of token and the hashing
  algorithm.

- The second part (yyyyy) is the **payload,** which, typically, in the case of authentication,
  contains user information.

- The third part (zzzzz) is the **signature,** which is used to verify that the token hasn't been changed along the way.

Here is an example of a JWT:

```
eyJhbGciOiJIUzI1NiIsInR5cCI6IkpXVCJ9.
eyJzdWIiOiIxMjM0NTY3ODtZSI6IkpvaG4gRG9lIiwiaWF0IjoxNTE2MjM5MDIyfQ.
SflKxwRJSMeKKF2QT4fwpMeJf36POk6yJV_adQssw5c
```

The following diagram shows a simplified representation of the authentication process using a JWT:

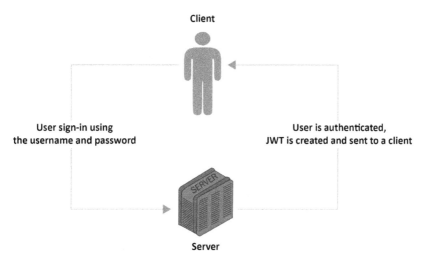

Figure 5.9: JWT authentication process

After successful authentication, the requests sent by the client should always contain the JWT that was received in the authentication.

We will use jjwt (https://github.com/jwtk/jjwt), which is the JWT library for Java and Android for creating and parsing JWTs. Therefore, we have to add the following dependencies to the build.gradle file:

```
dependencies {
    implementation 'org.springframework.boot:spring-boot-starter-web'
    implementation 'org.springframework.boot:spring-boot-starter-data-jpa'
    implementation 'org.springframework.boot:spring-boot-starter-data-rest'
    implementation 'org.springframework.boot:spring-boot-starter-security'
    implementation 'io.jsonwebtoken:jjwt-api:0.11.5'
    runtimeOnly 'io.jsonwebtoken:jjwt-impl:0.11.5', 'io.jsonwebtoken:jjwt-
```

```
    jackson:0.11.5'
developmentOnly 'org.springframework.boot:spring-boot-devtools'
runtimeOnly 'org.mariadb.jdbc:mariadb-java-client'
testImplementation 'org.springframework.boot:spring-boot-starter-test'
testImplementation 'org.springframework.security:spring-security-test'
}
```

 Remember to refresh the Gradle project from Eclipse after you have updated the dependencies.

The following steps demonstrate how to enable JWT authentication in our backend.

Securing the login

We will start with the login functionality:

1. First, we will create a class that generates and verifies a signed JWT. Create a new class called JwtService in the com.packt.cardatabase.service package. At the beginning of the class, we will define a few constants: EXPIRATIONTIME defines the expiration time of the token in milliseconds, PREFIX defines the prefix of the token, and the "Bearer" schema is typically used. A JWT is sent in the Authorization header and the content of the header looks like the following when using the Bearer schema:

    ```
    Authorization: Bearer <token>
    ```

    The JwtService source code looks like the following:

    ```
    package com.packt.cardatabase.service;

    import org.springframework.stereotype.Component;

    @Component
    public class JwtService {
      static final long EXPIRATIONTIME = 86400000;
      // 1 day in ms. Should be shorter in production.
      static final String PREFIX = "Bearer";
    }
    ```

2.   We will create a secret key using the jjwt library's secretKeyFor method. This is only for
     demonstration purposes. In a production environment, you should read your secret key
     from the application configuration. The getToken method then generates and returns the
     token. The getAuthUser method gets the token from the response Authorization header.
     Then, we will use the parserBuilder method provided by the jjwt library to create a
     JwtParserBuilder instance. The setSigningKey method is used to specify a secret key
     for token verification. The parseClaimsJws method removes the Bearer prefix from the
     Authorization header. Finally, we will use the getSubject method to get the username.
     The whole JwtService source code follows:

```java
package com.packt.cardatabase.service;

import io.jsonwebtoken.Jwts;
import io.jsonwebtoken.SignatureAlgorithm;
import io.jsonwebtoken.security.Keys;
import java.security.Key;
import org.springframework.http.HttpHeaders;
import org.springframework.stereotype.Component;
import jakarta.servlet.http.HttpServletRequest;
import java.util.Date;

@Component
public class JwtService {
  static final long EXPIRATIONTIME = 86400000;
  // 1 day in ms. Should be shorter in production.
  static final String PREFIX = "Bearer";

  // Generate secret key. Only for demonstration purposes.
  // In production, you should read it from the application
  // configuration.
  static final Key key = Keys.secretKeyFor (SignatureAlgorithm.
    HS256);

  // Generate signed JWT token
  public String getToken(String username) {
    String token = Jwts.builder()
    .setSubject(username)
    .setExpiration(new Date(System.currentTimeMillis() +
                            EXPIRATIONTIME))
```

```
  .signWith(key)
  .compact();

  return token;
}


// Get a token from request Authorization header,
// verify the token, and get username
public String getAuthUser(HttpServletRequest request) {
  String token = request.getHeader
     (HttpHeaders.AUTHORIZATION);

  if (token != null) {
    String user = Jwts.parserBuilder()
    .setSigningKey(key)
    .build()
    .parseClaimsJws(token.replace(PREFIX, ""))
    .getBody()
    .getSubject();

    if (user != null)
      return user;
  }
  return null;
  }
}
```

3.   Next, we will add a new class to store credentials for authentication. Here we can use a
     Java **record**, which was introduced in Java 14. A record is a good choice if you need a class
     that only holds data; you can avoid a lot of boilerplate code. Create a new record (**New
     | Record**) called AccountCredentials in the com.packt.cardatabase.domain package:

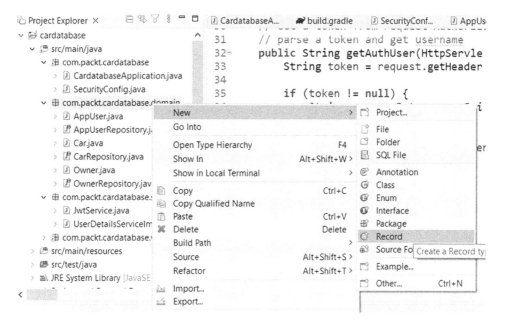

Figure 5.10: Create a new record

The record has two fields: username and password. Here is the source code for the record. As you can see, we don't have to write getters and setters when using it:

```
package com.packt.cardatabase.domain;


public record AccountCredentials(String username, String password)
{}
```

4. Now, we will implement the controller class for login. Login is done by calling the /login endpoint using the POST method and sending the username and password inside the request body. Create a class called LoginController inside the com.packt. cardatabase.web package. We have to inject a JwtService instance into the controller class because that is used to generate a signed JWT in the case of a successful login. The code is illustrated in the following snippet:

```
package com.packt.cardatabase.web;


import org.springframework.http.HttpHeaders;
import org.springframework.http.ResponseEntity;
import org.springframework.security.authentication.
  AuthenticationManager;
```

```java
import org.springframework.security.authentication.
  UsernamePasswordAuthenticationToken;
import org.springframework.security.core.Authentication;
import org.springframework.web.bind.annotation.RequestBody;
import org.springframework.web.bind.annotation.PostMapping;
import org.springframework.web.bind.annotation.RestController;
import com.packt.cardatabase.domain.AccountCredentials;
import com.packt.cardatabase.service.JwtService;

@RestController
public class LoginController {
    private final JwtService jwtService;
    private final AuthenticationManager authenticationManager;

    public LoginController(JwtService jwtService,
      AuthenticationManager authenticationManager) {
        this.jwtService = jwtService;
        this.authenticationManager = authenticationManager;
    }

    @PostMapping("/login")
    public ResponseEntity<?> getToken(@RequestBody
      AccountCredentials credentials) {
    // Generate token and send it in the response Authorization
    // header
    }
}
```

5. Next, we will implement the getToken method that handles the login functionality. We get a JSON object from the request body that contains the username and password. AuthenticationManager is used to perform authentication and it uses credentials that we get from the request. Then, we use the JwtService class' getToken method to generate a JWT. Finally, we build an HTTP response that contains the generated JWT in the Authorization header:

```java
// LoginController.java
@PostMapping("/login")
public ResponseEntity<?> getToken(@RequestBody AccountCredentials
```

```
    credentials) {
      UsernamePasswordAuthenticationToken creds = new
        UsernamePasswordAuthenticationToken(credentials.username(),
                                        credentials.password());
      Authentication auth = authenticationManager.authenticate(creds);

      // Generate token
      String jwts = jwtService.getToken(auth.getName());

      // Build response with the generated token
      return ResponseEntity.ok().header(HttpHeaders.AUTHORIZATION,
                    "Bearer" + jwts).header(HttpHeaders.
                    ACCESS_CONTROL_EXPOSE_HEADERS,
                    "Authorization").build();
  }
```

6. We have also injected `AuthenticationManager` into the `LoginController` class, therefore we have to add the following highlighted code to the `SecurityConfig` class:

```
package com.packt.cardatabase;

import org.springframework.context.annotation.Bean;
import org.springframework.context.annotation.Configuration;
import org.springframework.security.authentication.
  AuthenticationManager;
import org.springframework.security.config.annotation.
  authentication.configuration.AuthenticationConfiguration;
import org.springframework.security.config.annotation.
  authentication.builders.AuthenticationManagerBuilder;
import org.springframework.security.config.annotation.
  authentication.configuration.AuthenticationConfiguration;
import org.springframework.security.config.annotation.web.
  configuration.EnableWebSecurity;
import org.springframework.security.crypto.bcrypt.
  BCryptPasswordEncoder;
import com.packt.cardatabase.service.UserDetailsServiceImpl;

@Configuration
@EnableWebSecurity
```

```java
public class SecurityConfig {
    private final UserDetailsServiceImpl userDetailsService;

    public SecurityConfig(UserDetailsServiceImpl userDetailsService){
        this.userDetailsService = userDetailsService;
    }

    public void configureGlobal(AuthenticationManagerBuilder auth)
      throws Exception {
        auth.userDetailsService(userDetailsService)
          .passwordEncoder(new BCryptPasswordEncoder());
    }

    @Bean
    public PasswordEncoder passwordEncoder() {
        return new BCryptPasswordEncoder();
    }

    @Bean
    public AuthenticationManager uthenticationManager(
      AuthenticationConfiguration authConfig) throws Exception {
        return authConfig.getAuthenticationManager();
    }
}
```

7. In this step, we have to configure Spring Security functionality. Spring Security's SecurityFilterChain bean defines which paths are secured and which are not. Add the following filterChain method to the SecurityConfig class. In the method, we define that the POST method request to the /login endpoint is allowed without authentication and that requests to all other endpoints require authentication. We will also define that Spring Security will never create a session, and therefore we can disable cross-site request forgery (csrf). JWTs are designed to be stateless, which reduces the risk of session-related vulnerabilities. We will use Lambdas in the HTTP security configuration:

 In some other programming languages, Lambdas are called **anonymous functions**. The usage of Lambdas makes code more readable and reduces boilerplate code.

```java
// SecurityConfig.java
// Add the following import
import org.springframework.security.web.SecurityFilterChain;

// Add filterChain method
@Bean
public SecurityFilterChain filterChain(HttpSecurity http) throws
  Exception {
    http.csrf((csrf) -> csrf.disable())
        .sessionManagement((sessionManagement) -> sessionManagement.
            sessionCreationPolicy(SessionCreationPolicy.STATELESS))
        .authorizeHttpRequests((authorizeHttpRequests) ->
            authorizeHttpRequests.requestMatchers(HttpMethod.POST,
            "/login").permitAll().anyRequest().authenticated());

    return http.build();
}
```

8. Finally, we are ready to test our login functionality. Open Postman and make a POST request to the http://localhost:8080/login URL. Define a valid user inside the request body, for example, {"username":"user", "password":"user"} and select **JSON** from the drop-down list. Postman will then set the Content-Type header to application/json automatically. You should check from the **Headers** tab that the Content-Type header is set correctly. Now, you should see an Authorization header in the response that contains the signed JWT, like the one shown in the following screenshot:

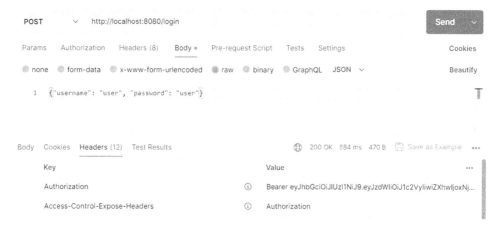

Figure 5.11: Login request

You can also test the login by using the wrong password and seeing that the response doesn't contain the Authorization header.

Securing the other requests

We have now finalized the login step, and we will move on to handling authentication for the rest of the incoming requests. In the authentication process, we are using **filters** that allow us to perform some operations before a request goes to the controller or before a response is sent to a client.

The following steps demonstrate the rest of the authentication process:

1. We will use a filter class to authenticate all other incoming requests. Create a new class called AuthenticationFilter in the root package. The AuthenticationFilter class extends Spring Security's OncePerRequestFilter interface, which provides a doFilterInternal method where we implement our authentication. We have to inject a JwtService instance into the filter class because it is needed to verify a token from the request. The SecurityContextHolder is where Spring Security stores the details of the authenticated user. The code is illustrated in the following snippet:

```
package com.packt.cardatabase;

import org.springframework.http.HttpHeaders;
import org.springframework.security.authentication.
  UsernamePasswordAuthenticationToken;
import org.springframework.security.core.Authentication;
import org.springframework.security.core.context.
  SecurityContextHolder;
import org.springframework.stereotype.Component;
import org.springframework.web.filter.OncePerRequestFilter;

import com.packt.cardatabase.service.JwtService;

import jakarta.servlet.FilterChain;
import jakarta.servlet.ServletException;
import jakarta.servlet.http.HttpServletRequest;
import jakarta.servlet.http.HttpServletResponse;

@Component
public class AuthenticationFilter extends OncePerRequestFilter {
    private final JwtService jwtService;
```

```java
    public AuthenticationFilter(JwtService jwtService) {
        this.jwtService = jwtService;
    }


    @Override
    protected void doFilterInternal(HttpServletRequest request,
            HttpServletResponse response, FilterChain filterChain)
        throws ServletException, java.io.IOException {
        // Get token from the Authorization header
        String jws = request.getHeader(HttpHeaders.AUTHORIZATION);
        if (jws != null) {
            // Verify token and get user
            String user = jwtService.getAuthUser(request);
            // Authenticate
            Authentication authentication =
            new UsernamePasswordAuthenticationToken(user, null,
                java.util.Collections.emptyList());

            SecurityContextHolder.getContext()
                .setAuthentication(authentication);
        }

        filterChain.doFilter(request, response);
    }
}
```

2. Next, we have to add our filter class to the Spring Security configuration. Open the SecurityConfig class and inject the AuthenticationFilter class that we just implemented, as shown in the highlighted code:

```java
private final UserDetailsServiceImpl userDetailsService;
private final AuthenticationFilter authenticationFilter;

public SecurityConfig(UserDetailsServiceImpl userDetailsService,
    AuthenticationFilter authenticationFilter) {
    this.userDetailsService = userDetailsService;
    this.authenticationFilter = authenticationFilter;
}
```

3. Then, modify the `filterChain` method in the `SecurityConfig` class and add the following lines of code:

```
//Add the following import
import org.springframework.security.web.authentication.
  UsernamePasswordAuthenticationFilter;

// Modify the filterChain method
@Bean
public SecurityFilterChain filterChain(HttpSecurity http) throws
  Exception {
    http.csrf((csrf) -> csrf.disable())
        .sessionManagement((sessionManagement) -> sessionManagement.
            sessionCreationPolicy(SessionCreationPolicy.STATELESS))
        .authorizeHttpRequests((authorizeHttpRequests) ->
            authorizeHttpRequests.requestMatchers(HttpMethod.POST,
            "/login").permitAll().anyRequest().authenticated())
        .addFilterBefore(authenticationFilter,
            UsernamePasswordAuthenticationFilter.class);

    return http.build();
}
```

4. Now, we are ready to test the whole workflow. After we run the application, we can first log in by calling the `/login` endpoint with the POST method and, in the case of a successful login, we will receive a JWT in the `Authorization` header. Remember to add a valid user inside the body and set the `Content-Type` header to `application/json` if it is not done automatically by Postman. The following screenshot illustrates the process:

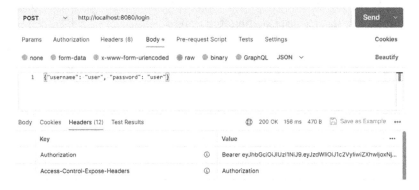

Figure 5.12: Login request

5. Following a successful login, we can call the other RESTful service endpoints by sending the JWT that was received from the login in the `Authorization` header. Copy the token from the login response (without the `Bearer` prefix) and add the `Authorization` header with the token in the `VALUE` column. Refer to the example in the following screenshot where a `GET` request to the `/cars` endpoint is done:

Figure 5.13: Authenticated GET request

 Each time the application is restarted, you must authenticate again because a new JWT is generated.

The JWT is not valid forever because an expiration date was set for it. In our case, we set a long expiration time for demonstration purposes. In production, the time should preferably be minutes, depending on the use case.

Handling exceptions

We should also handle exceptions in the authentication. At the moment, if you try to log in using the wrong password, you get a `403 Forbidden` status without any further clarification. Spring Security provides an `AuthenticationEntryPoint` interface that can be used to handle exceptions. Let's see how it works:

1. Create a new class named `AuthEntryPoint` in the root package that implements `AuthenticationEntryPoint`. We will implement the commence method, which gets an exception as a parameter. In the case of an exception, we set the response status to 401 Unauthorized and write an exception message to the response body. The code is illustrated in the following snippet:

```java
package com.packt.cardatabase;

import java.io.IOException;
import java.io.PrintWriter;
import jakarta.servlet.ServletException;
import jakarta.servlet.http.HttpServletRequest;
import jakarta.servlet.http.HttpServletResponse;
import org.springframework.http.MediaType;
import org.springframework.security.core.
  AuthenticationException;
import org.springframework.security.web.
  AuthenticationEntryPoint;
import org.springframework.stereotype.Component;

@Component
public class AuthEntryPoint implements AuthenticationEntryPoint {
  @Override
  public void commence(
    HttpServletRequest request, HttpServletResponse response,
    AuthenticationException authException) throws IOException,
    ServletException {
        response.setStatus (HttpServletResponse.SC_UNAUTHORIZED);
        response.setContentType (MediaType.APPLICATION_JSON_VALUE);
        PrintWriter writer = response.getWriter();
        writer.println("Error: " + authException.getMessage());
  }
}
```

2. Then, we have to configure Spring Security for the exception handling. Inject our AuthEntryPoint class into the SecurityConfig class, as shown in the following highlighted code:

```
// SecurityConfig.java
private final UserDetailsServiceImpl userDetailsService;
private final AuthenticationFilter authenticationFilter;
private final AuthEntryPoint exceptionHandler;

public SecurityConfig(UserDetailsServiceImpl userDetailsService,
    AuthenticationFilter authenticationFilter, AuthEntryPoint
    exceptionHandler) {
        this.userDetailsService = userDetailsService;
        this.authenticationFilter = authenticationFilter;
        this.exceptionHandler = exceptionHandler;
}
```

3. Then, modify the filterChain method as follows:

```
// SecurityConfig.java
@Bean
public SecurityFilterChain filterChain(HttpSecurity http) throws
    Exception {
        http.csrf((csrf) -> csrf.disable())
            .sessionManagement((sessionManagement) ->
                sessionManagement.sessionCreationPolicy(
                SessionCreationPolicy.STATELESS))
            .authorizeHttpRequests((authorizeHttpRequests) ->
                authorizeHttpRequests.requestMatchers(HttpMethod.POST,
                "/login").permitAll().anyRequest().authenticated())
            .addFilterBefore(authenticationFilter,
                UsernamePasswordAuthenticationFilter.class)
            .exceptionHandling((exceptionHandling) -> exceptionHandling.
                authenticationEntryPoint(exceptionHandler));
        return http.build();
}
```

4. Now, if you send a login POST request with the wrong credentials, you will get a 401 Unauthorized status in the response and an error message in the body, as shown in the following screenshot:

Figure 5.14: Bad credentials

Adding a CORS filter

We will also add a **cross-origin resource sharing (CORS)** filter to our security configuration class. CORS introduces certain headers that help the client and server decide if cross-origin requests should be allowed or denied. The CORS filter is needed for the frontend, which is sending requests from the other origin. The CORS filter intercepts requests, and if these are identified as cross-origin, it adds proper headers to the request. For that, we will use Spring Security's CorsConfigurationSource interface.

In this example, we will allow all origins' HTTP methods and headers. You can define a list of permissible origins, methods, and headers here if you require a more finely graded definition. Let's begin:

1. Add the following imports and methods to your SecurityConfig class to enable the CORS filter:

```
// SecurityConfig.java
// Add the following imports
import java.util.Arrays;
import org.springframework.web.cors.CorsConfiguration;
import org.springframework.web.cors.CorsConfigurationSource;
import org.springframework.web.cors.UrlBasedCorsConfigurationSource;
```

```java
// Add Global CORS filter inside the class
@Bean
public CorsConfigurationSource corsConfigurationSource() {
    UrlBasedCorsConfigurationSource source =
      new UrlBasedCorsConfigurationSource();
    CorsConfiguration config = new CorsConfiguration();
    config.setAllowedOrigins(Arrays.asList("*"));
    config.setAllowedMethods(Arrays.asList("*"));
    config.setAllowedHeaders(Arrays.asList("*"));
    config.setAllowCredentials(false);
    config.applyPermitDefaultValues();

    source.registerCorsConfiguration("/**", config);
    return source;
}
```

If you want to explicitly define the origins, you can set this in the following way:

```java
// localhost:3000 is allowed
config.setAllowedOrigins(Arrays.asList ("http://localhost:3000"));
```

2. We also have to add the `cors()` function to the `filterChain` method, as shown in the following code snippet:

```java
// SecurityConfig.java
// Add the following static import
import static org.springframework.security.config.Customizer.
  withDefaults;

// Modify filterChain method
@Bean
public SecurityFilterChain filterChain(HttpSecurity http) throws
  Exception {
    http.csrf((csrf) -> csrf.disable())
        .cors(withDefaults())
        .sessionManagement((sessionManagement) -> sessionManagement.
            sessionCreationPolicy(SessionCreationPolicy.STATELESS))
        .authorizeHttpRequests((authorizeHttpRequests) ->
            authorizeHttpRequests.requestMatchers(HttpMethod.POST,
            "/login").permitAll().anyRequest().authenticated())
```

```
        .addFilterBefore(authenticationFilter,
            UsernamePasswordAuthenticationFilter.class)
        .exceptionHandling((exceptionHandling) -> exceptionHandling.
            authenticationEntryPoint(exceptionHandler));

    return http.build();
}
```

Now, we have secured our backend. In the next section, we will introduce the basics of role-based security, which you can use to get more fine-grained access control in your Spring Boot application.

Role-based security

In Spring Security, **roles** can be used to define coarse-grained role-based security, and users can be assigned to one or multiple roles. Roles often have a hierarchical structure, for example, ADMIN, MANAGER, USER. Spring Security also provides **authorities**, which can be used for more fine-grained access control. We have defined simple roles for our users, ADMIN and USER, and we don't use role-based security in our sample backend application. This section introduces the different ways to implement role-based security in your Spring Boot applications.

You can define role-based access control at the request level in your security configuration class. In the following example code, we define which endpoints require specific roles for access. The /admin/** endpoint requires the ADMIN role for access and the /user/** endpoint requires the USER role for access. We use the Spring Security hasRole() method, which returns true if the user has the specified role:

```
@Bean
public SecurityFilterChain filterChain(HttpSecurity http) throws
  Exception {
    http.csrf((csrf) -> csrf.disable()).cors(withDefaults())
        .sessionManagement((sessionManagement) -> sessionManagement.
            sessionCreationPolicy(SessionCreationPolicy.STATELESS))
        .authorizeHttpRequests((authorizeHttpRequests) ->
            authorizeHttpRequests.requestMatchers("/admin/**").hasRole
            ("ADMIN").requestMatchers("/user/**").hasRole("USER")
            .anyRequest().authenticated())

    return http.build();
}
```

You can read more about request authorization in the Spring Boot documentation: `https://docs.spring.io/spring-security/reference/servlet/authorization/authorize-http-requests.html`.

Spring Security provides the @PreAuthorize, @PostAuthorize, @PreFilter, @PostFilter, and @Secured annotations, which are used to apply **method-level security**. Method-level security is not enabled by default in `spring-boot-starter-security`. You have to enable it in your Spring configuration class, for example, in top-level configuration, by using the @EnableMethodSecurity annotation:

```
import org.springframework.boot.CommandLineRunner;
import org.springframework.boot.SpringApplication;
import org.springframework.boot.autoconfigure.SpringBootApplication;
import org.springframework.security.config.annotation.method.
  configuration.EnableMethodSecurity;

@SpringBootApplication
@EnableMethodSecurity
public class CardatabaseApplication implements CommandLineRunner {
}
```

Then, you will be able to use the method-level security annotations in your methods. In the following example, users with the USER role can execute the updateCar() method and users with the ADMIN role can execute the deleteOwner() method. The @PreAuthorize annotation checks the rule before the method is executed. If the user does not have a specified role, Spring Security prevents method execution, and an AccessDeniedException is thrown:

```
@Service
public class CarService {
    @PreAuthorize("hasRole('USER')")
    public void updateCar(Car car) {
        // This method can be invoked by user with USER role.
    }

    @PreAuthorize("hasRole('ADMIN')")
    public void deleteOwner(Car car) {
        // This method can be invoked by user with ADMIN role.
    }
}
```

The @PreAuthorize annotation replaces the @Secured annotation, and its use is recommended instead.

The @PostAuthorize annotation can be used to check authorization after the method is executed. You can use this, for example, to check that the user has permission to access the object that the method returns, or you can filter the data returned based on the user's authorization.

The @PreFilter and @PostFilter annotations can be used to filter lists of objects, but they are not typically used for role-based access control. The rules used with these annotations are more fine-grained.

You can read more about method security in the Spring Security documentation: https://docs.spring.io/spring-security/reference/servlet/authorization/method-security.html.

In the next section, we will introduce the basics of OAuth with Spring Boot.

Using OAuth2 with Spring Boot

It is really challenging to implement fully secure authentication and authorization in your application. In a production environment, it is recommended that you do it using an OAuth2 provider. This actually simplifies the authentication process, and providers typically have excellent security practices.

These are not detailed instructions for implementing OAuth 2.0 authorization, but they will give you an idea of the process.

OAuth (Open Authorization) is a standard for secure access to protected resources on the internet. The OAuth standard version 2.0 is commonly used nowadays. There are several OAuth 2.0 providers that implement OAuth authorization for third-party applications. Some common providers are listed here:

- Auth0: https://auth0.com/
- Okta: https://www.okta.com/
- Keycloak: https://www.keycloak.org/

You can implement social logins using OAuth2, after which users can log in with their existing credentials from social media platforms such as Facebook. OAuth also defines mechanisms for revoking access tokens and handling token expiration.

If you want to use OAuth in your Spring Boot applications, the first step is to select an OAuth provider. All providers in the list above can be used with your Spring Boot applications.

In the OAuth2 process, the term **resource owner** refers typically to an end user and the **authorization server** is part of the OAuth provider's service. The **client** is an application that wants to get access to protected resources. The **resource server** commonly refers to an API that the client wants to use.

The simplified version of the OAuth2 authentication process with a REST API contains the following steps:

1. Authentication: The third-party application authenticates by requesting access to protected resources.

2. Authorization: The resource owner authorizes access to their resources, commonly through user login.

3. The authorization server authorizes the resource owner and redirects the user back to the client with an authorization code.

4. The client requests an access token from the authorization server using the authorization code. The access token format is not specified in the standard, and JWTs are quite commonly used.

5. The authorization server validates the access token. If the token is valid, the client application receives an access token.

6. The client can start to use the access token to access protected resources, for example, calling REST API endpoints.

After you have selected a provider and know how its service works, you have to configure your Spring Boot application. Spring Boot provides the `spring-boot-starter-oauth2-client` dependency for OAuth2 authentication and authorization. It is used to simplify OAuth 2.0 integration in your Spring Boot application. Quite a few OAuth providers have documentation for different technologies, such as Spring Boot.

The implementation will differ depending on the provider. Here are some useful links:

*   Auth0 has a good tutorial for how to add login to your Spring Boot application: `https://auth0.com/docs/quickstart/webapp/java-spring-boot/interactive`.

*   Baeldung provides a quick guide to using Keycloak with Spring Boot applications: `https://www.baeldung.com/spring-boot-keycloak`.

*   Spring also has a tutorial on how to implement social login using GitHub: `https://spring.io/guides/tutorials/spring-boot-oauth2`.

We recommend reading these to get a better idea of using OAuth 2.0 in your own applications.

Now, we have finished securing our backend using the JWT, and we will use this version when we start to develop our frontend.

Summary

In this chapter, we focused on making our Spring Boot backend more secure. We started by adding extra protection using Spring Security. Then, we implemented JWT authentication. JWTs are commonly used to secure RESTful APIs and it is a lightweight authentication method suitable for our needs. We also covered the basics of the OAuth 2.0 standard and how to start using it in your Spring Boot application.

In the next chapter, we will learn the basics of testing in Spring Boot applications.

Questions

1. What is Spring Security?
2. How can you secure your backend with Spring Boot?
3. What is a JWT?
4. How can you secure your backend with a JWT?
5. What is OAuth 2.0?

Further reading

Packt has other resources available for you to learn about Spring Security. For instance:

-   *Spring Security Core: Beginner to Guru,* by John Thompson (`https://www.packtpub.com/product/spring-security-core-beginner-to-guru-video/9781800560000`)

Learn more on Discord

To join the Discord community for this book – where you can share feedback, ask the author questions, and learn about new releases – follow the QR code below:

`https://packt.link/FullStackSpringBootReact4e`

6

Testing Your Backend

This chapter explains how to test your Spring Boot backend. The backend of an application is responsible for handling business logic and data storage. Proper testing of the backend ensures that the application works as intended, is secure, and is easier to maintain. We will create some unit and integration tests in relation to our backend, using the database application that we created earlier as a starting point.

In this chapter, we will cover the following topics:

- Testing in Spring Boot
- Creating test cases
- Test-driven development

Technical requirements

The Spring Boot application that we created in the previous chapters is required.

The following GitHub link will also be required: https://github.com/PacktPublishing/Full-Stack-Development-with-Spring-Boot-3-and-React-Fourth-Edition/tree/main/Chapter06.

Testing in Spring Boot

The Spring Boot test starter package is automatically added to the build.gradle file by **Spring Initializr** when we create our project. The test starter dependency can be seen in the following snippet:

```
testImplementation 'org.springframework.boot:spring-boot-starter-test'
```

The Spring Boot test starter provides lots of handy libraries for testing, such as **JUnit**, **Mockito**, and **AssertJ**. Mockito is a mocking framework that is often used alongside testing frameworks like JUnit. AssertJ is a popular library for writing assertions in Java testing. In this book, we will use **JUnit 5**. The **JUnit Jupiter** module is part of JUnit 5 and provides annotations for more flexible testing.

If you take a look at your project structure, you'll see that it already has its own package created for test classes:

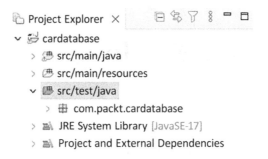

Figure 6.1: Test classes

By default, Spring Boot uses an in-memory database for testing. We are using **MariaDB** at this point in the book, but we can use H2 for testing if we add the following dependency to the build.gradle file:

```
testRuntimeOnly 'com.h2database:h2'
```

This specifies that the H2 database will only be used to run tests; otherwise, the application will use the MariaDB database.

 Remember to refresh your Gradle project in Eclipse after you have updated the build.gradle file.

Now, we can start to create test cases for our application.

Creating test cases

There are many different types of software tests, and each has its own specific objectives. Some of the most important test types are:

- **Unit tests**: Unit tests focus on the smallest component of software. This could be, for example, a function, and a unit test will ensure that it works correctly *in isolation*. **Mocking** is often used in unit testing to replace the dependencies of the unit that is being tested.

- **Integration tests**: Integration tests focus on the interaction between individual components, ensuring that individual components work together as expected.

- **Functional tests**: Functional testing focuses on business scenarios that are defined in functional specifications. Test cases are designed to verify that software meets the specified requirements.

- **Regression tests**: Regression tests are designed to verify that new code or code updates do not break existing functionality.

- **Usability tests**: Usability tests verify that software is user-friendly, intuitive, and easy to use from an end-user perspective. Usability tests focus more on the frontend and user experience.

For unit and integration testing, we are using **JUnit**, a popular Java-based unit testing library. Spring Boot has built-in support for JUnit, making it easy to write tests for your application.

The following source code shows an example skeleton for the Spring Boot test class. The @SpringBootTest annotation specifies that the class is a regular test class that runs Spring Boot-based tests. The @Test annotation before the method specifies to JUnit that the method can be run as a test case:

```
@SpringBootTest
public class MyTestsClass {
    @Test
    public void testMethod() {
        // Test case code
    }
}
```

Assertions in unit testing are statements that can be used to verify whether the actual output of a code unit matches the expected output. In our case, the assertions are implemented using the **AssertJ** library that the spring-boot-starter-test artifact automatically includes. The AssertJ library provides an assertThat() method that you can use to write assertions. You pass an object or a value to the method, allowing you to compare values with the actual assertions. The AssertJ library contains multiple assertions for different data types. The next sample demonstrates some example assertions:

```
// String assertion
assertThat("Learn Spring Boot").startsWith("Learn");
// Object assertion
```

```
assertThat(myObject).isNotNull();
// Number assertion
assertThat(myNumberVariable).isEqualTo(3);
// Boolean assertion
assertThat(myBooleanVariable).isTrue();
```

 You can find all the different assertions in the AssertJ documentation: `https://assertj.github.io/doc`.

We will now create our initial unit test case, which checks that our controller instance is correctly instantiated and is not null. Proceed as follows:

1. Open the `CardatabaseApplicationTests` test class that has already been made for your application by the Spring Initializr starter project. There is one test method called `contextLoads` in here, and this is where we will add the test. Write the following test, which checks that the instance of the controller was created and injected successfully. We use an AssertJ assertion to test that the injected controller instance is not null:

    ```java
    package com.packt.cardatabase;

    import static org.assertj.core.api.Assertions.assertThat;
    import org.junit.jupiter.api.Test;
    import org.springframework.beans.factory.annotation.Autowired;
    import org.springframework.boot.test.context.SpringBootTest;
    import com.packt.cardatabase.web.CarController;

    @SpringBootTest
    class CardatabaseApplicationTests {
        @Autowired
        private CarController controller;

        @Test
        void contextLoads() {
            assertThat(controller).isNotNull();
        }

    }
    ```

We use **field injection** here, which is well-suited for test classes because you will never instantiate your test classes directly. You can read more about dependency injection of test fixtures in the Spring documentation: `https://docs.spring.io/spring-framework/reference/testing/testcontext-framework/fixture-di.html`.

2. To run tests in Eclipse, activate the test class in the **Project Explorer** and right-click. Select **Run As | JUnit test** from the menu. You should now see the **JUnit** tab in the lower part of the Eclipse workbench. The test results are shown in this tab, and the test case has been passed, as illustrated in the following screenshot:

Figure 6.2: JUnit test run

3. You can use the `@DisplayName` annotation to give a more descriptive name to your test case. The name defined in the `@DisplayName` annotation is shown in the JUnit test runner. The code is illustrated in the following snippet:

```
@Test
@DisplayName("First example test case")
void contextLoads() {
    assertThat(controller).isNotNull();
}
```

Now, we will create integration tests for our owner repository to test **create**, **read**, **update**, and **delete** (**CRUD**) operations. This test verifies that our repository interacts correctly with a database. The idea is to simulate database interactions and verify that your repository methods behave as expected:

1. Create a new class called `OwnerRepositoryTest` in the root test package. Instead of the `@SpringBootTest` annotation, the `@DataJpaTest` annotation can be used if the test is focused on **Jakarta Persistence API (JPA)** components. When using this annotation, the H2 database and Spring Data are automatically configured for testing. SQL logging is also turned on. The code is illustrated in the following snippet:

```
package com.packt.cardatabase;

import static org.assertj.core.api.Assertions.assertThat;
```

```
import org.junit.jupiter.api.Test;
import org.springframework.beans.factory.annotation.Autowired;
import org.springframework.boot.test.autoconfigure.orm.jpa.
DataJpaTest;
import com.packt.cardatabase.domain.Owner;
import com.packt.cardatabase.domain.OwnerRepository;

@DataJpaTest
class OwnerRepositoryTest {
    @Autowired
    private OwnerRepository repository;
}
```

 In this example, we use the root package for all test classes and name our classes logically. Alternatively, you can create a similar package structure for your test classes as we did for our application classes.

2. We will add our first test case to test the addition of a new owner to the database. Add the following query to your OwnerRepository.java file. We will use this query in our test case:

```
Optional<Owner> findByFirstname(String firstName);
```

3. A new Owner object is created and saved to the database using the save method. Then, we check that the owner can be found. Add the following test case method code to your OwnerRepositoryTest class:

```
@Test
void saveOwner() {
    repository.save(new Owner("Lucy", "Smith"));
    assertThat(
        repository.findByFirstname("Lucy").isPresent()
    ).isTrue();
}
```

4. The second test case will test the deletion of the owner from the database. A new Owner object is created and saved to the database. Then, all owners are deleted from the database, and finally, the count() method should return zero. The following source code shows the test case method. Add the following method code to your OwnerRepositoryTest class:

```
@Test
void deleteOwners() {
    repository.save(new Owner("Lisa", "Morrison"));
    repository.deleteAll();
    assertThat(repository.count()).isEqualTo(0);
}
```

5. Run the test cases and check the Eclipse **JUnit** tab to find out whether the tests passed.
    The following screenshot shows that they have indeed passed:

Figure 6.3: Repository test cases

Next, we will demonstrate how to test your RESTful web service JWT authentication functionality.
We will create an integration test that sends an actual HTTP request to the login endpoint and
verifies the response:

1. Create a new class called `CarRestTest` in the root test package. To test the controllers or
    any endpoint that is exposed, we can use a `MockMvc` object. By using the `MockMvc` object,
    the server is not started, but the tests are performed in the layer where Spring handles
    HTTP requests, and therefore it mocks the real situation. `MockMvc` provides the `perform`
    method to send these requests. To test authentication, we have to add credentials to the
    request body. We print request and response details to the console using the `andDo()`
    method. Finally, we check that the response status is `Ok` using the `andExpect()` method.
    The code is illustrated in the following snippet:

    ```
    package com.packt.cardatabase;

    import static org.springframework.test.web.servlet.
    request.MockMvcRequestBuilders.post;
    import static org.springframework.test.web.
    servlet.result.MockMvcResultHandlers.print;
    import static org.springframework.test.web.servlet.result.
    MockMvcResultMatchers.status;
    import org.junit.jupiter.api.Test;
    import org.springframework.beans.factory.annotation.Autowired;
    ```

```java
import org.springframework.boot.test.autoconfigure.web.servlet.
AutoConfigureMockMvc;
import org.springframework.boot.test.context.SpringBootTest;
import org.springframework.http.HttpHeaders;
import org.springframework.test.web.servlet.MockMvc;

@SpringBootTest
@AutoConfigureMockMvc
class CarRestTest {
    @Autowired
    private MockMvc mockMvc;

    @Test
    public void testAuthentication() throws Exception {
    // Testing authentication with correct credentials
        this.mockMvc
            .perform(post("/login")
            .content("{\"username\":\"admin\",\"password\""
                    +":\"admin\"}")
            .header(HttpHeaders.CONTENT_TYPE,"application/json"))
            .andDo(print()).andExpect(status().isOk());
    }
}
```

2. Now, when we run the authentication tests, we will see that the test passes, as the following screenshot confirms:

Figure 6.4: Login test

3. You can run all tests at once by selecting the test package from the Project Explorer and running the JUnit tests (**Run As | JUnit test**). In the image below, you can see the result when all test cases have been passed:

Figure 6.5: Running tests

Testing with Gradle

All tests run automatically when you build your project using Gradle. We will go into more detail about building and deployment later in this book. In this section, we will only cover some basics:

1. You can run different predefined Gradle tasks using Eclipse. Open the **Window | Show View | Other...** Menu. That opens the **Show View** window, where you should select **Gradle Tasks**:

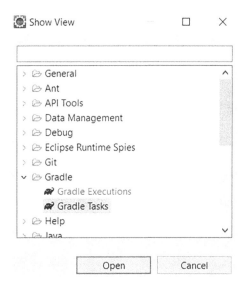

Figure 6.6: Gradle tasks

2. You should see the list of Gradle tasks, as shown in the following image. Open the `build` folder and double-click the **build** task to run it:

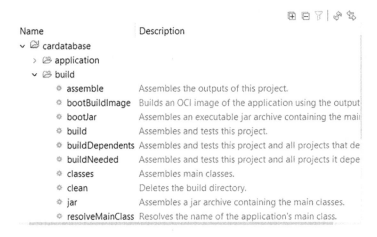

Figure 6.7: Build task

The Gradle build task creates a `build` folder in your project, where your Spring Boot project is built. The build process runs all the tests from your project. If any of the tests fail, the build process also fails. The build process creates a test summary report (an `index.html` file), which you can find in the `build\reports\tests\test` folder. If any of your tests fail, you can find the reason from the summary report. In the image below, you can see an example of a test summary report:

Figure 6.8: Test summary

3. The build task creates an executable `jar` file in the `\build\libs` folder. You can now run your built Spring Boot application using the following command in the `\build\libs` folder (you should have the JDK installed):

```
java -jar .\cardatabase-0.0.1-SNAPSHOT.jar
```

Now, you can write unit and integration tests for your Spring Boot application. You have also learned how to run tests using the Eclipse IDE.

Test-driven development

Test-driven development (TDD) is a practice in software development where you write tests before writing the actual code. The idea is to ensure that your code meets the criteria or requirements that are set. Let's see one example of how TDD works in practice.

Our goal is to implement a service class that manages messages in our application. You can see the common steps of TDD below:

 The following code is not fully functioning. It is just an example for you to get a better idea of the TDD process.

1. The first functionality to be implemented is a service that can be used to add new messages. Therefore, in TDD, we will create a test for adding new messages to a list of messages. In the test code, we first create an instance of the message service class. Then, we create a test message that we want to add to the list. We call the addMsg method of the messageService instance, passing the msg as an argument. This method is responsible for adding messages to a list. Finally, the assertion checks if the message added to the list matches the expected message, "Hello world":

```
import org.junit.jupiter.api.Test;
import org.springframework.boot.test.context.SpringBootTest;
import static org.junit.jupiter.api.Assertions.assertEquals;

@SpringBootTest
public class MessageServiceTest {

    @Test
    public void testAddMessage() {
        MessageService messageService = new MessageService();
        String msg = "Hello world";

        Message newMsg = messageService.addMsg(msg);
```

```
            assertEquals(msg, newMsg.getMessage());
        }
    }
```

2.   Now, we can run the test. It should fail because we haven't implemented our service yet.

3.   Next, we will implement the `MessageService`, which should contain the `addMsg()` function that we are testing in our test case:

```
@Service
public class MessageService {
    private List<Message> messages = new ArrayList<>();

    public Message addMsg(String msg) {
        Message newMsg = new Message(msg);
        messages.add(newMSg);
        return newMsg;
    }
}
```

4.   Now, if you run the test again, it should pass if your code works as expected.

5.   If the test does not pass, you should refactor your code until it does.

6.   Repeat these steps for each new feature.

TDD is an iterative process that helps to ensure that your code works and that new features don't break other parts of the software. This is also called **regression testing**. By writing a test before implementing the functionality, we can catch bugs early in the development phase. Developers should understand feature requirements and expected outcomes before actual development.

At this point, we have covered the basics of testing in Spring Boot applications, and you have gained the knowledge you need to implement more test cases for your applications.

Summary

In this chapter, we focused on testing the Spring Boot backend. We used JUnit for testing and implemented test cases for JPA and RESTful web service authentication. We created one test case for our owner repository to verify that repository methods behave as expected. We also tested the authentication process by using our RESTful API. Remember that testing is an ongoing process throughout the development life cycle. You should update and add tests to cover new features and changes when your application evolves. Test-driven development is one way of doing this.

In the next chapter, we will set up the environment and tools related to frontend development.

Questions

1. How can you create unit tests with Spring Boot?

2. What is the difference between unit and integration tests?

3. How can you run and check the results of unit tests?

4. What is TDD?

Further reading

There are many other good resources available to learn about Spring Security and testing. A few are listed here:

- *JUnit and Mockito Unit Testing for Java Developers*, by Matthew Speake (`https://www.packtpub.com/product/junit-and-mockito-unit-testing-for-java-developers-video/9781801078337`)

- *Mastering Software Testing with JUnit 5*, by Boni García (`https://www.packtpub.com/product/mastering-software-testing-with-junit-5/9781787285736`)

- *Java Programming MOOC: Introduction to testing*, by the University of Helsinki (`https://java-programming.mooc.fi/part-6/3-introduction-to-testing`)

- *Master Java Unit Testing with Spring Boot and Mockito*, by In28Minutes Official (`https://www.packtpub.com/product/master-java-unit-testing-with-spring-boot-and-mockito-video/9781789346077`)

Learn more on Discord

To join the Discord community for this book – where you can share feedback, ask the author questions, and learn about new releases – follow the QR code below:

`https://packt.link/FullStackSpringBootReact4e`

Part II

Frontend Programming with React

7

Setting Up the Environment and Tools – Frontend

This chapter describes the development environment and tools that are needed for React so that you can start frontend development. In this chapter, we will create a simple starter React app by using the Vite frontend tooling.

In this chapter, we will cover the following topics:

- Installing Node.js
- Installing Visual Studio Code
- Creating and running a React app
- Debugging a React app

Technical requirements

The following GitHub link will be required: https://github.com/PacktPublishing/Full-Stack-Development-with-Spring-Boot-3-and-React-Fourth-Edition/tree/main/Chapter07.

Installing Node.js

Node.js is an open-source, JavaScript-based, server-side environment. It is available for multiple operating systems, such as Windows, macOS, and Linux, and is required to develop React apps.

The Node.js installation package can be found at https://nodejs.org/en/download/. Download the latest **Long-Term Support (LTS)** version for your operating system. In this book, we are using the Windows 10 operating system, and you can get the Node.js MSI installer for it, which makes installation really straightforward.

When you execute the installer, you will go through the installation wizard, and you can do so using the default settings:

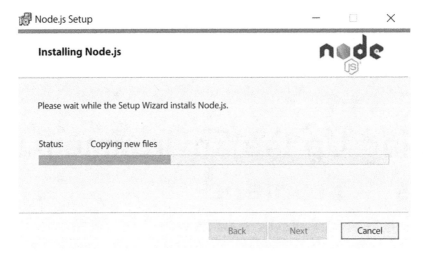

Figure 7.1: Node.js installation

Once the installation is complete, we can check that everything proceeded correctly. Open PowerShell, or whatever terminal you are using, and type the following commands:

```
node --version
npm --version
```

These commands should show you the installed versions of Node.js and npm:

```
PS C:\> node --version
v18.16.0
PS C:\> npm --version
9.2.0
PS C:\>
```

Figure 7.2: Node.js and npm versions

npm comes with the Node.js installation and is a package manager for JavaScript. We will use this a lot in the following chapters when we install different Node.js modules in our React app.

 There is another package manager called **Yarn** that you can use as well, but we will use npm because it comes with the Node.js installation. Yarn has some advantages, such as better overall performance due to its caching mechanism.

Next, we will install a code editor.

Installing Visual Studio Code

Visual Studio Code (VS Code) is an open-source code editor for multiple programming languages. It was developed by Microsoft. There are many different code editors available, such as Atom and Sublime, and you can use something other than VS Code if you are familiar with it.

 Eclipse, which we used for backend development, is optimized for Java development. VS Code can also be used for Java and Spring Boot development, so it is possible to use only one editor for both backend and frontend development if you prefer.

VS Code is available for Windows, macOS, and Linux, and you can download it from `https://code.visualstudio.com/`. Installation for Windows is done with the MSI installer, and you can execute the installation with default settings.

The following screenshot shows the workbench for VS Code. On the left-hand side is the activity bar, which you can use to navigate between different views. Next to the activity bar is a sidebar that contains different views, such as the project file explorer. The editor takes up the rest of the workbench:

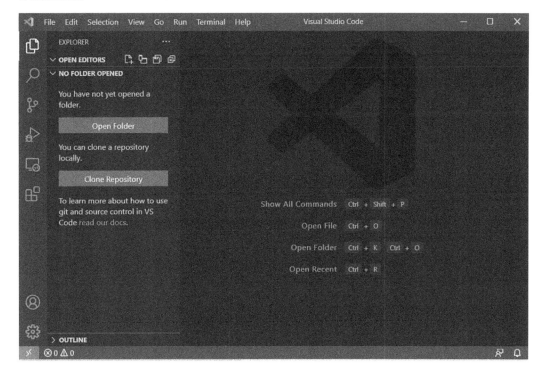

Figure 7.3: VS Code workbench

VS Code provides an integrated terminal that you can use to create and run React apps. The terminal can be found in the **View | Terminal** menu. You can use this in later chapters when we create more React apps.

VS Code extensions

There are a lot of extensions available for different programming languages and frameworks. If you open **Extensions** from the activity bar, you can search for different ones.

One really useful extension for React development is **Reactjs code snippets**, which we recommend installing. It has multiple code snippets available for React.js apps, which makes the development process faster. VS Code code snippet extensions can significantly enhance your workflow by saving time, promoting consistency, and reducing errors.

The following screenshot shows the Reactjs code snippets installation page:

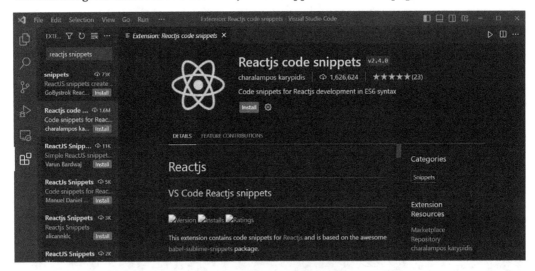

Figure 7.4: React js code snippets

The **ESLint** extension helps you find typos and syntax errors quickly and makes formatting source code easier:

Figure 7.5: ESLint extension

ESLint (`https://eslint.org/`) is an open-source linter for JavaScript, and it helps you to find and fix problems in your source code. ESLint can highlight errors and warnings directly within the VS Code editor to help you identify and fix issues as you write code. Errors and warnings are shown in red or yellow underlines, and if you hover over these lines, you can see information about the specific error or warning. VS Code also provides a **Problems** panel that shows all ESLint errors and warnings. ESLint is flexible, and it can be configured using the `.eslintrc` file. You can define which rules are enabled and at what error level.

Prettier is a code formatter. With the Prettier extension, you can get automatic code formatting:

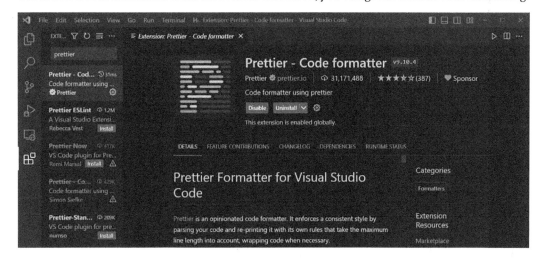

Figure 7.6: Prettier extension

You can set it in VS Code so that code is formatted automatically after you save it, by going to **Settings** from the **File | Preferences** menu and then searching for **Format On Save**.

These are just a few examples of the great extensions you can get for VS Code. We recommend you install all of them and test them out yourself.

In the next section, we will create our first React app and learn how to run and modify it.

Creating and running a React app

Now that we have Node.js and our code editor installed, we are ready to create our first React.js app. We will use the **Vite** frontend tool (https://vitejs.dev/) for this. There are excellent React frameworks available, like Next.js or Remix, that can be used as well, but Vite is a good option to learn React basics. Vite provides a really fast development server, and you don't have to do any complex configuration to start coding.

In the past, **Create React App** (CRA) was the most popular tool for creating React projects, but its usage has decreased, and it is no longer recommended by official documentation. Vite offers many advantages over CRA (such as its faster development server).

 We are using Vite version 4.3 in this book. You should verify the commands against the Vite documentation if you are using some other version. Also, check the Node.js version requirements, and upgrade your Node.js installation if your package manager warns you about it.

Here are the steps you need to follow to make your first React project using Vite:

1. Open PowerShell, or another terminal that you are using, and move to a folder where you want to create your project.

2. Type the following npm command, which uses the latest version of Vite:

```
npm create vite@latest
```

To use the same Vite major version that we are using in this book, you can also specify the Vite version in the command:

```
npm create vite@4.3
```

The command starts the project creation wizard. If this is the first time you are creating a Vite project, you will get a message prompting you to install the create-vite package. Press *y* to proceed.

3. In the first phase, type your project name – in this case, myapp:

```
PS C:\> npm create vite@latest
? Project name: » myapp
```

Figure 7.7: Project name

4. Then, you will select a **framework**. In this phase, select the **React** framework. Note that Vite isn't tied to React and can be used to bootstrap projects in lots of different frontend frameworks:

```
PS C:\> npm create vite@latest
√ Project name: ... myapp
? Select a framework: » - Use arrow-keys. Return to submit.
    Vanilla
    Vue
>   React
    Preact
    Lit
    Svelte
    Others
```

Figure 7.8: Framework selection

5. In the final step, you will select a **variant**. We'll first learn the basics of React with JavaScript and later move on to TypeScript. So, in this phase, we will select **JavaScript**:

```
PS C:\> npm create vite@latest
√ Project name: ...  myapp
√ Select a framework: » React
? Select a variant: » - Use arrow-keys. Return to submit.
>   JavaScript
    TypeScript
    JavaScript + SWC
    TypeScript + SWC
```

Figure 7.9: Project variant

 SWC (Speedy Web Compiler) is a fast JavaScript and TypeScript compiler written in Rust. It is a faster alternative to Babel, which is normally used.

6. Once the app has been created, move into your app folder:

```
cd myapp
```

7. Then, install dependencies using the following command:

```
npm install
```

8. Finally, run your app using the following command, which starts the app in development mode:

```
npm run dev
```

Now, you should see the following message in your terminal:

Figure 7.10: Run your project

9. Open your browser and navigate to the URL that is shown in your terminal after the **Local:** text (in the example, it is http://localhost:5173/, but it might be different in your case):

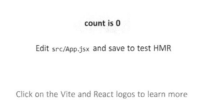

Figure 7.11: React app

10. You can stop the development server by pressing *q* in your terminal.

 To build a minified version of your app for production, you can use the npm run build command, which builds your app in the build folder. We will look more closely at deployment in *Chapter 17, Deploying Your Application*.

Modifying a React app

Now, we will learn how to modify the React app that we created using Vite. We will use VS Code, which we installed earlier:

1. Open your React project folder with VS Code by selecting **File | Open folder**. You should see the app's structure in the file explorer. The most important folder in this phase is the src folder, which contains the JavaScript source code:

Figure 7.12: Project structure

You can also open VS Code by typing the code . command into the terminal. This command opens VS Code and the folder where you are located.

2.   Open the App.jsx file from the src folder in the code editor. Modify the text inside the <h1> element to Hello React and save the file. You don't need to know anything else about this file at the moment. We will go deeper into this topic in *Chapter 8, Getting Started with React*:

```
function App() {
  const [count, setCount] = useState(0)

  return (
    <div className="App">
      <div>
        <a href="https://vitejs.dev" target="_blank">
          <img src={viteLogo} className="logo" alt="Vite logo" />
        </a>
        <a href="https://reactjs.org" target="_blank">
          <img src={reactLogo} className="logo react" alt="React logo" />
        </a>
      </div>
      <h1>Hello React</h1>
      <div className="card">
        <button onClick={() => setCount((count) => count + 1)}>
          count is {count}
        </button>
        <p>
          Edit <code>src/App.jsx</code> and save to test HMR
        </p>
      </div>
      <p className="read-the-docs">
        Click on the Vite and React logos to learn more
      </p>
    </div>
  )
```

Figure 7.13: App.js code

3. Now, if you look at the browser, you should immediately see that the header text has changed. Vite provides the **Hot Module Replacement** (**HMR**) feature, which updates a React component automatically when you modify its source code or styles in your React project, without the need for manual page refreshing:

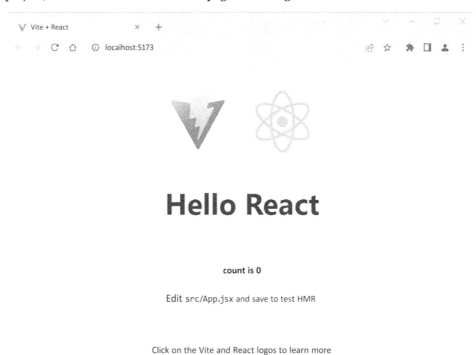

Figure 7.14: Modified React app

Debugging a React app

To debug React apps, we should also install **React Developer Tools**, which is available for Chrome, Firefox, and Edge browsers. Chrome plugins can be installed from the Chrome Web Store (`https://chrome.google.com/webstore/category/extensions`), while Firefox add-ons can be installed from the Firefox add-ons site (`https://addons.mozilla.org`). After you have installed React Developer Tools, you should see a new **Components** tab in your browser's developer tools once you navigate to your React app.

You can open the developer tools by pressing *Ctrl + Shift + I* (or *F12*) in the Chrome browser. The following screenshot shows the developer tools in the browser. The **Components** tab shows a visual representation of the React component tree, and you can use the search bar to find components. If you select a component in the component tree, you will see more specific information about it in the right-hand panel:

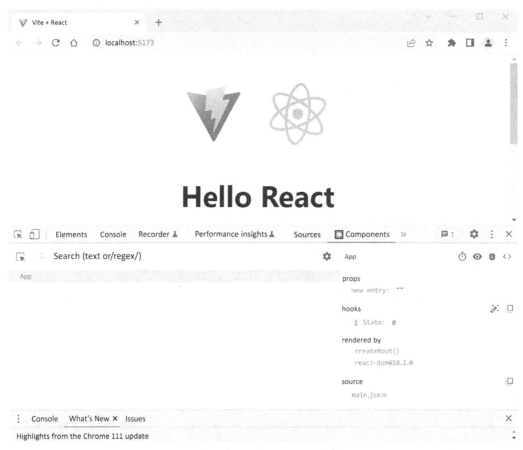

Figure 7.15: React Developer Tools

We will see that the browser's developer tools are really important, and it is useful to open them during development so that you can see errors and warnings immediately. The **Console** in developer tools is where you can log messages, warnings, and errors from your JavaScript or TypeScript code. The **Network** tab shows all the requests made by a web page, including their status codes, response times, and content. This is good for optimizing the performance of your web app and diagnosing network-related issues.

Summary

In this chapter, we installed everything that is needed to start our frontend development with React. First, we installed Node.js and the VS Code editor. Then, we used Vite to create our first React app. Finally, we ran the app, demonstrated how to modify it, and introduced debugging tools. We will continue to use Vite in the following chapters.

In the next chapter, we will familiarize ourselves with the basics of React programming.

Questions

1. What are Node.js and npm?
2. How do you install Node.js?
3. What is VS Code?
4. How do you install VS Code?
5. How do you create a React app with Vite?
6. How do you run a React app?
7. How do you make basic modifications to your app?

Further reading

Here are some useful resources that will extend the knowledge we have learned in this chapter:

*   *React 18 Design Patterns and Best Practices*, by Carlos Santana Roldán (https://www.packtpub.com/product/react-18-design-patterns-and-best-practices-fourth-edition/9781803233109)
*   *JavaScript in Visual Studio Code*, by Microsoft (https://code.visualstudio.com/docs/languages/javascript)
*   *TypeScript in Visual Studio Code*, by Microsoft (https://code.visualstudio.com/docs/languages/typescript)

Learn more on Discord

To join the Discord community for this book – where you can share feedback, ask the author questions, and learn about new releases – follow the QR code below:

`https://packt.link/FullStackSpringBootReact4e`

8

Getting Started with React

This chapter describes the basics of React programming. We will cover the skills that are required to create basic functionalities for our React frontend. In JavaScript, we use the **ECMAScript 2015 (ES6)** syntax because it provides many features that make coding cleaner.

In this chapter, we will look at the following topics:

- Creating React components
- Useful ES6 features
- JSX and styling
- Props and state
- Conditional rendering
- React hooks
- The Context API
- Handling lists, events, and forms with React

Technical requirements

For our work, React version 18 or higher will be required. We set up our environment correctly in *Chapter 7*.

You can find more resources at the GitHub link for this chapter: `https://github.com/PacktPublishing/Full-Stack-Development-with-Spring-Boot-3-and-React-Fourth-Edition/tree/main/Chapter08`.

Creating React components

React is a JavaScript library for **user interfaces (UIs)**. Since version 15, React has been developed under the MIT license. React is component-based, and the components are independent and re-usable. Components are the basic building blocks of React. When you start to develop a UI with React, it is good to start by creating **mock interfaces**. That way, it will be easy to identify what kinds of components you have to create and how they interact.

From the following mock UI, we can see how the UI can be split into components. In this case, there will be an application root component, a search bar component, a table component, and a table row component:

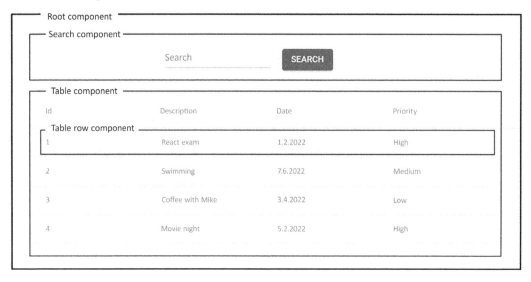

Figure 8.1: React components

The components can then be arranged in a **tree hierarchy**, as shown in the following screenshot:

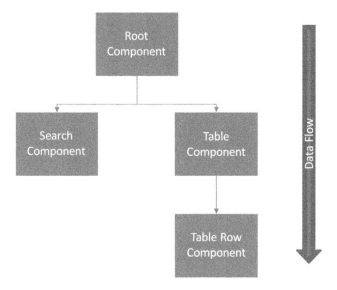

Figure 8.2: Component tree

The **root component** has two **child components**: the search component and the table compo-nent. The table component has one child component: the table row component. The important thing to understand with React is that the data flow goes from a parent component to a child component. We will learn later how data can be passed from a parent component to a child component using props.

React uses the **virtual document object model (VDOM)** for selective re-rendering of the UI, which makes it more cost-effective. The **document object model (DOM)** is a programming interface for web documents that represents the web page as a structured tree of objects. Each object in a tree corresponds to a part of the document. Using the DOM, programmers can create documents, navigate their structure, and add, modify, or delete elements and content. The VDOM is a light-weight copy of the DOM, and manipulation of the VDOM is much faster than it is with the real DOM. After the VDOM is updated, React compares it to a snapshot that was taken of the VDOM before updates were run. After the comparison, React will know which parts have been changed, and only these parts will be updated to the real DOM.

A React component can be defined either by using a JavaScript function – a **functional compo-nent** – or the ES6 JavaScript class – a **class component**. We will go more deeply into ES6 in the next section.

Here is some simple component source code that renders the Hello World text. This first code block uses a JavaScript function:

```
// Using JavaScript function
function App() {
    return <h1>Hello World</h1>;
}
```

The mandatory return statement in the React function component defines what the component looks like.

Alternatively, the following code uses the ES6 class to create a component:

```
// Using ES6 class
class App extends React.Component {
    render() {
        return <h1>Hello World</h1>;
    }
}
```

The class component contains the required render() method, which shows and updates the rendered output of the component. If you compare the functional and class App components, you can see that the render() method is not needed in the functional component. Before React version 16.8, you had to use class components to be able to use states. Now, you can use hooks to create states with functional components as well. We will learn about states and hooks later in this chapter.

In this book, we will create components using functions, which means we have to write less code. Functional components are a modern way to write React components, and we recommend avoiding using classes.

 The name of the React component should start with a capital letter. It is also rec-ommended to use the PascalCase naming convention, whereby each word starts with a capital letter.

Imagine we are making changes to our example component's `return` statement and adding a new `<h2>` element to it, as follows:

```
function App() {
  return (
    <h1>Hello World</h1>
    <h2>This is my first React component</h2>
  );
}
```

Now, if the app is run, we will see an **Adjacent JSX elements must be wrapped in an enclosing tag** error, as indicated in the following screenshot:

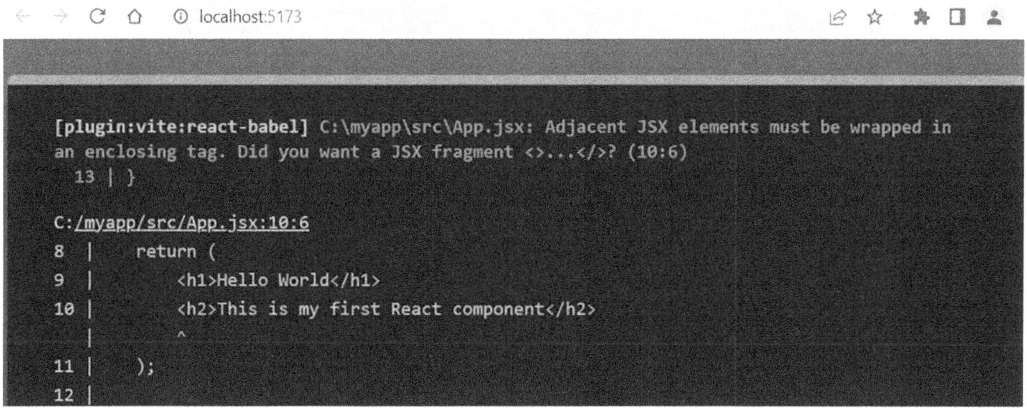

Figure 8.3: Adjacent JSX elements error

If your component returns multiple elements, you have to wrap these inside one parent element. To fix this error, we have to wrap the header elements in one element, such as a `div`, as illustrated in the following code snippet:

```
// Wrap elements inside the div
function App() {
  return (
    <div>
      <h1>Hello World</h1>
      <h2>This is my first React component</h2>
    </div>
  );
}
```

We can also use a React **fragment**, as shown in the following code snippet. Fragments don't add any extra nodes to the DOM tree:

```
// Using fragments
function App() {
  return (
    <React.Fragment>
      <h1>Hello World</h1>
      <h2>This is my first React component</h2>
    </React.Fragment>
  );
}
```

There is also shorter syntax for fragments, which looks like empty JSX tags. This is shown in the following code snippet:

```
// Using fragments short syntax
function App() {
  return (
    <>
      <h1>Hello World</h1>
      <h2>This is my first React component</h2>
    </>
  );
}
```

Examining our first React app

Let's look more carefully at the first React app we created in *Chapter 7, Setting Up the Environment and Tools – Frontend*, using Vite.

The source code of the `main.jsx` file in the root folder looks like this:

```
import React from 'react'
import ReactDOM from 'react-dom/client'
import App from './App'
import './index.css'

ReactDOM.createRoot(document.getElementById('root')).render(
  <React.StrictMode>
```

```
      <App />
    </React.StrictMode>,
  )
```

At the beginning of the file, there are `import` statements that load components and assets to our file. For example, the second line imports the `react-dom` package from the `node_modules` folder, and the third line imports the `App` component (the `App.jsx` file in the `src` folder). The fourth line imports the `index.css` style sheet that is in the same folder as the `main.jsx` file.

The `react-dom` package provides DOM-specific methods for us. To render the React component to the DOM, we can use the `render` method from the `react-dom` package. `React.StrictMode` is used to find potential problems in your React app and these are printed in the browser console. Strict Mode only runs in development mode and renders your components extra time, so it has time to find bugs.

The **root API** is used to render React components inside a browser DOM node. In the following example, we first create a root by passing the DOM element to the `createRoot` method. The root calls the `render` method to render an element to the root:

```
import ReactDOM from 'react-dom/client';
import App from './App';

const container = document.getElementById('root');

// Create a root
const root = ReactDOM.createRoot(container);

// Render an element to the root
root.render(<App />);
```

The container in the root API is the `<div id="root"></div>` element, which can be found in the `index.html` file inside the project root folder. Look at the following `index.html` file:

```
<!DOCTYPE html>
<html lang="en">
  <head>
    <meta charset="UTF-8" />
    <link rel="icon" type="image/svg+xml" href="/vite.svg" />
    <meta name="viewport" content="width=device-width, initial-scale=1.0" />
```

```
      <title>Vite + React</title>
    </head>
    <body>
      <div id="root"></div>
      <script type="module" src="/src/main.jsx"></script>
    </body>
</html>
```

The following source code shows the App.jsx component from our first React app. You can see that import also applies to assets, such as images and style sheets. At the end of the source code, there is an export default statement that exports the component, and it can be made available to other components by using the import statement:

```
import { useState } from 'react'
import reactLogo from './assets/react.svg'
import viteLogo from '/vite.svg'
import './App.css'

function App() {
  const [count, setCount] = useState(0)

  return (
    <div className="App">
      <div>
        <a href="https://vitejs.dev" target="_blank">
          <img src={viteLogo} className="logo" alt="Vite logo" />
        </a>
        <a href="https://reactjs.org" target="_blank">
          <img src={reactLogo} className="logo react" alt="React logo" />
        </a>
      </div>
      <h1>Hello React</h1>
      <div className="card">
        <button onClick={() => setCount((count) => count + 1)}>
          count is {count}
        </button>
        <p>
          Edit <code>src/App.jsx</code> and save to test HMR
```

```
        </p>
      </div>
      <p className="read-the-docs">
        Click on the Vite and React logos to learn more
      </p>
    </div>
  )
}


export default App
```

 You can see that in the App component that Vite has created, we don't have semi-colons at the end of statements. It is optional in JavaScript but, in this book, we will use semicolons to terminate statements when we start to create our own React components.

There can only be one export default statement per file, but there can be multiple named export statements. Default exports are commonly used to export React components. Named exports are commonly used to export specific functions or objects from a module.

The following example shows how to import default and named exports:

```
import React from 'react' // Import default value
import { name } from … //  Import named value
```

The exports look like this:

```
export default React // Default export
export { name }  //  Named export
```

Now that we have covered the basics of React components, let's take a look at the basic features of ES6.

Useful ES6 features

ES6 was released in 2015, and it introduced a lot of new features. ECMAScript is a standardized scripting language, and JavaScript is one implementation of it. In this section, we will go through the most important features released in ES6 that we will be using in the following sections.

Constants and variables

Constants, or immutable variables, can be defined by using a const keyword, as shown in the following code snippet. When using the const keyword, the variable content cannot be reassigned:

```
const PI = 3.14159;
```

Now, you will get an error if you try to reassign the PI value, as indicated in the following screenshot:

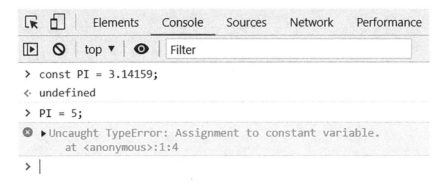

Figure 8.4: Assignment to constant variable

The const is block-scoped. This means that the const variable can only be used inside the block in which it is defined. In practice, the block is the area between curly brackets {}. If const is defined outside of any function or block, it becomes a global variable, and you should try to avoid this situation. Global variables make code harder to understand, maintain, and debug. The following sample code shows how the scope works:

```
let count = 10;

if (count > 5) {
  const total = count * 2;
  console.log(total); // Prints 20 to console
}

console.log(total); // Error, outside the scope
```

The second console.log statement gives an error because we are trying to use the total variable outside its scope.

The following example demonstrates what happens when const is an object or array:

```
const myObj = {foo:  3};
myObj.foo = 5; // This is ok
```

When const is an object or array, its properties or elements can be updated.

The let keyword allows you to declare *mutable* block-scoped variables. The variable declared using let can be used inside the block in which it is declared (it can also be used inside sub-blocks).

Arrow functions

The traditional way of defining a function in JavaScript is by using a function keyword. The following function takes one argument and returns the argument value multiplied by 2:

```
function(x) {
  return x * 2;
}
```

When we use the ES6 arrow function, the function looks like this:

```
x => x * 2
```

As we can see, by using the arrow function, we have made the declaration of the same function more compact. The function is a so-called **anonymous function**, and we can't call it. Anonymous functions are often used as an argument for other functions. In JavaScript, functions are *first-class citizens* and you can store functions in variables, as illustrated here:

```
const calc = x => x * 2
```

Now, you can use the variable name to call the function, like this:

```
calc(5); // returns 10
```

When you have more than one argument, you have to wrap the arguments in parentheses and separate the arguments with a comma to use the arrow function effectively. For example, the following function takes two parameters and returns their sum:

```
const calcSum = (x, y) => x + y
// function call
calcSum(2, 3); // returns 5
```

If the function body is an expression, then you don't need to use the return keyword. The expression is always implicitly returned from the function. When you have multiple lines in the function body, you have to use curly brackets and a return statement, as follows:

```
const calcSum = (x, y) => {
  console.log('Calculating sum');
  return x + y;
}
```

If the function doesn't have any arguments, then you should use empty parentheses, like so:

```
const sayHello = () => "Hello"
```

We are going to use lots of arrow functions later in our frontend implementation.

Template literals

Template literals can be used to concatenate strings. The traditional way to concatenate strings is to use the + operator, as follows:

```
let person = {firstName: 'John', lastName: 'Johnson'};
let greeting = "Hello " + ${person.firstName} + " " + ${person.lastName};
```

With template literals, the syntax looks like this. You have to use backticks (` `) instead of single or double quotes:

```
let person = {firstName: 'John', lastName: 'Johnson'};
let greeting = `Hello ${person.firstName} ${person.lastName}`;
```

Next, we will learn how to use object destructuring.

Object destructuring

The object destructuring feature allows you to extract values from an object and assign them to a variable. You can use a single statement to assign multiple properties of an object to individual variables. For example, if you have this object:

```
const person = {
  firstName: 'John',
  lastName: 'Johnson',
  email: 'j.johnson@mail.com'
};
```

You can destructure it using the following statement:

```
const { firstName, lastName, email } = person;
```

It creates three variables, firstName, lastName, and email, which get their values from the person object.

Without object destructuring, you have to access each property individually, as shown in the following code snippet:

```
const firstName = person.firstName;
const lastName = person.lastName;
const email = person.email;
```

Next, we will learn how to create classes using JavaScript ES6 syntax.

Classes and inheritance

Class definition in ES6 is similar to other object-oriented languages such as Java or C#. We saw an ES6 class when we looked at how to create React class components earlier. But, as we said earlier, classes are no longer recommended for creating React components.

The keyword for defining classes is class. A class can have fields, constructors, and class methods. The following sample code shows an ES6 class:

```
class Person {
  constructor(firstName, lastName) {
    this.firstName = firstName;
    this.lastName = lastName;
  }
}
```

Inheritance is performed with an extends keyword. The following sample code shows an Employee class that inherits a Person class. This means that it inherits all fields from the parent class and can have its own fields that are specific to Employee. In the constructor, we first call the parent class constructor by using the super keyword. That call is required by the rest of the code, and you will get an error if it is missing:

```
class Employee extends Person {
  constructor(firstName, lastName, title, salary) {
    super(firstName, lastName);
    this.title = title;
```

```
        this.salary = salary;
    }
}
```

Although ES6 is already quite old, some of its features are still only partially supported by modern web browsers. **Babel** is a JavaScript compiler that is used to compile ES6 (or newer versions)
to an older version that is compatible with all browsers. You can test the compiler on the Babel
website (`https://babeljs.io`). The following screenshot shows the arrow function compiling
back to the older JavaScript syntax:

Figure 8.5: Babel

Now that we have learned about the basics of ES6, let's take a look at what JSX and styling are
all about.

JSX and styling

JavaScript XML (JSX) is the syntax extension for JavaScript. It is not mandatory to use JSX with
React, but there are some benefits that make development easier. For example, JSX prevents
injection attacks because all values are escaped in JSX before they are rendered. The most useful
feature is that you can embed JavaScript expressions in JSX by wrapping them with curly brackets;
this technique will be used a lot in the following chapters. JSX is compiled into regular JavaScript
by Babel.

In the following example, we can access a component's props when using JSX:

```
function App(props) {
    return <h1>Hello World {props.user}</h1>;
}
```

   Component props are covered in the next section.

You can also pass a JavaScript expression as props, as shown in the following code snippet:

```
<Hello count={2+2} />
```

You can use both inline and external styling with React JSX elements. Here are two examples of inline styling. This first one defines the style inside the div element:

```
<div style={{ height: 20, width: 200 }}>
  Hello
</div>
```

The second example creates a style object first, which is then used in the div element. The object name should use the *camelCase* naming convention:

```
const divStyle = { color: 'red', height: 30 };

const MyComponent = () => (
  <div style={divStyle}>Hello</div>
);
```

As shown in a previous section, you can import a style sheet into a React component. To reference classes from an external **CSS** file, you should use a className attribute, as shown in the following code snippet:

```
import './App.js';
...
<div className="App-header"> This is my app</div>
```

In the next section, we will learn about React props and state.

Props and state

Props and **state** are the input data for rendering a component. The component is re-rendered when the props or state change.

Props

Props are inputs to components, and they are a mechanism to pass data from a parent component to its child component. Props are JavaScript objects, so they can contain multiple key-value pairs.

Props are immutable, so a component cannot change its props. Props are received from the parent component. A component can access props through the `props` object that is passed to the function component as a parameter. For example, let's take a look at the following component:

```
function Hello() {
    return <h1>Hello John</h1>;
}
```

The component just renders a static message, and it is not reusable. Instead of using a hardcoded name, we can pass a name to the `Hello` component by using props, like this:

```
function Hello(props) {
    return <h1>Hello {props.user}</h1>;
}
```

The parent component can send props to the `Hello` component in the following way:

```
<Hello user="John" />
```

Now, when the `Hello` component is rendered, it shows the `Hello John` text.

You can also pass multiple props to a component, as shown here:

```
<Hello firstName="John" lastName="Johnson" />
```

Now, you can access both props in the component using the props object, as follows:

```
function Hello(props) {
    return <h1>Hello {props.firstName} {props.lastName}</h1>;
}
```

Now, the component output is `Hello John Johnson`.

You can also use object destructuring to destructure a props object in the following way:

```
function Hello({ firstName, lastName }) {
    return <h1>Hello {firstName} {lastName}</h1>;
}
```

State

In React, the component **state** is an internal data store that holds information that can change over time. The state also affects the rendering of the component. When the state is updated, React schedules a re-render of the component. When the component re-renders, the state retains its latest values. State allows components to be dynamic and responsive to user interactions or other events.

It's generally a good practice to avoid introducing unnecessary states in your React components. Unnecessary states increase the complexity of your components and can cause unwanted side effects. Sometimes, a local variable can be a better option. But you have to understand that *changes to local variables won't trigger re-rendering*. Each time a component re-renders, local variables are reinitialized, and their values don't persist between renders.

The state is created using the useState hook function. It takes one argument, which is the initial value of the state, and returns an array of two elements. The first element is the name of the state, and the second element is a function that is used to update the state value. The syntax of the useState function is shown in the following code snippet:

```
const [state, setState] = React.useState(initialValue);
```

The next code example creates a state variable called name, and the initial value is Jim:

```
const [name, setName] = React.useState('Jim');
```

You can also import the useState function from React, like so:

```
import React, { useState } from 'react';
```

Then, you don't need to type the React keyword, as indicated here:

```
const [name, setName] = useState('Jim');
```

The value of the state can now be updated by using the setName function, as illustrated in the following code snippet. This is the only way to modify the state value:

```
// Update name state value
setName('John');
```

You should never update the state value directly using the = operator. If you update the state directly, as shown next, React won't re-render the component and you will also get an error because you cannot reassign the const variable:

```
// Don't do this, UI won't re-render
name = 'John';
```

If you have multiple states, you can call the useState function multiple times, as shown in the following code snippet:

```
// Create two states: firstName and lastName
const [firstName, setFirstName] = useState('John');
const [lastName, setLastName] = useState('Johnson');
```

Now, you can update states using the setFirstName and setLastName functions, as shown in the following code snippet:

```
// Update state values
setFirstName('Jim');
setLastName('Palmer');
```

You can also define state using an object, as follows:

```
const [name, setName] = useState({
  firstName: 'John',
  lastName: 'Johnson'
});
```

Now, you can update both the firstName and lastName state object parameters using the setName function, as follows:

```
setName({ firstName: 'Jim', lastName: 'Palmer' })
```

If you want to do a partial update of the object, you can use the **spread operator**. In the following example, we use the object spread syntax (. . .) that was introduced in ES2018. It clones the name state object and updates the firstName value to be Jim:

```
setName({ ...name, firstName: 'Jim' })
```

A state can be accessed by using the state name, as shown in the next example. The scope of the state is the component, so it cannot be used outside the component in which it is defined:

```
// Renders Hello John
import React, { useState } from 'react';

function MyComponent() {
  const [firstName, setFirstName] = useState('John');

  return <div>Hello {firstName}</div>;
}
```

If your state is an object, then you can access it in the following way:

```
const [name, setName] = useState({
  firstName: 'John',
  lastName: 'Johnson'
});


return <div>Hello {name.firstName}</div>;
```

We have now learned the basics of state and props, and we will learn more about states later in this chapter.

Stateless components

The React **stateless component** is just a pure JavaScript function that takes props as an argument and returns a React element. Here's an example of a stateless component:

```
function HeaderText(props) {
  return (
    <h1>
      {props.text}
    </h1>
  )
}


export default HeaderText;
```

Our HeaderText example component is also called a **pure component**. A component is said to be pure if its return value is consistently the same given the same input values. React provides React.memo(), which optimizes the performance of pure functional components. In the following code snippet, we wrap our component using memo():

```
import React, { memo } from 'react';

function HeaderText(props) {
  return (
    <h1>
      {props.text}
    </h1>
  )
```

```
    }

    export default memo(HeaderText);
```

Now, the component is rendered and **memoized**. In the next render, React renders a memoized result if the props are not changed. The `React.memo()` phrase also has a second argument, `arePropsEqual()`, which you can use to customize rendering conditions, but we will not cover that here. The one benefit of using functional components is unit testing, which is straightforward because their return values are always the same for the same input values.

Conditional rendering

You can use a conditional statement to render different UIs if a condition is `true` or `false`. This feature can be used, for example, to show or hide some elements, handle authentication, and so on.

In the following example, we will check if `props.isLoggedin` is `true`. If so, we will render the `<Logout />` component; otherwise, we render the `<Login />` component. This is now implemented using two separate `return` statements:

```
function MyComponent(props) {
    const isLoggedin = props.isLoggedin;

    if (isLoggedin) {
      return (
        <Logout />
      )
    }

    return (
      <Login />
    )
}
```

You can also implement this by using `condition ? true : false` logical operators, and then you need only one `return` statement, as illustrated here:

```
function MyComponent(props) {
    const isLoggedin = props.isLoggedin;
    return (
      <>
```

```
        { isLoggedin ? <Logout /> : <Login /> }
    </>
  );
}
```

React hooks

Hooks were introduced in React version 16.8. Hooks allow you to use state and some other React features in functional components. Before hooks, you had to write class components if states or complex component logic were needed.

There are certain important rules for using hooks in React. You should always call hooks at the top level in your React function component. You shouldn't call hooks inside loops, conditional statements, or nested functions. Hook names begin with the word use, followed by the purpose they serve.

useState

We are already familiar with the useState hook function that is used to declare states. Let's look at one more example of using the useState hook. We will create an example counter that contains a button, and when it is pressed, the counter is increased by 1, as illustrated in the following screenshot:

Figure 8.6: Counter component

1. First, we create a Counter component and declare a state called count with the initial value 0. The value of the counter state can be updated using the setCount function. The code is illustrated in the following snippet:

    ```
    import { useState } from 'react';

    function Counter() {
      // count state with initial value 0
    ```

```
      const [count, setCount] = useState(0);
      return <div></div>;
    };


    export default Counter;
```

2. Next, we render a button element that increments the state by 1. We use the onClick event attribute to call the setCount function, and the new value is the current value plus 1. We will also render the counter state value. The code is illustrated in the following snippet:

```
import { useState }  from 'react';

function Counter() {
  const [count, setCount] = useState(0);


  return (
    <div>
      <p>Counter = {count}</p>
      <button onClick={() => setCount(count + 1)}>
        Increment
      </button>
    </div>
  );
};


export default Counter;
```

3. Now, our Counter component is ready, and the counter is incremented by 1 each time the button is pressed. When the state is updated, React re-renders the component and we can see the new count value.

 In React, events are named using camelCase, for example, **onClick**.

Note that the function must be *passed* to an event handler, and then React will call the function only when the user clicks the button. We use an arrow function in the following example because it is more compact to write and improves code readability. If you call the function *in* the event handler, then the function is called when the component is rendered, which can cause an infinite loop:

```
// Correct -> Function is called when button is pressed
<button onClick={() => setCount(count + 1)}>

// Wrong -> Function is called in render -> Infinite loop
<button onClick={setCount(count + 1)}>
```

State updates are asynchronous, so you have to be careful when a new state value depends on the current state value. To be sure that the latest value is used, you can pass a function to the update function. You can see an example of this here:

```
setCount(prevCount => prevCount + 1)
```

Now, the previous value is passed to the function, and the updated value is returned and saved to the count state.

 There is also a hook function called useReducer that is recommended when you have a complex state, but we won't cover that in this book.

Batching

React uses **batching** in state updates to reduce re-renders. Before React version 18, batching only worked in states updated during browser events – for example, a button click. The following example demonstrates the idea of batch updates:

```
import { useState } from 'react';

function App() {
  const [count, setCount] = useState(0);
  const [count2, setCount2] = useState(0);

  const increment = () => {
    setCount(count + 1); // No re-rendering yet
    setCount2(count2 + 1);
    // Component re-renders after all state updates
```

```
  }

  return (
    <>
      <p>Counters: {count} {count2}</p>
      <button onClick={increment}>Increment</button>
    </>
  );
};


export default App;
```

From React version 18 onward, all state updates will be batched. If you don't want to use batch updates in some cases, you can use the react-dom library's flushSync API to avoid batching. For example, you might have a case where you want to update some state before updating the next one. It can be useful when incorporating third-party code, such as browser APIs.

Here's the code you'd need to do this:

```
import { flushSync } from "react-dom";

const increment = () => {
  flushSync( () => {
    setCount(count + 1); // No batch update
  });
}
```

You should use flushSync only if it is needed, because it can affect the performance of your React app.

useEffect

The useEffect hook function can be used to perform side effects in the React function component. The side effect can be, for example, a fetch request. The useEffect hook takes two arguments, as shown here:

```
useEffect(callback, [dependencies])
```

The callback function contains side-effect logic, and [dependencies] is an optional array of dependencies.

The following code snippet shows the previous counter example, but we have added the useEffect hook. Now, when the button is pressed, the count state value increases, and the component is re-rendered. After each render, the useEffect callback function is invoked and we can see **Hello from useEffect** in the console, as illustrated in the following code snippet:

```
import { useState, useEffect } from 'react';

function Counter() {
  const [count, setCount] = useState(0);

  // Called after every render
  useEffect(() => {
    console.log('Hello from useEffect')
  });

  return (
    <>
      <p>{count}</p>
      <button onClick={() => setCount(count + 1)}>Increment
      </button>
    </>
  );
};

export default Counter;
```

In the following screenshot, we can see what the console now looks like, and we can see that the useEffect callback is invoked after each render. The first log row is printed after the initial render, and the rest are printed after the button is pressed two times and the component is re-rendered due to state updates:

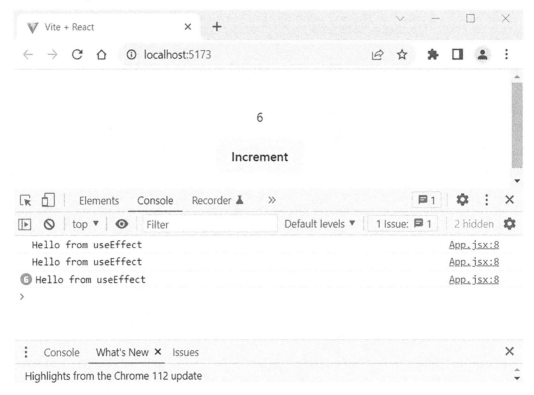

Figure 8.7: useEffect

The useEffect hook has a second optional argument (a dependency array) that you can use to prevent it from running in every render. In the following code snippet, we define that if the count state value is changed (meaning that the previous and current values differ), the useEffect callback function will be invoked. We can also define multiple states in the second argument. If any of these state values are changed, the useEffect hook will be invoked:

```
// Runs when count value is changed and component is re-rendered
useEffect(() => {
  console.log('Counter value is now ' + count);
}, [count]);
```

If you pass an empty array as the second argument, the `useEffect` callback function runs only after the first render, as shown in the following code snippet:

```
// Runs only after the first render
useEffect(() => {
  console.log('Hello from useEffect')
}, []);
```

Now, you can see that **Hello from useEffect** is printed only once after the initial render, and if you press the button, the text is not printed. The message is printed twice after the first render due to React Strict Mode. Strict Mode renders your component twice in development mode to find bugs and does not impact the production build:

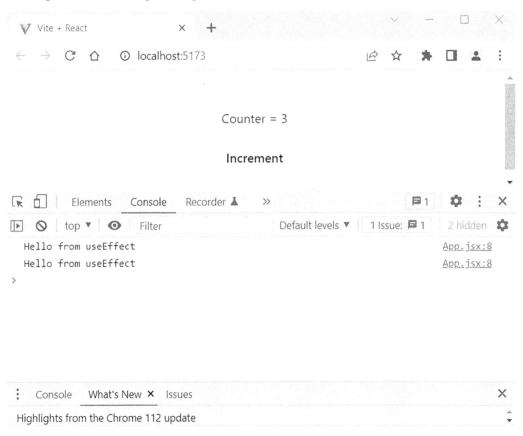

Figure 8.8: useEffect with an empty array

The useEffect function can also return a cleanup function that will run before every effect, as shown in the following code snippet. With this mechanism, you can clean up each effect from the previous render before running the effect next time. It is useful when you are setting up subscriptions, timers, or any resource that needs to be cleaned up to prevent unexpected behavior. The cleanup function is also executed after your component is removed from the page (or **unmounted**):

```
useEffect(() => {
  console.log('Hello from useEffect');
  return () => {
    console.log('Clean up function');
  });
}, [count]);
```

If you run the counter app with these changes, you can see what happens in the console, as shown in the following screenshot. The component is rendered twice at the beginning due to Strict Mode. After the initial render, the component is unmounted (removed from the DOM), and therefore, the cleanup function is called:

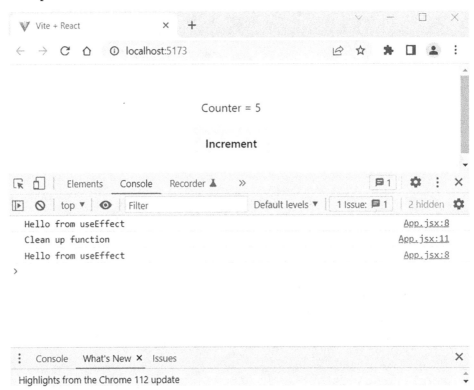

Figure 8.9: Cleanup function

useRef

The useRef hook returns a mutable ref object that can be used, for example, to access DOM nodes. You can see it in action here:

```
const ref = useRef(initialValue)
```

The ref object returned has a current property that is initialized with the argument passed (initialValue). In the next example, we create a ref object called inputRef and initialize it to null. Then, we use the JSX element's ref property and pass our ref object to it. Now, it contains our input element, and we can use the current property to execute the input element's focus function. Now, when the button is pressed, the input element is focused:

```
import { useRef } from 'react';
import './App.css';

function App() {
  const inputRef = useRef(null);

  return (
    <>
      <input ref={inputRef} />
      <button onClick={() => inputRef.current.focus()}>
        Focus input
      </button>
    </>
  );
}


export default App;
```

In this section, we have learned the basics of React hooks, and we will use them in practice when we start to implement our frontend. There are other useful hook functions available in React, and next you will learn how to create your own hooks.

Custom hooks

You can build your own hooks in React. As we have seen already, hooks' names should start with the use word, and they are JavaScript functions. Custom hooks can also call other hooks. With custom hooks, you can reduce your component code complexity.

Let's go through a simple example of creating a custom hook:

1. We will create a useTitle hook that can be used to update a document title. We will define it in its own file called useTitle.js. First, we define a function, and it gets one argument named title. The code is illustrated in the following snippet:

```
// useTitle.js
function useTitle(title) {
}
```

2. Next, we will use a useEffect hook to update the document title each time the title argument is changed, as follows:

```
import { useEffect } from 'react';

function useTitle(title) {
  useEffect(() => {
    document.title = title;
  }, [title]);
}

export default useTitle;
```

3. Now, we can start to use our custom hook. Let's use it in our counter example and print the current counter value into the document title. First, we have to import the useTitle hook into our Counter component, like this:

```
import useTitle from './useTitle';

function Counter() {
  return (
    <>
    </>
  );
};

export default Counter;
```

4. Then, we will use the useTitle hook to print the count state value into the document title. We can call our hook function in the top level of the Counter component function, and every time the component is rendered, the useTitle hook function is called and we can see the current count value in the document title. The code is illustrated in the following snippet:

```jsx
import React, { useState } from 'react';
import useTitle from './useTitle';

function App() {
  const [count, setCount] = useState(0);
  useTitle(`You clicked ${count} times`);

  return (
    <>
      <p>Counter = {count}</p>
      <button onClick={ () => setCount(count + 1) }>
        Increment
      </button>
    </>
  );
};

export default App;
```

5. Now, if you click the button, the count state value is also shown in the document title using our custom hook, as illustrated in the following screenshot:

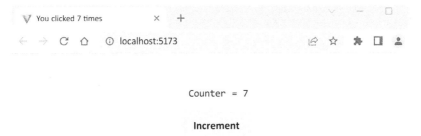

Figure 8.10: Custom hook

You now have basic knowledge of React hooks and how you can create your own custom hooks.

The Context API

Passing data using props can be cumbersome if your component tree is deep and complex. You have to pass data through all components down the component tree. **The Context API** solves this problem, and it is recommended for use with *global* data that you might need in multiple components throughout your component tree – for example, a theme or authenticated user.

Context is created using the `createContext` method, which takes an argument that defines the default value. You can create your own file for the context, and the code looks like this:

```
import React from 'react';

const AuthContext = React.createContext('');

export default AuthContext;
```

Next, we will use a context provider component, which makes our context available for other components. The context provider component has a `value` prop that will be passed to consuming components. In the following example, we have wrapped `<MyComponent />` using the context provider component, so the `userName` value is available in our component tree under `<MyComponent />`:

```
import React from 'react';
import AuthContext from './AuthContext';
import MyComponent from './MyComponent';

function App() {
  // User is authenticated and we get the username
  const userName = 'john';

  return (
    <AuthContext.Provider value={userName}>
      <MyComponent />
    </AuthContext.Provider>
  );
};

export default App;
```

Now, we can access the value provided in any component in the component tree by using the `useContext()` hook, as follows:

```
import React from 'react';
import AuthContext from './AuthContext';

function MyComponent() {
  const authContext = React.useContext(AuthContext);

  return(
    <>
      Welcome {authContext}
    </>
  );
}


export default MyComponent;
```

The component now renders the `Welcome john` text.

Handling lists with React

For list handling, we will learn about the JavaScript `map()` method, which is useful when you have to manipulate a list. The `map()` method creates a new array containing the results of calling a function on each element in the original array. In the following example, each array element is multiplied by 2:

```
const arr = [1, 2, 3, 4];
const resArr = arr.map(x => x * 2); // resArr = [2, 4, 6, 8]
```

The following example code demonstrates a component that transforms an array of integers into an array of list items and renders these inside the `ul` element:

```
import React from 'react';

function MyList() {
  const data = [1, 2, 3, 4, 5];

  return (
    <>
```

```
    <ul>
      {
      data.map((number) =>
        <li>Listitem {number}</li>)
      }
    </ul>
  </>
  );
};


export default MyList;
```

The following screenshot shows what the component looks like when it is rendered. If you open the console, you can see a warning (**Each child in a list should have a unique "key" prop**):

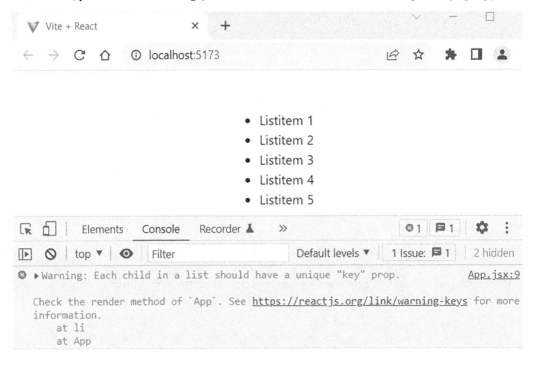

Figure 8.11: React list component

List items in React need a **unique key** that is used to detect rows that have been updated, added, or deleted. The map() method also has index as a second argument, which we use to handle the warning:

```
function MyList() {
  const data = [1, 2, 3, 4, 5];

  return (
    <>
      <ul>
        {
        data.map((number, index) =>
          <li key={index}>Listitem {number}</li>)
        }
      </ul>
    </>
  );
};

export default MyList;
```

Now, after adding the key, there is no warning in the console.

 The usage of index is not recommended because it can cause bugs if the list is re-ordered or if you add or delete list items. Instead of that, you should use a unique key from the data if that exists. There are also libraries available that you can use to generate unique IDs, like **uuid** (https://github.com/uuidjs/uuid).

If the data is an array of objects, it would be nicer to present it in table format. We do this in roughly the same way as we did with the list, but now we just map the array to table rows (tr elements) and render these inside the table element, as shown in the following component code. Now we have a unique ID in the data so we can use it as a key:

```
function MyTable() {
  const data = [
    {id: 1, brand: 'Ford', model: 'Mustang'},
    {id: 2, brand: 'VW', model: 'Beetle'},
    {id: 3, brand: 'Tesla', model: 'Model S'}];
```

```
    return (
      <>
        <table>
          <tbody>
          {
          data.map((item) =>
            <tr key={item.id}>
              <td>{item.brand}</td><td>{item.model}</td>
            </tr>)
          }
          </tbody>
        </table>
      </>
    );
  };


  export default MyTable;
```

The following screenshot shows what the component looks like when it is rendered. You should see the data in the HTML table:

Figure 8.12: React table

Now, we have learned how to handle list data using the map() method and how to render it using, for example, an HTML table element.

Handling events with React

Event handling in React is similar to handling DOM element events. The difference compared to HTML event handling is that event naming uses *camelCase* in React. The following sample component code adds an event listener to a button and shows an alert message when the button is pressed:

```
function MyComponent() {
  // This is called when the button is pressed
  const handleClick = () => {
    alert('Button pressed');
  }
  return (
    <>
      <button onClick={handleClick}>Press Me</button>
    </>
  );
};


export default MyComponent;
```

As we learned earlier in the counter example, you have to pass a function to the event handler instead of calling it. Now, the handleClick function is defined outside the return statement, and we can refer to it using the function name:

```
// Correct
<button onClick={handleClick}>Press Me</button>

// Wrong
<button onClick={handleClick()}>Press Me</button>
```

In React, you cannot return false from the event handler to prevent the default behavior. Instead, you should call the event object's preventDefault() method. In the following example, we are using a form element, and we want to prevent form submission:

```
function MyForm() {
  // This is called when the form is submitted
  const handleSubmit = (event) => {
```

```
    event.preventDefault(); // Prevents default behavior
    alert('Form submit');
  }

  return (
    <form onSubmit={handleSubmit}>
      <input type="submit" value="Submit" />
    </form>
  );
};
export default MyForm;
```

Now, when you press the **Submit** button, you can see the alert and the form will not be submitted.

Handling forms with React

Form handling is a little bit different with React. An HTML form will navigate to the next page when it is submitted. In React, often, we want to invoke a JavaScript function that has access to form data after submission, and avoid navigating to the next page. We already covered how to avoid submission in the previous section using preventDefault().

Let's first create a minimalistic form with one input field and a **Submit** button. In order to get the value of the input field, we use the onChange event handler. We use the useState hook to create a state variable called text. When the value of the input field is changed, the new value will be saved to the state. This component is called a **controlled component** because form data is handled by React. In an uncontrolled component, the form data is handled only by the DOM.

The setText(event.target.value) statement gets the value from the input field and saves it to the state. Finally, we will show the typed value when a user presses the **Submit** button. Here is the source code for our first form:

```
import { useState } from 'react';

function MyForm() {
  const [text, setText] = useState('');

  // Save input element value to state when it has been changed
  const handleChange = (event) => {
```

```
    setText(event.target.value);
  }

  const handleSubmit = (event) => {
    alert(`You typed: ${text}`);
    event.preventDefault();
  }

  return (
    <form onSubmit={handleSubmit}>
      <input type="text" onChange={handleChange}
          value={text}/>
      <input type="submit" value="Press me"/>
    </form>
  );
};

export default MyForm;
```

Here is a screenshot of our form component after the **Submit** button has been pressed:

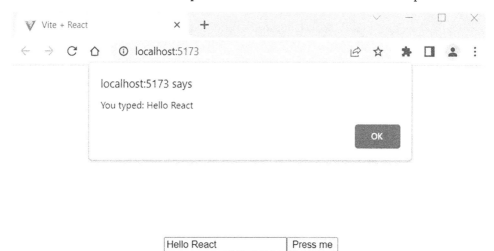

Figure 8.13: Form component

You can also write an inline onChange handler function using JSX, as shown in the following example. This is quite common practice if you have a simple event handler function, and it makes your code more readable:

```
return (
  <form onSubmit={handleSubmit}>
    <input
      type="text"
      onChange={event => setText(event.target.value)}
      value={text}/
    >
    <input type="submit" value="Press me"/>
  </form>
);
```

Now is a good time to look at React Developer Tools, which are useful for debugging React apps.

 If you haven't installed React Developer Tools yet, you can find the instructions in *Chapter 7, Setting Up the Environment and Tools – Frontend.*

If we open the React Developer Tools **Components** tab with our React form app and type something into the input field, we can see how the value of the state changes, and we can inspect the current value of both the props and the state.

The following screenshot shows how the state changes when we type something into the input field:

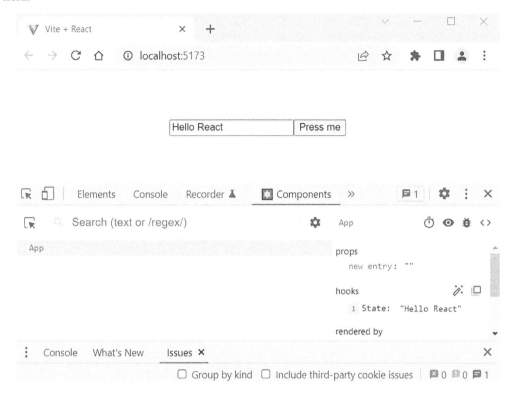

Figure 8.14: React Developer Tools

Typically, we have more than one input field in the form. Let's look at how we can handle that using an object state. First, we introduce a state called user using the useState hook, as shown in the following code snippet. The user state is an object with three attributes: firstName, lastName, and email:

```
const [user, setUser] = useState({
  firstName: '',
  lastName: '',
  email: ''
});
```

One way to handle multiple input fields is to add as many change handlers as we have input fields, but this creates a lot of boilerplate code, which we want to avoid. Therefore, we add name attributes to our input fields. We can utilize these in the change handler to identify which input field triggers the change handler. The name attribute value of the input element must be the same as the name of the state object property in which we want to save the value, and the value attribute should be object.property, for example, in the last name input element. The code is illustrated here:

```
<input type="text" name="lastName" onChange={handleChange}
   value={user.lastName}/>
```

Now, if the input field that triggers the handler is the last name field, then event.target.name is lastName, and the typed value will be saved to the state object's lastName field. Here, we will also use the object spread notation that was introduced in the *Props and state* section. In this way, we can handle all input fields with the one change handler:

```
const handleChange = (event) => {
  setUser({...user, [event.target.name]:
      event.target.value});
}
```

Here is the full source code for the component:

```
import { useState } from 'react';

function MyForm() {
  const [user, setUser] = useState({
    firstName: '',
    lastName: '',
    email: ''
  });
```

```
    // Save input box value to state when it has been changed
    const handleChange = (event) => {
      setUser({...user, [event.target.name]:
          event.target.value});
    }

    const handleSubmit = (event) => {
      alert(`Hello ${user.firstName} ${user.lastName}`);
      event.preventDefault();
    }

    return (
      <form onSubmit={handleSubmit}>
        <label>First name </label>
        <input type="text" name="firstName" onChange=
            {handleChange}
          value={user.firstName}/><br/>
        <label>Last name </label>
        <input type="text" name="lastName" onChange=
            {handleChange}
          value={user.lastName}/><br/>
        <label>Email </label>
        <input type="email" name="email" onChange=
            {handleChange}
          value={user.email}/><br/>
        <input type="submit" value="Submit"/>
      </form>
    );
};

export default MyForm;
```

Here is a screenshot of our form component after the **Submit** button has been pressed:

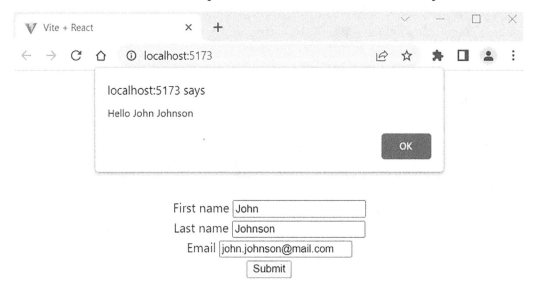

Figure 8.15: React form component

In the previous example, it is better to create one object state because all three values belong to one user. It could also be implemented using separate states instead of one state and object. The following code snippet demonstrates this. Now, we have three states, and in the input element's onChange event handler, we call the correct update function to save values into the states. In this case, we don't need the name input element's name attribute:

```
import { useState } from 'react';

function MyForm() {
  const [firstName, setFirstName] = useState('');
  const [lastName, setLastName] = useState('');
  const [email, setEmail] = useState('');

  const handleSubmit = (event) => {
    alert('Hello ${firstName} ${lastName}');
    event.preventDefault();
  }

  return (
    <form onSubmit={handleSubmit}>
```

```
      <label>First name </label>
      <input
        onChange={e => setFirstName(e.target.value)}
        value={firstName}/><br/>
      <label>Last name </label>
      <input
        onChange={e => setLastName(e.target.value)}
        value={lastName}/><br/>
      <label>Email </label>
      <input
        onChange={e => setEmail(e.target.value)}
        value={email}/><br/>
      <input type="submit" value="Press me"/>
    </form>
  );
};

export default MyForm;
```

We now know how to handle forms with React, and we will use these skills later when we implement our frontend.

Summary

In this chapter, we started to learn about React, which we will be using to build our frontend. In our frontend development, we will use ES6, which makes our code cleaner, as we saw in the chapter. Before starting to develop with React, we covered the basics, such as the React component, JSX, props, state, and hooks. We then went through the features we need for further development. We learned about conditional rendering and context, as well as how to handle lists, forms, and events with React.

In the next chapter, we will focus on TypeScript with React. We will learn the basics of TypeScript and how to use it in our React projects.

Questions

1. What is a React component?
2. What are states and props?
3. How does data flow in a React app?

4. What is the difference between stateless and stateful components?

5. What is JSX?

6. How are React hooks named?

7. How does context work?

Further reading

Here are some other good resources for learning about React:

-   *React – The Complete Guide*, by Maximilian Schwarzmüller (`https://www.packtpub.com/product/react-the-complete-guide-includes-hooks-react-router-and-redux-2021-updated-second-edition-video/9781801812603`)

-   *The Ultimate React Course 2023*, by Jonas Schmedtmann (`https://www.udemy.com/course/the-ultimate-react-course/`)

Learn more on Discord

To join the Discord community for this book – where you can share feedback, ask the author questions, and learn about new releases – follow the QR code below:

`https://packt.link/FullStackSpringBootReact4e`

Introduction to TypeScript

This chapter introduces TypeScript. We will cover the basic skills that are required to use TypeScript with React and create our first React app with TypeScript.

In this chapter, we will look at the following topics:

- Understanding TypeScript
- Using TypeScript features with React
- Creating a React app with TypeScript

Technical requirements

For our work, React version 18 or higher will be required.

You can find more resources at the GitHub link for this chapter: `https://github.com/PacktPublishing/Full-Stack-Development-with-Spring-Boot-3-and-React-Fourth-Edition/tree/main/Chapter09`.

Understanding TypeScript

TypeScript (`https://www.typescriptlang.org/`) is a strongly typed superset of JavaScript, developed by Microsoft. TypeScript adoption has grown a lot in recent years and it is widely used in the industry. It has an active development community and is supported by most popular libraries. In the JetBrains 2022 Developer Ecosystem report, TypeScript was named the fastest-growing programming language (`https://www.jetbrains.com/lp/devecosystem-2022/`).

TypeScript offers several advantages compared to JavaScript, mostly due to strong typing:

- TypeScript allows you to define **types** for variables, functions, and classes. This allows you to catch errors early in the development process.

- TypeScript improves the scalability of your app, as well as making your code easier to maintain.

- TypeScript improves code readability and makes your code more self-documenting.

Compared to JavaScript, the TypeScript learning curve can be steeper if you are not familiar with static typing.

The easiest way to try TypeScript is to use an online environment such as *TypeScript Playground* (`https://www.typescriptlang.org/play`). If you want to code TypeScript locally, you can install the TypeScript compiler on your computer using npm. This will not be needed for our React project because Vite comes with built-in TypeScript support. TypeScript is transpiled to plain JavaScript and can then be executed in a JavaScript engine.

The following npm command installs the latest version of TypeScript globally, allowing you to use TypeScript anywhere in your terminal:

```
npm install -g typescript
```

You can check the installation by checking the TypeScript version number:

```
tsc --version
```

 If you are using Windows PowerShell, you might get an error stating that **running scripts is disabled on this system**. In this case, you have to change the execution policy to be able to run the installation command. You can read more at `https://go.microsoft.com/fwlink/?LinkID=135170`.

Like JavaScript, TypeScript has good IDE support that makes your coding more productive, with features like linting and code autocompletion – for example, IntelliSense in Visual Studio Code.

Common types

TypeScript will automatically define the type of a variable when you initialize it. This is called **type inference**. In the following example, we declare a message variable and assign it to a string value. If we try to reassign it with another type, we get an error, as shown in the following image:

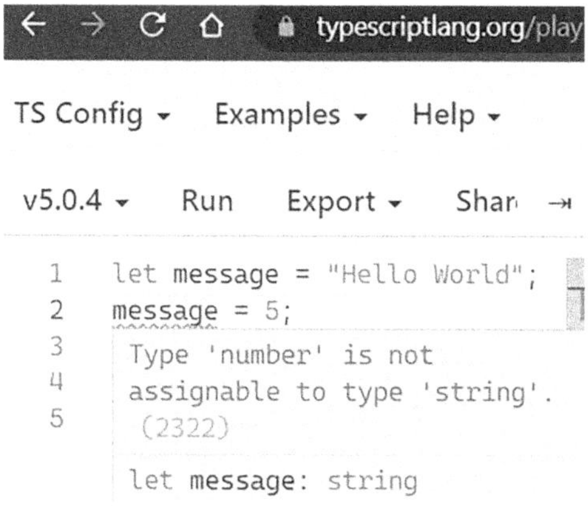

Figure 9.1: Type inference

TypeScript has the following primitive types: `string`, `number`, and `boolean`. The `number` type represents both integer and floating-point numbers. You can also set an explicit type for a variable using the following syntax:

```
let variable_name: type;
```

The following code demonstrates explicit typing:

```
let email: string;
let age: number;
let isActive: boolean;
```

The variables' types can be checked using the `typeof` keyword, which returns a string representing the type of the variable it is applied to:

```
// Check variable type
console.log(typeof email); // Output is "string"
typeof email === "string" // true
typeof age === "string" // false
```

If you don't know the type of a variable, you can use the unknown type. It can be used when you get a value, for example, from some external source, and you don't know its type:

```
let externalValue: unknown;
```

When a value is assigned to the unknown variable, you can check the type using the `typeof` keyword.

TypeScript also provides the any type. If you define a variable using the any type, TypeScript doesn't perform a type check or inference on that variable. You should avoid using the any type whenever possible, since it negates the effectiveness of TypeScript.

Arrays can be declared in the same way as in JavaScript, but you have to define the type of the elements in the array:

```
let arrayOfNums: number[] = [1, 2, 3, 4];
let animals: string[] = ["Dog", "Cat", "Tiger"];
```

You can also use the Array generic type (Array<TypeOfElement>) in the following way:

```
let arrayOfNums: Array<number> = [1, 2, 3, 4];
let animals: Array<string> = ["Dog", "Cat", "Tiger"];
```

Type inference also works with objects. If you create the following object, TypeScript creates an object with these inferred types: id: number, name: string, and email: string:

```
const student = {
  id: 1,
  name: "Lisa Smith ",
  email: "lisa.s@mail.com ",
};
```

You can also define an object using the interface or type keyword, which describes the object's shape. The type and interface are quite similar, and most of the time you are free to choose which one you use:

```
// Using interface
interface Student {
    id: number;
    name: string;
    email: string;
};
// Or using type
type Student = {
    id: number;
    name: string;
    email: string;
};
```

Then, you can declare an object that conforms to the Student interface or type:

```
const myStudent: Student = {
    id: 1,
    name: "Lisa Smith ",
    email: "lisa.s@mail.com ",
};
```

 You can read more about the difference between type and interface in the Type-
Script documentation: https://www.typescriptlang.org/docs/handbook/2/
everyday-types.html#differences-between-type-aliases-and-interfaces.

Now, if you try to create an object that doesn't match the interface or type, you will get an error.
In the next image, we create an object where the id property value is string, but it is defined as
number in the interface:

```
TS Config ▾   Examples ▾   Help ▾                          Settings

v5.0.4 ▾   Run   Export ▾   Shar  →     .JS  .D.TS  Errors ❶Logs  Plugins

  1  interface Student {
  2      id: number;
  3      name: string;               Errors in code
  4      email: string;
  5  };                               Type 'string' is not assignable to
  6                                   type 'number'.
  7  const myStudent: Student = {
  8      id: "1",
  9      name: "Lisa Smith",
 10      email: "lisa.s@mail.com",
 11  };
 12
 13
```

Figure 9.2: Interface

You can define optional properties by using the question mark (?) at the end of the property name.
In the following example, we mark email to be optional. Now, you can create a student object
without an email because it is an optional property:

```
type Student = {
    id: number;
    name: string;
    email?: string;
```

```
};
// Student object without email
const myStudent: Student = {
    id: 1,
    name: "Lisa Smith"
}
```

The **optional chaining operator** (?.) can be used to safely access object properties and methods that can be null or undefined without causing an error. It is really useful with optional properties. Let's look at the following type, where address is optional:

```
type Person = {
    name: string,
    email: string;
    address?: {
        street: string;
        city: string;
    }
}
```

You can create an object based on the Person type that doesn't have the address property defined:

```
const person: Person = {
    name: "John Johnson",
    email: "j.j@mail.com"
}
```

Now, if you try to access the address property, an error is thrown:

```
// Error is thrown
console.log(person.address.street);
```

However, if you use optional chaining, the value undefined is printed to the console and an error is not thrown:

```
// Output is undefined
console.log(person.address?.street);
```

There are also many ways to compose types in TypeScript. You can use the | operator to create a **union type**, a type that handles different types. For example, the following example defines a type that can contain a string or number:

```
type InputType = string | number;
// Use your type
let name: InputType = "Hello";
let age: InputType = 12;
```

You can also use union types to define sets of strings or numbers, as shown in the following example:

```
type Fuel = "diesel" | "gasoline" | "electric ";
type NoOfGears = 5 | 6 | 7;
```

Now, we can use our union types in the following way:

```
type Car = {
  brand: string;
  fuel: Fuel;
  gears: NoOfGears;
}
```

If you create a new Car object and try to assign some other value than what is defined in the Fuel or NoOfGears union types, you will get an error.

Functions

When you define functions, you can set parameter types in the following way:

```
function sayHello(name: string) {
  console.log("Hello " + name);
}
```

If you now try to call the function using a different parameter type, you will get an error:

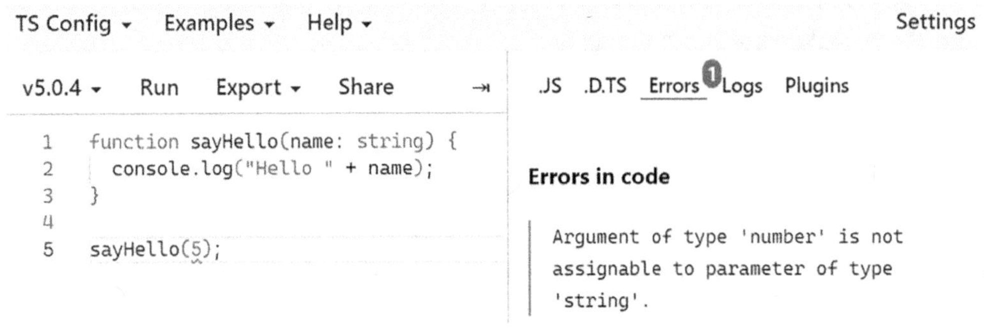

TS Config ▾   Examples ▾   Help ▾   Settings

v5.0.4 ▾   Run   Export ▾   Share   ⇥   .JS   .D.TS   Errors ❶ Logs   Plugins

```
1   function sayHello(name: string) {
2     console.log("Hello " + name);
3   }
4
5   sayHello(5);
```

Errors in code

Argument of type 'number' is not
assignable to parameter of type
'string'.

Figure 9.3: Function call

If a function parameter type is not defined, it implicitly has an any type. You can also use union types in function parameters:

```
function checkId(id: string | number) {
  if (typeof id === "string ")
    // do something
  else
    // do something else
}
```

A function's return type can be declared in the following way:

```
function calcSum(x: number, y: number): number {
  return x + y;
}
```

Arrow functions work in the same way in TypeScript, for example:

```
const calcSum = (x:number, y:number): number => x + y;
```

If the arrow function returns nothing, you can use the void keyword:

```
const sayHello = (name: string): void => console.log("Hello " + name);
```

Now, you have encountered some TypeScript basics, and we will learn how to apply these new skills in our React apps.

Using TypeScript features with React

TypeScript is a valuable addition to your React projects, especially when they grow in complexity. In this section, we will learn how we can get prop and state type validation in our React components and detect potential errors early in development.

State and props

In React, you have to define the type of component props. We have already learned that component props are JavaScript objects, so we can use type or interface to define the prop type.

Let's look at one example where a component receives a name (string) and age (number) prop:

```
function HelloComponent({ name, age }) {
  return(
    <>
      Hello {name}, you are {age} years old!
    </>
  );
}


export default HelloComponent;
```

Now, we can render our HelloComponent and pass props to it:

```
// imports...
function App() {
  return(
    <HelloComponent name="Mary" age={12} />
  )
}


export default App;
```

If we use TypeScript, we can first create a type that describes our props:

```
type HelloProps = {
  name: string;
  age: number;
};
```

Then, we can use our HelloProps type in the component props:

```
function HelloComponent({ name, age }: HelloProps) {
  return(
    <>
      Hello {name}, you are {age} years old!
    </>
  );
}


export default HelloComponent;
```

Now, if we pass props using the wrong type, we will get an error. This is great because, now, we can catch potential errors in the development phase:

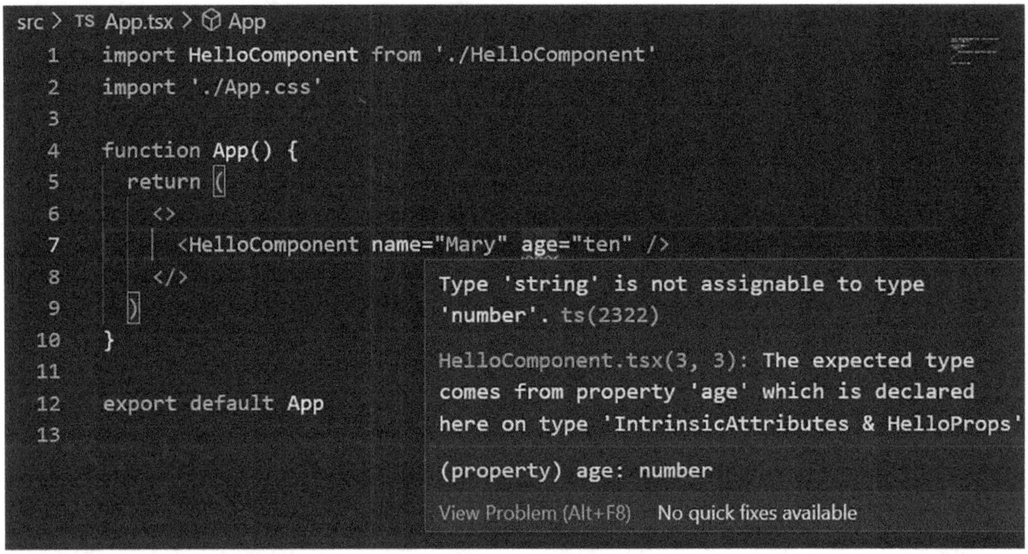

```
src > TS App.tsx > ⊘ App
  1    import HelloComponent from './HelloComponent'
  2    import './App.css'
  3
  4    function App() {
  5      return (
  6        <>
  7          <HelloComponent name="Mary" age="ten" />
  8        </>
  9      )
 10    }
 11
 12    export default App
 13
```

Type 'string' is not assignable to type 'number'. ts(2322)

HelloComponent.tsx(3, 3): The expected type comes from property 'age' which is declared here on type 'IntrinsicAttributes & HelloProps'

(property) age: number

View Problem (Alt+F8)   No quick fixes available

Figure 9.4: Typing props

If we had used JavaScript instead, we wouldn't have seen an error in this phase. In JavaScript, if we had passed a string as the age prop instead of a number, it would still have worked, but we might have encountered unexpected behavior or errors if we had tried to perform numerical operations on it later on.

If there are optional props, you can mark these using the question mark in your type where you define the props – for example, if age is optional:

```
type HelloProps = {
  name: string;
```

```
  age?: number;
};
```

Now, you can use your component with or without age props.

If you want to pass a function using the props, you can define it in your type using the following syntax:

```
// Function without parameters
type HelloProps = {
  name: string;
  age: number;
  fn: () => void;
};

// Function with parameters
type HelloProps = {
  name: string;
  age: number;
  fn: (msg: string) => void;
};
```

Quite often, you will want to use the same type in multiple files in your app. In that case, it is a good practice to extract types into their own file and export them:

```
// types.ts file
export type HelloProps = {
  name: string;
  age: number;
};
```

Then, you can import the type into any component where you need it:

```
// Import type and use it in your component
import { HelloProps } from ./types;

function HelloComponent({ name, age }: HelloProps) {
  return(
    <>
      Hello {name}, you are {age} years old!
    </>
```

```
  );
}


export default HelloComponent;
```

As we touched on in *Chapter 8*, you can also use the arrow function to create a functional component. There is a standard React type, `FC` (**function component**), that we can use with arrow functions. This type takes a generic argument that specifies the prop type, which is `HelloProps` in our case:

```
import React from 'react';
import { HelloProps } from './types';

const HelloComponent: React.FC<HelloProps> = ({ name, age }) => {
  return (
    <>
      Hello {name}, you are {age} years old!
    </>
  );
};


export default HelloComponent;
```

Now, you have learned how to define prop types in your React app, so we will move on to states. When you create states using the `useState` hook we learned about in *Chapter 8*, type inference handles typing when you are using common primitive types. For example:

```
// boolean
const [isReady, setReady] = useState(false);

// string
const [message, setMessage] = useState("");

// number
const [count, setCount] = useState(0);
```

If you try to update the state using a different type, you will get an error:

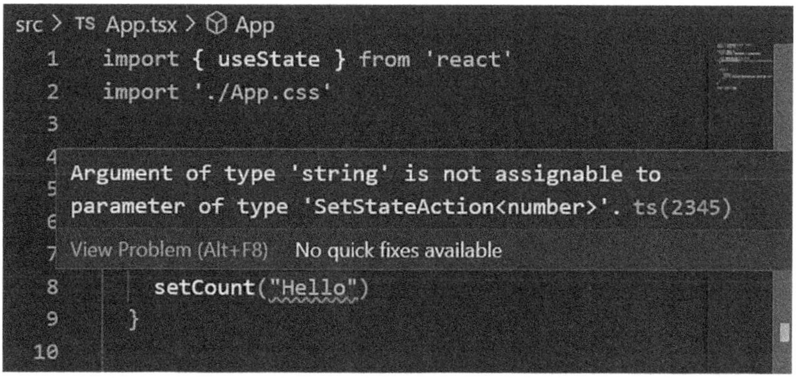

```
src > TS App.tsx > ⊘ App
  1    import { useState } from 'react'
  2    import './App.css'
  3
  4
       Argument of type 'string' is not assignable to
  5
       parameter of type 'SetStateAction<number>'. ts(2345)
  6
  7    View Problem (Alt+F8)    No quick fixes available
  8          setCount("Hello")
  9      }
 10
```

Figure 9.5: Typing state

You can also explicitly define state types. You have to do this if you want to initialize your state to null or undefined. In this case, you can use the union operator, and the syntax is the following:

```
const [message, setMessage] = useState<string | undefined>(undefined);
```

If you have a complex state, you can use a type or interface. In the following example, we create a type that describes a user. Then, we create a state and initialize it with an empty User object. If you want to allow null values, you can use a union to allow either a User object or a null value:

```
type User = {
  id: number;
  name: string;
  email: number;
};

// Use type with state, the initial value is an empty User object
const [user, setUser] = useState<User>({} as User);

// If null values are accepted
const [user, setUser] = useState<User | null>(null);
```

Events

In *Chapter 8*, we learned how to read user input in a React app. We used the input element's onChange event handler to save typed data to the state. When using TypeScript, we have to define the types of events. In the following screenshot, you can see that we get an error if types are not defined:

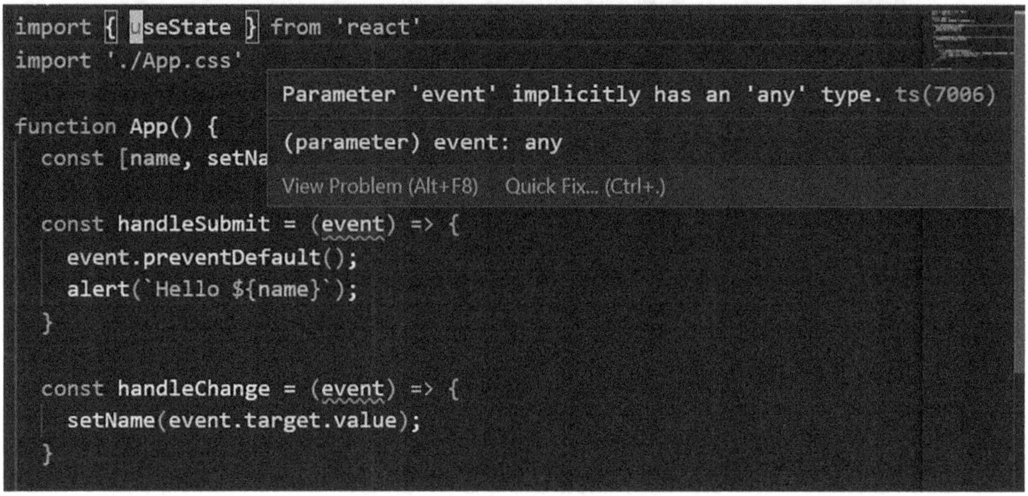

```
import { useState } from 'react'
import './App.css'
                          Parameter 'event' implicitly has an 'any' type. ts(7006)

function App() {
  const [name, setNa    (parameter) event: any

                          View Problem (Alt+F8)   Quick Fix... (Ctrl+.)

  const handleSubmit = (event) => {
    event.preventDefault();
    alert(`Hello ${name}`);
  }

  const handleChange = (event) => {
    setName(event.target.value);
  }
```

Figure 9.6: Typing events

Let's see how we can handle an input element's change event. Let's see one example where the input element code in the return statement looks like the following:

```
<input
  type="text"
  onChange={handleChange}
  value={name}
/>
```

The event handler function is called when the user types something into the input element, and the code looks like this:

```
const handleChange = (event) => {
  setName(event.target.value);
}
```

Now, we have to define the type of the event. For this, we can use the predefined React.ChangeEvent type.

 You can read the complete list of event types in the React TypeScript CheatSheet: https://react-typescript-cheatsheet.netlify.app/docs/basic/getting-started/forms_and_events/.

We want to handle a change event on an input element, so the type is the following:

```
const handleChange = (event: React.ChangeEvent<HTMLInputElement>) => {
  setName(event.target.value);
}
```

The form submission handler function handles the form submission. This function should take an event parameter of the type React.FormEvent<HTMLFormElement>:

```
const handleSubmit = (event: React.FormEvent<HTMLFormElement>) => {
  event.preventDefault();
  alert(`Hello ${name}`);
}
```

Now, we know how to handle events when using TypeScript in our React apps. Next, we will learn how to actually create a React app that uses TypeScript.

Creating a React app with TypeScript

Now, we will create a React app using Vite, and we will use TypeScript instead of JavaScript. We will use TypeScript later when we develop the frontend for our car backend. As we mentioned earlier, Vite comes with built-in TypeScript support:

1. Create a new React app using the following command:

```
npm create vite@latest
```

2. Next, name your project tsapp, and select the **React** framework and the **TypeScript** variant:

Figure 9.7: React TypeScript app

3. Then, move to your app folder, install dependencies, and run your app using the following commands:

```
cd tsapp
npm install
npm run dev
```

4. Open your app folder in VS Code, and you will see that the filename of our App component is App.tsx:

Figure 9.8: App.tsx

The file extension of TypeScript React files is .tsx (combining JSX with TypeScript). The regular file extension of TypeScript files is .ts.

5. Locate the tsconfig.json file in the root of your project. This is a configuration file used by TypeScript to specify compiler options, such as the target version of the compiled JavaScript output or the module system that is used. We can use the default settings defined by Vite.

    Let's create the React app that we used as an example in an earlier section, when we defined types for events. The user can enter a name, and when the button is pressed, a hello message is shown using an alert:

6. First, we will remove the code from the App.tsx file's return statement and leave only fragments. After also removing all unused imports (except the useState import), your code should look like the following:

```
import { useState } from 'react';
import './App.css';

function App() {
  return (
    <>
    </>
  )
}

export default App;
```

7. Next, create a state to store the value that the user enters into the input element:

```
function App() {
  const [name, setName] = useState("");

  return (
    <>
    </>
  )
}
```

8. After that, add two input elements to the `return` statement, one that collects user input and another that submits the form:

```tsx
// App.tsx return statement
return (
  <>
    <form onSubmit={handleSubmit}>
      <input
        type="text"
        value={name}
        onChange={handleChange}
      />
      <input type="submit" value="Submit"/>
    </form>
  </>
)
```

9. Next, create the event handler functions, `handleSubmit` and `handleChange`. Now, we also have to define the types of the events:

```tsx
// imports
function App() {
  const [name, setName] = useState("");

  const handleChange = (event: React.ChangeEvent<HTMLInputElement>) =>
  {
    setName(event.target.value);
  }

  const handleSubmit = (event: React.FormEvent<HTMLFormElement>) =>
  {
    event.preventDefault();
    alert(`Hello ${name}`);
  }
// continue...
```

10. Run the app using the `npm run dev` command.

11. Try typing your name into the input element and pressing the **Submit** button. You should see the hello message showing your name:

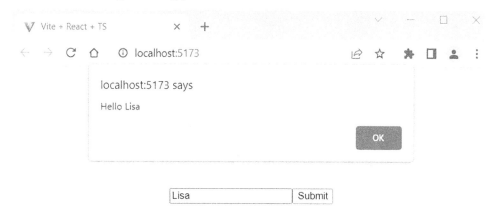

Figure 9.9: React TypeScript app

Vite and TypeScript

Vite transpiles TypeScript files to JavaScript, but it doesn't perform type checking. Vite uses **esbuild** to transpile TypeScript files because that is much faster than the TypeScript compiler (`tsc`).

The VS Code IDE handles type checking for us, and you should fix all errors that are shown in the IDE. You can also use a Vite plugin called `vite-plugin-checker` (https://github.com/fi3ework/vite-plugin-checker). Type checking is done when we build a Vite app to production, and all errors should be fixed before the production build. We will build our Vite app later in this book.

Summary

In this chapter, we started to learn TypeScript and how to use it in our React apps. Now, we know how to use common types in TypeScript and how to define types for React component props and states. We also learned to define types for events, and created our first React app with TypeScript using Vite.

In the next chapter, we will focus on networking with React. We will also use the GitHub REST API to learn how to consume a RESTful web service with React.

Questions

1. What is TypeScript?
2. How do we define variable types?

3. How do we define types in functions?

4. How do we define types for React props and states?

5. How do we define types for events?

6. How do we create a React TypeScript app using Vite?

Further reading

Here are some other useful resources for learning about React with TypeScript:

- React TypeScript Cheatsheets (`https://react-typescript-cheatsheet.netlify.app/`)

- *Learn React with TypeScript, Second Edition*, by Carl Rippon (`https://www.packtpub.com/product/learn-react-with-typescript-second-edition/9781804614204`)

- *Mastering TypeScript*, by Nathan Rozentals (`https://www.packtpub.com/product/mastering-typescript-fourth-edition/9781800564732`)

Learn more on Discord

To join the Discord community for this book – where you can share feedback, ask the author questions, and learn about new releases – follow the QR code below:

`https://packt.link/FullStackSpringBootReact4e`

10

Consuming the REST API with React

This chapter explains networking with React. This is a really important skill that we need in most React apps. We will learn about promises, which make asynchronous code cleaner and more readable. For networking, we will use the fetch and Axios libraries. As an example, we will use the OpenWeather and GitHub REST APIs to demonstrate how to consume RESTful web services with React. We will also see the React Query library in action.

In this chapter, we will cover the following topics:

- Promises
- Using the fetch API
- Using the Axios library
- Practical examples
- Handling race conditions
- Using the React Query library

Technical requirements

The following GitHub link will be required: https://github.com/PacktPublishing/Full-Stack-Development-with-Spring-Boot-3-and-React-Fourth-Edition/tree/main/Chapter10.

Promises

The traditional way to handle an asynchronous operation is to use **callback functions** for the success or failure of the operation. If the operation succeeds, the `success` function is called; otherwise, the `failure` function is called. The following (abstract) example shows the idea of using a callback function:

```
function doAsyncCall(success,  failure) {
  // Do some API call

  if (SUCCEED)
    success(resp);
  else
    failure(err);
}

success(response) {
  // Do something with response
}

failure(error) {
  // Handle error
}

doAsyncCall(success, failure);
```

Nowadays, **promises** are a fundamental part of asynchronous programming in JavaScript. A promise is an object that represents the result of an asynchronous operation. The use of promises simplifies the code when you're executing asynchronous calls. Promises are non-blocking. If you are using an older library for asynchronous operations that doesn't support promises, the code becomes much more difficult to read and maintain. In that case, you will end up with multiple nested callbacks that are really hard to read. Error handling will also be hard because you will have to check for errors in each callback.

With promises, we can execute asynchronous calls if the API or library we are using to send requests supports promises. In the following example, an asynchronous call is made. When the response is returned, the callback function inside the then method is executed, taking the response as an argument:

```
doAsyncCall()
.then(response => // Do something with the response)
```

The then method returns a promise. A promise can be in one of three states:

- **Pending**: Initial state
- **Fulfilled (or Resolved)**: Successful operation
- **Rejected**: Failed operation

The following code demonstrates a simple promise object, where setTimeout simulates an asynchronous operation:

```
const myPromise = new Promise((resolve, reject) => {
  setTimeout(() => {
    resolve("Hello");
  }, 500);
});
```

The promise is in the **pending** state when the promise object is created and while the timer is running. After 500 milliseconds, the resolve function is called with the value "Hello" and the promise enters the **fulfilled** state. If there is an error, the promise state changes to **rejected**, and that can be handled using the catch() function, which we'll show later.

You can chain many instances of then together, which means that you can run multiple asynchronous operations one after another:

```
doAsyncCall()
.then(response => // Get some data from the response)
.then(data => // Do something with the data
```

You can also add error handling to promises by using catch(). The catch() is executed if any error occurs in the preceding then chain:

```
doAsyncCall()
.then(response => // Get some data from the response)
.then(data => // Do something with data)
.catch(error => console.error(error))
```

async and await

There is a more modern way to handle asynchronous calls that involves async/await, which was introduced in ECMAScript 2017. The async/await method is based on promises. To use async/await, you must define an async() function that can contain await expressions.

The following is an example of an asynchronous call containing async/await. As you can see, you can write the code in a similar way to synchronous code:

```
const doAsyncCall = async () => {
  const response = await fetch('http://someapi.com');
  const data = await response.json();
  // Do something with the data
}
```

The fetch() function returns a promise, but now it is handled using await instead of the then method.

For error handling, you can use try...catch with async/await, as shown in the following example:

```
const doAsyncCall = async () => {
  try {
    const response = await fetch('http://someapi.com');
    const data = await response.json();
    // Do something with the data
  }
  catch(err) {
    console.error(err);
  }
}
```

Now that we understand promises, we can start learning about the fetch API, which we can use to make requests in our React apps.

Using the fetch API

With the fetch API, you can make web requests. The idea of the fetch API is similar to the traditional XMLHttpRequest or jQuery Ajax API, but the fetch API also supports promises, which makes it more straightforward to use. You don't have to install any libraries if you are using fetch and it is supported by modern browsers natively.

The fetch API provides a fetch() method that has one mandatory argument: the path of the resource you are calling. In the case of a web request, it will be the URL of the service. For a simple GET method call, which returns a response, the syntax is as follows:

```
fetch('http://someapi.com')
.then(response => response.json())
.then(data => console.log(data))
.catch(error => console.error(error))
```

The fetch() method returns a promise that contains the response. You can use the json() method to extract the JSON data from a response, and this method also returns a promise.

The response that is passed to the first then statement is an object that contains the properties ok and status, which we can use to check whether the request was successful. The ok property value is true if the response status is in the form 2XX:

```
fetch('http://someapi.com')
.then(response => {
  if (response.ok)
    // Successful request -> Status 2XX
  else
    // Something went wrong -> Error response
})
.then(data => console.log(data))
.catch(error => console.error(error))
```

To use another HTTP method, such as POST, you must define it in the second argument of the fetch() method. The second argument is an object where you can define multiple request settings. The following source code makes the request using the POST method:

```
fetch('http://someapi.com', {method: 'POST'})
.then(response => response.json())
.then(data => console.log(data))
.catch(error => console.error(error))
```

You can also add headers inside the second argument. The following `fetch()` call contains the `'Content-Type':'application/json'` header. It is recommended that you add the `'Content-Type'` header because then the server can interpret the request body correctly:

```
fetch('http://someapi.com',
  {
    method: 'POST',
    headers: {'Content-Type':'application/json'}
  }
.then(response => response.json())
.then(data => console.log(data))
.catch(error => console.error(error))
```

If you have to send JSON-encoded data inside the request body, the syntax to do so is as follows:

```
fetch('http://someapi.com',
{
  method: 'POST',
  headers: {'Content-Type':'application/json'},
  body: JSON.stringify(data)
}
.then(response => response.json())
.then(data => console.log(data))
.catch(error => console.error(error))
```

The `fetch` API is not the only way to execute requests in the React app. There are other libraries that you can use as well. In the next section, we will learn how to use one such popular library: `axios`.

Using the Axios library

You can also use other libraries for network calls. One very popular library is `axios` (https://github.com/axios/axios), which you can install in your React app with npm:

```
npm install axios
```

You must add the following `import` statement to your React component before using it:

```
import axios from 'axios';
```

The axios library has some benefits, such as automatic transformation of the JSON data, so you don't need the `json()` function when using axios. The following code shows an example call being made using axios:

```
axios.get('http://someapi.com')
.then(response => console.log(response))
.catch(error => console.log(error))
```

The axios library has its own call methods for the different HTTP methods. For example, if you want to make a POST request and send an object in the body, axios provides the axios.post() method:

```
axios.post('http://someapi.com', { newObject })
.then(response => console.log(response))
.catch(error => console.log(error))
```

You can also use the axios() function and pass a configuration object that specifies the request details, such as the method, header, data, and URL:

```
const response = await axios({
  method: 'POST',
  url: 'https://myapi.com/api/cars',
  headers: { 'Content-Type': 'application/json' },
  data: { brand: 'Ford', model: 'Ranger' },
});
```

The example code above sends a POST request to the https://myapi.com/api/cars endpoint. The request body contains an object and Axios automatically stringifies the data.

Now, we are ready to look at a few practical examples involving networking with React.

Practical examples

In this section, we will go through two examples of using public REST APIs in your React apps. In the first example, we use the OpenWeather API to fetch the current weather for London and render it in the component. In the second example, we use the GitHub API and allow the user to fetch repositories by keyword.

OpenWeather API

First, we will make a React app that shows the current weather in London. We will show the temperature, description, and weather icon in our app. This weather data will be fetched from **OpenWeather** (https://openweathermap.org/).

You need to register with OpenWeather to get an API key. A free account will be sufficient for our needs. Once you have registered, navigate to your account information to find the **API keys** tab. There, you'll see the API key that you need for your React weather app:

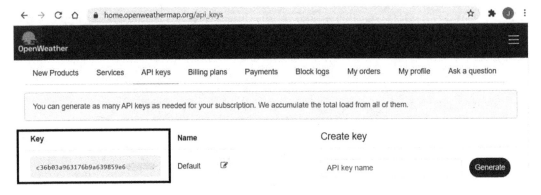

Figure 10.1: The OpenWeather API key

 Your API key will be activated automatically, up to 2 hours after your successful registration, so you may have to wait a while before you can use it in this section.

Let's create a new React app with Vite:

1. Open a terminal in Windows or Terminal in macOS/Linux, and type the following command:

    ```
    npm create vite@latest
    ```

2. Name your app weatherapp and select the **React** framework and **JavaScript** variant.

3. Navigate to the weatherapp folder and install dependencies:

    ```
    cd weatherapp
    npm install
    ```

4. Start your app with the following command:

    ```
    npm run dev
    ```

5. Open your project folder with VS Code and open the App.jsx file in the editor view. Remove all the code inside the fragment (<></>)and remove unused imports. Now, your source code should look as follows:

```
import './App.css'

function App() {
  return (
    <>
    </>
  );
}

export default App;
```

6. First, we must add the states that are needed to store response data. We will show the temperature, description, and weather icon in our app. We have three related values, so it is better to create one state that is an object instead of creating multiple individual states:

```
import { useState } from 'react';
import './App.css';

function App() {
  const [weather, setWeather] = useState({
      temp: '', desc: '', icon: ''
  });

  return (
    <>
    </>
  );
}

export default App;
```

7. When you are using a REST API, you should inspect the response so you can see the format of the JSON data. Here is the address that returns the current weather for London: https://api.openweathermap.org/data/2.5/weather?q=London&units=Metric&API key=YOUR_KEY.

If you copy the URL into a browser, you can view the JSON response data:

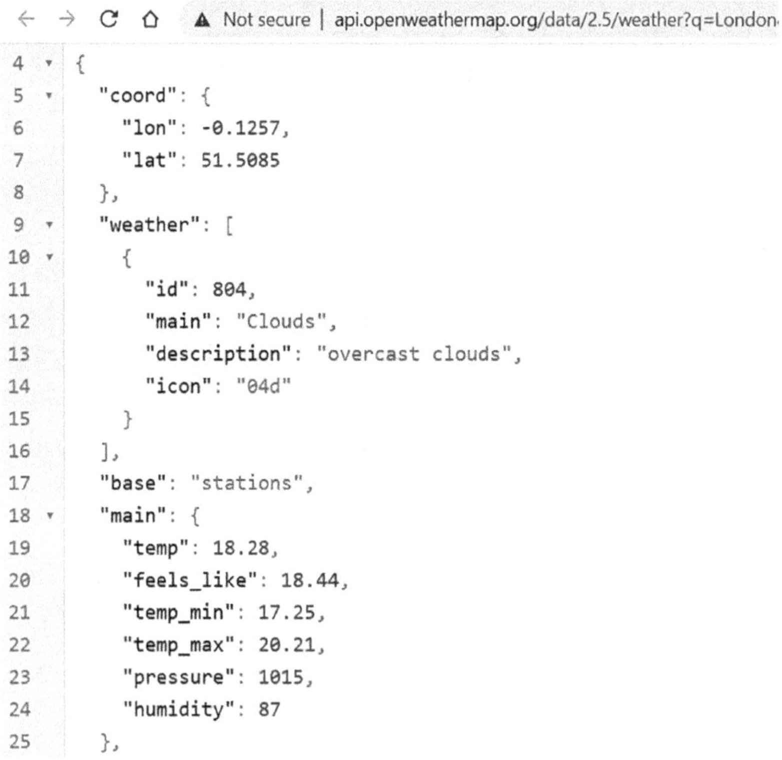

```
 4  ▾  {
 5  ▾      "coord": {
 6              "lon": -0.1257,
 7              "lat": 51.5085
 8          },
 9  ▾      "weather": [
10  ▾          {
11                  "id": 804,
12                  "main": "Clouds",
13                  "description": "overcast clouds",
14                  "icon": "04d"
15              }
16          ],
17          "base": "stations",
18  ▾      "main": {
19              "temp": 18.28,
20              "feels_like": 18.44,
21              "temp_min": 17.25,
22              "temp_max": 20.21,
23              "pressure": 1015,
24              "humidity": 87
25          },
```

Figure 10.2: Get weather by city

From the response, you can see that `temp` can be accessed using `main.temp`. You can also see that `description` and `icon` are inside the `weather` array, which has only one element, and that we can access it using `weather[0].description` and `weather[0].icon`.

8. We will implement the `fetch` call in the next few steps, inside the `useEffect` hook function. Import `useEffect` from React:

    ```
    import { useState, useEffect } from 'react';
    ```

9. The REST API call is executed using `fetch` in the `useEffect` hook function, using an empty array as the second argument. Therefore, the fetch is done once, after the first render. After a successful response, we save the weather data to the states. Once the state values have been changed, the component will be re-rendered. The following is the source code for the `useEffect` hook function. It will execute the `fetch()` function once after the first render (Note! Use your own API key in the code.):

```
useEffect(() => {
  fetch('https://api.openweathermap.org/data/2.5/
         weather?q=London&APIKey=YOUR_API_KEY&units=metric')
  .then(response => response.json())
  .then(result => {
    setWeather({
      temp: result.main.temp,
      desc: result.weather[0].main,
      icon: result.weather[0].icon
    });
  })
  .catch(err => console.error(err))
}, [])
```

10. Once you have added the `useEffect` function, the request is executed after the first render. We can check that everything has been done correctly using React Developer Tools. Open your app in a browser and open your React Developer Tools **Components** tab. Now, you can see that the states have been updated with the values from the response:

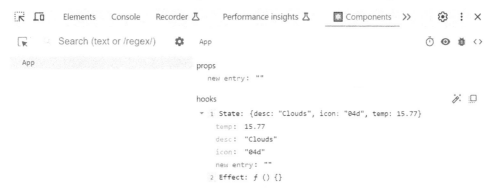

Figure 10.3: Weather component

You can also check that the request status is `200 OK` from the **Network** tab.

11. Finally, we will implement the `return` statement to show the weather values. We will use **conditional rendering** here; otherwise, we will get an error because we don't have image code in the first render call and the image upload won't succeed.

To show the weather icon, we must add `https://openweathermap.org/img/wn/` before the icon code, and `@2x.png` after the icon code.

You can find information about icons in the OpenWeather documentation:
`https://openweathermap.org/weather-conditions`.

Then, we can set the concatenated image URL as the img element's src attribute. Temperature and description are shown in the paragraph element. °C is the degrees Celsius symbol:

```
if (weather.icon) {
  return (
    <>
      <p>Temperature: {weather.temp} °C</p>
      <p>Description: {weather.desc}</p>
      <img src={`http://openweathermap.org/img/wn/${weather.
              icon}@2x.png`}
        alt="Weather icon" />
    </>
  );
}
else {
  return <div>Loading...</div>
}
```

12. Now, your app should be ready. When you open it in a browser, it should look as follows:

Temperature: 9.84 °C

Description: Clouds

Figure 10.4: WeatherApp

The source code for the entire App.jsx file is as follows:

```jsx
import { useState, useEffect } from 'react';
import './App.css'

function App() {
  const [weather, setWeather] = useState({temp: '', desc: '', icon: ''});

  useEffect(() => {
    fetch('https://api.openweathermap.org/data/2.5/weather?q=\
        London&APIKey=YOUR_API_KEY&units=metric')
    .then(response => response.json())
    .then(result => {
      setWeather({
        temp: result.main.temp,
        desc: result.weather[0].main,
        icon: result.weather[0].icon
      });
    })
    .catch(err => console.error(err))
  }, [])

  if (weather.icon) {
    return (
      <>
        <p>Temperature: {weather.temp} °C</p>
        <p>Description: {weather.desc}</p>
        <img src={
            `https://openweathermap.org/img/wn/${weather.icon}@2x.png`
        }
        alt="Weather icon" />
      </>
    );
  }
  else {
    return <>Loading...</>
  }
}

export default App
```

In our example, we checked that the weather icon was loaded to check if the fetch was completed. This is not the optimal solution because if the fetch ends in an error, our component still renders a loading message. The boolean state is used a lot in scenarios like this, but it doesn't solve the problem either. The best solution would be a status that indicates the exact state of the request (pending, resolved, rejected). You can read more about this in Kent C. Dodds' blog post, *Stop using isLoading Booleans*: `https://kentcdodds.com/blog/stop-using-isloading-booleans`. This problem is solved by the React Query library, which we will use later in this chapter.

GitHub API

In the second example, we are going to create an app that uses the GitHub API to fetch repositories by keyword. The user enters a keyword, and we fetch repositories that contain that keyword. We will use the `axios` library for web requests, and we will also practice using TypeScript in this example.

Let's first see how you can send a `GET` request using `axios` with TypeScript. You can make a `GET` request and specify the expected data type using TypeScript generics, as shown in the following example:

```
import axios from 'axios';

type MyDataType = {
  id: number;
  name: string;
}

axios.get<MyDataType>(apiUrl)
.then(response => console.log(response.data))
.catch(err => console.error(err));
```

If you try to access some field that is not present in the expected data type, you will get an error early in the development phase. At this point, it is important to understand that TypeScript is compiled to JavaScript and all type information is removed. Therefore, TypeScript doesn't have a direct impact on runtime behavior. If a REST API returns data of a different type than expected, TypeScript won't catch this as a runtime error.

Now, we can start to develop our GitHub app:

1. Create a new React app called restgithub using Vite, selecting the **React** framework and **TypeScript** variant.
2. Install dependencies, start the app, and open the project folder with VS Code.
3. Install axios using the following npm command in your project folder:

```
npm install axios
```

4. Remove the extra code inside the fragment <></> from the App.tsx file. Your App.tsx code should look as follows:

```
import './App.css';

function App() {
  return (
    <>
    </>
  );
}

export default App;
```

The URL of the GitHub REST API to search repositories is as follows: https://api.github.com/search/repositories?q={KEYWORD}.

 You can find the GitHub REST API documentation at https://docs.github.com/en/rest.

Let's inspect the JSON response by typing the URL into a browser and using the `react` keyword:

```
←  →  C  ⌂      🔒 api.github.com/search/repositories?q=react

7    ▾    "items": [
8    ▾       {
9               "id": 10270250,
10              "node_id": "MDEwOlJlcG9zaXRvcnkxMDI3MDI1MA==",
11              "name": "react",
12              "full_name": "facebook/react",
13              "private": false,
14    ▾         "owner": {
15                "login": "facebook",
16                "id": 69631,
17                "node_id": "MDEyOk9yZ2FuaXphdGlvbjY5NjMx",
18                "avatar_url": "https://avatars.githubusercontent.com/u/69631?v=4",
19                "gravatar_id": "",
20                "url": "https://api.github.com/users/facebook",
21                "html_url": "https://github.com/facebook",
22                "followers_url": "https://api.github.com/users/facebook/followers",
23                "following_url": "https://api.github.com/users/facebook/following{/other_user}",
24                "gists_url": "https://api.github.com/users/facebook/gists{/gist_id}",
25                "starred_url": "https://api.github.com/users/facebook/starred{/owner}{/repo}",
26                "subscriptions_url": "https://api.github.com/users/facebook/subscriptions",
27                "organizations_url": "https://api.github.com/users/facebook/orgs",
28                "repos_url": "https://api.github.com/users/facebook/repos",
29                "events_url": "https://api.github.com/users/facebook/events{/privacy}",
30                "received_events_url": "https://api.github.com/users/facebook/received_events",
31                "type": "Organization",
32                "site_admin": false
33              },
34              "html_url": "https://github.com/facebook/react",
35              "description": "A declarative, efficient, and flexible JavaScript library for building user interfaces.",
```

Figure 10.5: GitHub REST API

From the response, we can see that repositories are returned as a JSON array called `items`. From the individual repositories, we will show the `full_name` and `html_url` values.

5. We will present the data in the table and use the `map()` function to transform the values into table rows, as shown in *Chapter 8*. The `id` can be used as a key for a table row.

   We are going to make the REST API call with the keyword from the user input. One way to implement this is to create an input field and button. The user types the keyword into the input field, and the REST API call is made when the button is pressed.

    We can't make the REST API call in the `useEffect()` hook function because, in that phase, the user input isn't available when the component is rendered the first time.

We will create two states, one for the user input and one for the data from the JSON response. When we are using TypeScript, we have to define a type for the repository, as shown in the following code. The repodata state is an array of Repository type because repositories are returned as JSON arrays in the response. We only need to access three fields; therefore, only these fields are defined in the type. We will also import axios, which we'll use later when sending a request:

```
import { useState } from 'react';
import axios from 'axios';
import './App.css';

type Repository = {
  id: number;
  full_name: string;
  html_url: string;
};

function App() {
  const [keyword, setKeyword] = useState('');
  const [repodata, setRepodata] = useState<Repository[]>([]);

  return (
    <>
    </>
  );
}

export default App;
```

6. Next, we will implement the input field and the button in the return statement. We also have to add a change listener to our input field to be able to save the input value to a state called keyword. The button has a click listener, which invokes the function that will make the REST API call with the given keyword:

```
const handleClick = () => {
  // REST API call
}
```

```
return (
  <>
    <input
      value={keyword}
      onChange={e => setKeyword(e.target.value)}
    />
    <button onClick={handleClick}>Fetch</button>
  </>
);
```

7. In the handleClick() function, we will concatenate the url and keyword states using
    template literals (Note! Use backticks ` `). We will use the axios.get() method to send
    a request. As we learned earlier, Axios does not require the .json() method to be called
    on the response. Axios automatically parses the response data, and then we save the
    items array from the response data to the repodata state. We also use catch() to handle
    errors. Since we are using TypeScript, we will define the expected data type in the GET
    request. We have seen that the response is an object that contains an item property. The
    content of the item property is an array of repository objects; therefore, the data type is
    <{ items: Repository[] }>:

```
const handleClick = () => {
  axios.get<{ items: Repository[] }> (`https://api.github.com/
             search/repositories?q=${keyword}`)
  .then(response => setRepodata(response.data.items))
  .catch(err => console.error(err))
}
```

8. In the `return` statement, we will use the `map()` function to transform the `data` state into table rows. The `url` property of a repository will be the `href` value of the `<a>` element. Each repository has a unique `id` property, which we can use as a key for a table row. We use conditional rendering to handle cases where the response doesn't return any repositories:

```
return (
  <>
    <input
      value={keyword}
      onChange={e => setKeyword(e.target.value)}
    />
    <button onClick={handleClick}>Fetch</button>
    {repodata.length === 0 ? (
      <p>No data available</p>
    ) : (
      <table>
        <tbody>
          {repodata.map(repo => (
            <tr key={repo.id}>
              <td>{repo.full_name}</td>
              <td>
                <a href={repo.html_url}>{repo.html_url}</a>
              </td>
            </tr>
          ))}
        </tbody>
      </table>
    )}
  </>
);
```

9. The following screenshot shows the final app upon using the `react` keyword in the REST API call:

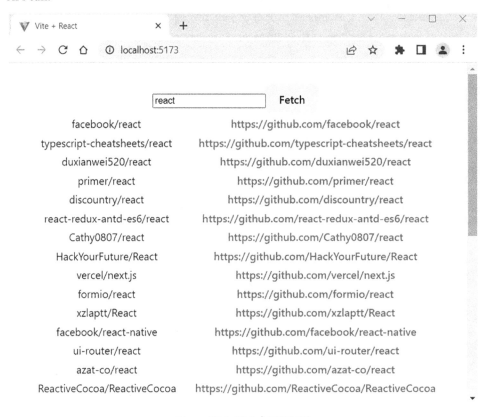

Figure 10.6: GitHub REST API

The source code for the `App.jsx` file looks as follows:

```
import { useState } from 'react';
import axios from 'axios';
import './App.css';

type Repository = {
  id: number;
  full_name: string;
  html_url: string;
};

function App() {
```

```
    const [keyword, setKeyword] = useState('');
    const [repodata, setRepodata] = useState<Repository[]>([]);

    const handleClick = () => {
      axios.get<{ items: Repository[]
        }>(`https://api.github.com/search/repositories?q=${keyword}`)
      .then(response => setRepodata(response.data.items))
      .catch(err => console.error(err));
    }


    return (
      <>
        <input
          value={keyword}
          onChange={e => setKeyword(e.target.value)}
        />
        <button onClick={handleClick}>Fetch</button>
        {repodata.length === 0 ? (
          <p>No data available</p>
        ) : (
          <table>
            <tbody>
              {repodata.map((repo) => (
                <tr key={repo.id}>
                  <td>{repo.full_name}</td>
                  <td>
                    <a href={repo.html_url}>{repo.html_url}</a>
                  </td>
                </tr>
              ))}
            </tbody>
          </table>
        )}
      </>
    );
}

export default App;
```

There is an API rate limit (number of daily requests without authentication) for the GitHub API, so if your code stops working, the reason might be here. The search endpoint that we are using has a limit of 10 requests per minute. If you exceed the limit, you have to wait one minute.

Handling race conditions

If your component makes several requests quickly, it can lead to a **race condition** that can create unpredictable or incorrect results. Network requests are asynchronous; therefore, requests don't necessarily finish in the same order as they were sent.

The following example code sends a network request when the `props.carid` value changes:

```
import { useEffect, useState } from 'react';

function CarData(props) {
  const [data, setData] = useState({});

  useEffect(() => {
    fetch(`https://carapi.com/car/${props.carid}`)
    .then(response => response.json())
    .then(cardata => setData(cardata))
  }, [props.carid]);

  if (data) {
    return <div>{data.car.brand}</div>;
  } else {
    return null;
  }
continue...
```

Now, if `carid` changes quickly multiple times, the data that is rendered might not be from the last request that was sent.

We can use the `useEffect` cleanup function to avoid race conditions. First, we create a boolean variable named `ignore` inside the `useEffect()`, with an initial value of `false`. Then, we update the `ignore` variable value to `true` in the cleanup function. In the state update, we check the value of the `ignore` variable, and the state is updated only if the value is `false`, which means that no new value has replaced `props.carid` and the effect is not cleaned up:

```
import { useEffect, useState } from 'react';

function CarData(props) {
  const [data, setData] = useState({});

  useEffect(() => {
    let ignore = false;
    fetch(`https://carapi.com/car/${props.carid}`)
    .then(response => response.json())
    .then(cardata => {
      if (!ignore) {
        setData(cardata)
      }
    });
      return () => {
        ignore = true;
      };
  }, [props.carid]);

  if (data) {
    return <div>{data.car.brand}</div>;
  } else {
    return null;
  }
}
continue...
```

Now, each time a component is re-rendered, the cleanup function is called and `ignore` is updated to `true`, and the effect is cleaned up. Only the result from the last request is rendered, and we can avoid race conditions.

React Query, which we will start to use next, provides some mechanisms for handling race conditions, such as concurrency control. It takes care that only one request is sent at a time for a given query key.

Using the React Query library

In proper React apps where you make a lot of network calls, the use of third-party networking libraries is recommended. The two most popular libraries are **React Query** (https://tanstack. com/query), also known as **Tanstack Query**, and **SWR** (https://swr.vercel.app/). These libraries provide a lot of useful features, such as data caching and performance optimization.

In this section, we will learn how you can use React Query to fetch data in your React app. We will create a React app that fetches repositories from the GitHub REST API using the react keyword:

1. First, create a React app called `gitapi` using Vite and select the **React** framework and **JavaScript** variant. Install dependencies and move to your project folder.

2. Next, install React Query and axios using the following commands in your project folder (Note! In this book, we are using Tanstack Query v4):

    ```
    // Install v4
    npm install @tanstack/react-query@4
    npm install axios
    ```

3. Remove the extra code inside the fragment `<></>` from the `App.jsx` file. Your `App.jsx` code should look as follows:

    ```jsx
    import './App.css';

    function App() {
      return (
        <>
        </>
      );
    }

    export default App;
    ```

4. React Query provides the `QueryClientProvider` and `QueryClient` components, which handle data caching. Import these components into your App component. Then, create an instance of `QueryClient` and render `QueryClientProvider` in our App component:

    ```jsx
    import './App.css';
    import { QueryClient, QueryClientProvider } from
      '@tanstack/react-query';

    const queryClient = new QueryClient();

    function App() {

      return (
        <>
          <QueryClientProvider client={queryClient}>
    ```

```
          </QueryClientProvider>
        </>
    )
  }
```

```
export default App;
```

React Query provides the useQuery hook function, which is used to invoke network requests. The syntax is the following:

```
const query = useQuery({ queryKey: ['repositories'], queryFn:
  getRepositories })
```

Note that:

- queryKey is a unique key for a query and it is used for caching and refetching data.
- queryFn is a function to fetch data, and it should return a promise.

The query object that the useQuery hook returns contains important properties, such as the status of the query:

```
const { isLoading, isError, isSuccess } = useQuery({ queryKey:
  ['repositories'], queryFn: getRepositories })
```

The possible status values are the following:

- isLoading: The data is not yet available.
- isError: The query ended with an error.
- isSuccess: The query ended successfully and query data is available.

The query object's data property contains the data that the response returns.

With this information, we can continue our GitHub example using useQuery.

5. We will create a new component for fetching data. Create a new file called Repositories.jsx in the src folder, and fill it with the following starter code:

```
function Repositories() {
  return (
    <> </>
  )
}
```

```
export default Repositories;
```

6. Import the useQuery hook and create a function called getRepositories() that invokes
    axios.get() on the GitHub REST API. Here, we use async/await with Axios. Call the
    useQuery hook function and make the value of the queryFn property our fetch function,
    getRepositories:

```
import { useQuery } from '@tanstack/react-query';
import axios from 'axios';

function Repositories() {
  const getRepositories = async () => {
    const response = await axios.get("https://api.github\
      .com/search/repositories?q=react");
    return response.data.items;
  }

  const { isLoading, isError, data } = useQuery({
    queryKey: ['repositories'],
    queryFn: getRepositories,
  })

  return (
    <></>
  )
}

export default Repositories;
```

7. Next, implement the conditional rendering. The repositories are rendered when the data
    is available. We also render a message if the REST API call ends with an error:

```
// Repositories.jsx
if (isLoading) {
  return <p>Loading...</p>
}

if (isError) {
  return <p>Error...</p>
}

else {
```

```
    return (
      <table>
        <tbody>
        {
        data.map(repo =>
          <tr key={repo.id}>
            <td>{repo.full_name}</td>
            <td>
              <a href={repo.html_url}>{repo.html_url}</a>
            </td>
          </tr>)
        }
      </tbody>
      </table>
    )
  }
```

8. In the final step, import our `Repositories` component into the `App` component and render it inside the `QueryClientProvider` component:

```
// App.jsx
import './App.css'
import Repositories from './Repositories'
import { QueryClient, QueryClientProvider } from '@tanstack/react-
  query'

const queryClient = new QueryClient()

function App() {
  return (
    <>
      <QueryClientProvider client={queryClient}>
        <Repositories />
      </QueryClientProvider>
    </>
  )
}

export default App
```

9. Now, your app should look like the following, and repositories are fetched using the React Query library. We also managed to handle request status easily using its built-in features. We don't need any states to store response data because React Query handles data management and caching:

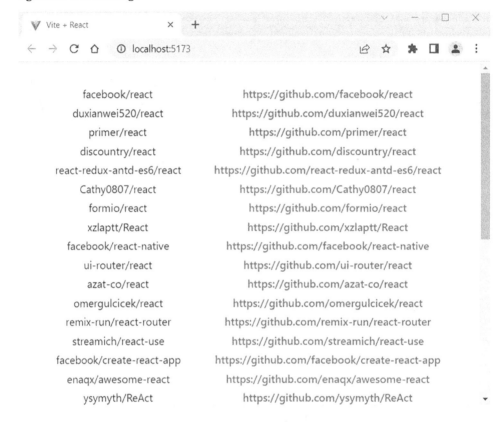

Figure 10.7: Tanstack Query

You should also see that refetching is done automatically by React Query when the browser is **refocused** (when the user returns to the application's window or tab). This is a good feature; you can see the updated data each time you refocus the browser. You can change this default behavior globally or per query.

 Refetching is also done automatically when the network is reconnected, or a new instance of the query is mounted (component is inserted into the DOM).

React Query has an important property called staleTime that defines how long data is considered fresh before it becomes stale and triggers a re-fetch in the background. By default, staleTime is 0, which means that data becomes stale immediately after a successful query. By setting the staleTime value, you can avoid unnecessary re-fetches if your data is not changing so often. The following example shows how you can set staleTime in your query:

```
const { isLoading, isError, data } = useQuery({
    queryKey: ['repositories'],
    queryFn: getRepositories,
    staleTime: 60 * 1000, // in milliseconds -> 1 minute

})
```

There is also a cacheTime property that defines when inactive queries are garbage collected, and the default time is 5 minutes.

React Query simplifies handling data mutations by providing a useMutation hook for creating, updating, and deleting data, along with built-in error handling and cache invalidation. Below is an example of useMutation that adds a new car. Now, because we want to add a new car, we use the axios.post() method:

```
// import useMutation
import { useMutation } from '@tanstack/react-query'
// usage
const mutation = useMutation({
    mutationFn: (newCar) => {
        return axios.post('api/cars', newCar);
    },
    onError: (error, variables, context) => {
        // Error in mutation
    },
    onSuccess: (data, variables, context) => {
        // Successful mutation
    },
})
```

 In the case of updating or deleting, you can use the axios.put(), axios.patch(), or axios.delete() methods.

The `mutationFn` property value is a function that sends a `POST` request to the server and returns a promise. React Query mutation also provides side effects, such as `onSuccess` and `onError`, that can be used in mutations. `onSuccess` is used to define a callback function that can perform any necessary actions, such as updating the UI or displaying a success message, based on a successful mutation response. `onError` is used to specify a callback function that will be executed if the mutation operation encounters an error.

Then, we can execute mutation in the following way:

```
mutation.mutate(newCar);
```

`QueryClient` provides an `invalidateQueries()` method that can be used to invalidate queries in the cache. If the query is invalidated in the cache, it will be fetched again. In the previous example, we used `useMutation` to add a new car to the server. If we have a query that fetches all cars and the query ID is `cars`, we can invalidate it in the following way after the new car has been added successfully:

```
import { useQuery, useMutation, useQueryClient } from
  '@tanstack/react-query'

const queryClient = useQueryClient();

// Fetch all cars
const { data } = useQuery({
  queryKey: ['cars'], queryFn: fetchCars
})

// Add a new car
const mutation = useMutation({
  mutationFn: (newCar) => {
    return axios.post('api/cars', newCar);
  },
  onError: (error, variables, context) => {
    // Error in mutation
  },
  onSuccess: (data, variables, context) => {
    // Invalidate cars query -> refetch
    queryClient.invalidateQueries({ queryKey: ['cars'] });
  },
})
```

This means that the cars will be fetched again after a new car has been added to the server.

By using React Query, we have to write less code to get proper error handling, data caching, and so on, due to the built-in functionalities that it provides. Now that we have learned about networking with React, we can utilize these skills in our frontend implementation.

Summary

In this chapter, we focused on networking with React. We started with promises, which make asynchronous network calls easier to implement. This is a cleaner way to handle calls, and it's much better than using traditional callback functions.

In this book, we are using the Axios and React Query libraries for networking in our frontend. We went through the basics of using these libraries. We implemented two React example apps using the fetch API and Axios to call REST APIs, and we presented the response data in the browser. We learned about race conditions and looked at how to fetch data using the React Query library.

In the next chapter, we will look at some useful React components that we are going to use in our frontend.

Questions

1. What is a promise?
2. What are fetch and axios?
3. What is React Query?
4. What are the benefits of using a networking library?

Further reading

There are other good resources available for learning about promises and asynchronous operations. A couple are as follows:

- *Using promises*, by MDN web docs (https://developer.mozilla.org/en-US/docs/Web/JavaScript/Guide/Using_promises)
- *Fetch Standard* (https://fetch.spec.whatwg.org/)

Learn more on Discord

To join the Discord community for this book – where you can share feedback, ask the author questions, and learn about new releases – follow the QR code below:

`https://packt.link/FullStackSpringBootReact4e`

11

Useful Third-Party Components for React

React is component-based, and we can find a lot of useful third-party components that we can use in our apps. In this chapter, we will look at several components that we are going to use in our frontend. We will examine how to find suitable components and how you can then use them in your own apps.

In this chapter, we will cover the following topics:

- Installing third-party React components
- Working with AG Grid
- Using the Material UI component library
- Managing routing with React Router

Technical requirements

Node.js must be installed. The following GitHub link for this chapter will also be required: `https://github.com/PacktPublishing/Full-Stack-Development-with-Spring-Boot-3-and-React-Fourth-Edition/tree/main/Chapter11`.

Installing third-party React components

There are lots of useful React components available for different purposes. You can save time by not doing everything from scratch. Well-known third-party components are also well tested, and there is good community support for them.

Our first task is to find a suitable component for our needs. One good site to search for components on is **JS.coach** (`https://js.coach/`). You just have to type in a keyword, search, and select **React** from the list of libraries.

In the following screenshot, you can see search results for table components for React:

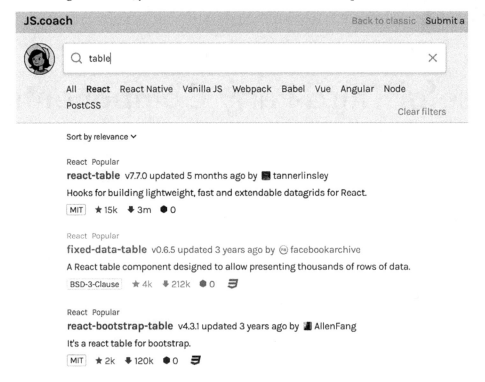

Figure 11.1: JS.coach

 Another good source for React components is `awesome-react-components`: `https://github.com/brillout/awesome-react-components`.

Components often have good documentation that helps you use them in your own React app. Let's see how we can install a third-party component in our app and start to use it:

1. Navigate to the **JS.coach** site, type `date` in the search input field, and filter by **React**.
2. In the search results, you will see a list component called `react-date-picker` (with two hyphens). Click the component link to see more detailed information about the component.

3. You should find the installation instructions on the info page, and some simple examples of how to use the component. You should also check that the development of a component is still active. The info page often provides the address of a component's website or GitHub repository, where you can find the full documentation. You can see the info page for react-date-picker in the following screenshot:

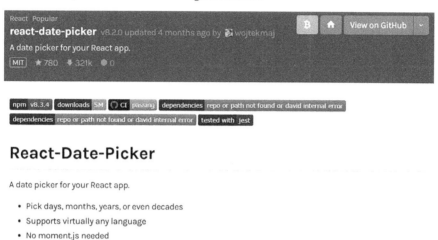

Figure 11.2: react-date-picker info page

4. As you can see from the component's info page, components are installed using the npm package. The syntax of the command to install components looks like this:

```
npm install component_name
```

Or, if you use yarn, it looks like this:

```
yarn add component_name
```

The npm install and yarn add commands save the component's dependency to the package.json file that is in the root folder of your React app.

Now, we will install the react-date-picker component to the myapp React app that we created in *Chapter 7, Setting Up the Environment and Tools – Frontend*. Move to your app root folder and type the following command:

```
npm install react-date-picker
```

5. If you open the `package.json` file from your app root folder, you can see that the component has now been added to the `dependencies` section, as illustrated in the following code snippet:

```
"dependencies": {
  "react": "^18.2.0",
  "react-dom": "^18.2.0"
  "react-date-picker": "^10.0.3",
},
```

As shown, you can find the installed version number from the `package.json` file.

If you want to install a specific version of a component, you can use the following command:

```
npm install component_name@version
```

And if you want to remove an installed component from your React app, you can use the following command:

```
npm uninstall component_name
```

Or, if you use yarn:

```
yarn remove component_name
```

You can see what components are outdated by using the following command in your project root directory. If the output is empty, all components are in the latest version:

```
npm outdated
```

You can update all outdated components by using the following command in your project root directory:

```
npm update
```

You should first ensure that there are no changes that might break your existing code. Proper components have a changelog or release notes available, where you can see what has changed in the new version.

6. Installed components are saved to the `node_modules` folder in your app. If you open that folder, you should find the `react-date-picker` folder, as illustrated in the following screenshot:

Figure 11.3: node_modules

You can get the list of your project dependencies by using the following npm command:

```
npm list
```

If you push your React app source code to GitHub, you should not include the node_modules folder because it contains a significant number of files. The Vite project contains a .gitignore file that excludes the node_modules folder from the repository. A section of the .gitignore file looks like this, and you can see that node_modules is found in the file:

```
# Logs
logs
*.log
npm-debug.log*
yarn-debug.log*
yarn-error.log*
pnpm-debug.log*
lerna-debug.log*

node_modules
dist
dist-ssr
*.local
```

The idea is that when you clone a React app from the GitHub repository, you type the npm install command, which reads dependencies from the package.json file and downloads them to your app.

7. To start using your installed component, import it into the file(s) where you want to use it. The code to achieve this is illustrated in the following snippet:

    ```
    import DatePicker from 'react-date-picker';
    ```

You have now learned how to install React components in your React app. Next, we will start to use a third-party component in our React app.

Working with AG Grid

AG Grid (https://www.ag-grid.com/) is a flexible data grid component for React apps. It is like a spreadsheet that you can use to present your data, and it can contain interactivity. It has many useful features, such as filtering, sorting, and pivoting. We will use the Community version, which is free (under an MIT license).

Let's modify the GitHub **REST API** app that we created in *Chapter 10, Consuming the REST API with React*. Proceed as follows:

1. To install the ag-grid community component, open the command line or terminal and move to the restgithub folder, which is the root folder of the app. Install the component by typing the following command:

    ```
    npm install ag-grid-community ag-grid-react
    ```

2. Open the App.tsx file with **Visual Studio Code** (**VS Code**) and remove the table element inside the return statement. The App.tsx file should now look like this:

    ```
    import { useState } from 'react';
    import axios from 'axios';
    import './App.css';

    type Repository = {
      id: number;
      full_name: string;
    ```

```
      html_url: string;
};

function App() {
  const [keyword, setKeyword] = useState('');
  const [repodata, setRepodata] = useState<Repository[]>([]);

  const handleClick = () => {
    axios.get<{ items: Repository[]
      }>(`https://api.github.com/search/repositories?q=${keyword}`)
      .then(response => setRepodata(response.data.items))
      .catch(err => console.error(err));
  }


  return (
    <>
      <input
        value={keyword}
        onChange={e => setKeyword(e.target.value)} />
      <button onClick={handleClick}>Fetch</button>
    </>
  );
}

export default App;
```

3. Import the `ag-grid` component and stylesheets by adding the following lines of code at the beginning of the `App.tsx` file:

```
import { AgGridReact } from 'ag-grid-react';
import 'ag-grid-community/styles/ag-grid.css';
import 'ag-grid-community/styles/ag-theme-material.css';
```

`ag-grid` provides different predefined styles. We are using a Material Design style.

4. Next, we will add the imported `AgGridReact` component to the `return` statement. To fill the ag-grid component with data, you have to pass the `rowData` prop to the component. Data can be an array of objects, so we can use our state, `repodata`. The ag-grid component should be wrapped inside the `div` element that defines the style. The code is illustrated in the following snippet:

```
return (
    <div className="App">
      <input value={keyword}
        onChange={e => setKeyword(e.target.value)} />
      <button onClick={fetchData}>Fetch</button>
      <div className="ag-theme-material"
        style={{height: 500, width: 850}}>
        <AgGridReact
          rowData={repodata}
        />
      </div>
    </div>
  );
```

5. Next, we will define columns for the ag-grid. We will define a state called `columnDefs`, which is an array of column definition objects. ag-grid provides a `ColDef` type that we can use here. In a column object, you have to define the data accessor by using the required `field` props. The `field` value is the property name in the REST API response data that the column should display:

```
// Import ColDef type
import { ColDef } from 'ag-grid-community';

// Define columns
const [columnDefs] = useState<ColDef[]>([
    {field: 'id'},
    {field: 'full_name'},
    {field: 'html_url'},
]);
```

6. Finally, we will use the AG Grid `columnDefs` prop to define these columns, as follows:

```
<AgGridReact
  rowData={data}
  columnDefs={columnDefs}
/>
```

7. Run the app and open it in a web browser. The table looks quite nice by default, as shown in the following screenshot:

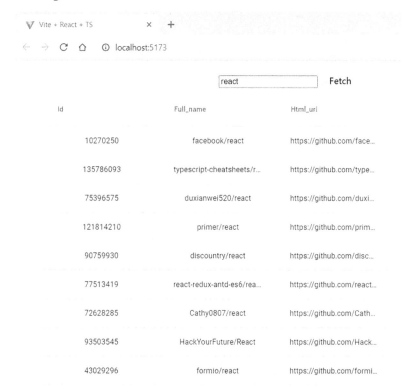

Figure 11.4: ag-grid component

8. Sorting and filtering are disabled by default, but you can enable them using the `sortable` and `filter` props in ag-grid columns, as follows:

```
const [columnDefs] = useState<ColDef[]>([
  {field: 'id', sortable: true, filter: true},
  {field: 'full_name', sortable: true, filter: true},
  {field: 'html_url', sortable: true, filter: true}
]);
```

Now, you can sort and filter any columns in the grid by clicking the column header, as illustrated in the following screenshot:

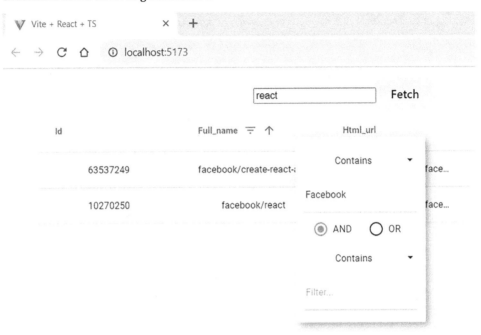

Figure 11.5: ag-grid filtering and sorting

9. You can also enable paging and set the page size in ag-grid by using the pagination and paginationPageSize props, as follows:

```
<AgGridReact
  rowData={data}
  columnDefs={columnDefs}
  pagination={true}
  paginationPageSize={8}
/>
```

Now, you should see pagination in your table, as illustrated in the following screenshot:

Id	Full_name ↑	Html_url
72628285	Cathy0807/react	https://github.com/Cath...
23338716	JedWatson/react-select	https://github.com/Jed...
3606624	ReactiveCocoa/Reactive...	https://github.com/Reac...
68626716	StephenGrider/ReactNat...	https://github.com/Step...
350770929	academind/react-compl...	https://github.com/acad...
26704639	akiran/react-slick	https://github.com/akira...
138648247	alpersonalwebsite/react	https://github.com/alper...
34526884	ant-design/ant-design	https://github.com/ant-d...

1 to 8 of 30 |<   <   Page 1 of 4   >   >|

Figure 11.6: ag-grid pagination

> You can find documentation for different grid and column props from
> the AG Grid website: `https://www.ag-grid.com/react-data-grid/`
> `column-properties/`.

10. The `cellRenderer` prop can be used to customize the content of a table cell. The following
    example shows how you can render a button in a grid cell:

```
// Import ICellRendererParams
import { ICellRendererParams } from 'ag-grid-community';

// Modify columnDefs
const columnDefs = useState<ColDef[]>([
  {field: 'id', sortable: true, filter: true},
  {field: 'full_name', sortable: true, filter: true},
  {field: 'html_url', sortable: true, filter: true},
  {
```

```
      field: 'full_name',
      cellRenderer: (params: ICellRendererParams) => (
        <button
          onClick={() => alert(params.value)}>
          Press me
        </button>
      ),
    },
  ]);
```

The function in the cell renderer accepts params as an argument. The type of params is
ICellRendererParams, which we have to import. The params.value will be the value of
the full_name cell, which is defined in the field property of the column definition. If you
need access to all values in a row, you can use params.row, which is the whole row object.
This is useful if you need to pass a whole row of data to some other component. When the
button is pressed, it will open an alert that shows the value of the full_name cell.

Here is a screenshot of the table with buttons:

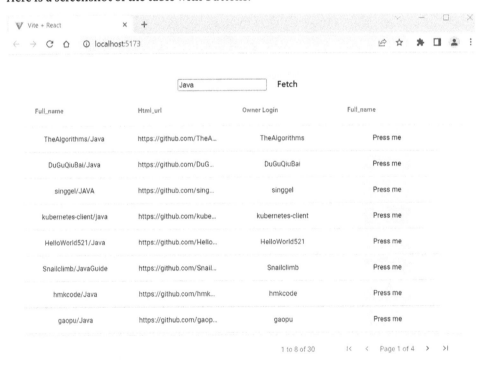

Figure 11.7: Grid with buttons

If you press any button, you should see an alert that shows the value of the full_name cell.

11. The button column has a Full_name header because, by default, the field name is used as the header name. If you want to use something else, you can use the headerName prop in the column definition, as shown in the following code:

```
const columnDefs: ColDef[] = [
  { field: 'id', sortable: true, filter: true },
  { field: 'full_name', sortable: true, filter: true },
  { field: 'html_url', sortable: true, filter: true },
  {
    headerName: 'Actions',
    field: 'full_name',
    cellRenderer: (params: ICellRendererParams) => (
      <button
        onClick={() => alert(params.value)}>
        Press me
      </button>
    ),
  },
];
```

In the next section, we will start to use the Material UI component library, which is one of the most popular React component libraries.

Using the Material UI component library

Material UI (https://mui.com/), or **MUI**, is the React component library that implements Google's Material Design language (https://m2.material.io/design). Material Design is one of the most popular design systems today. MUI contains a lot of different components – such as buttons, lists, tables, and cards – that you can use to achieve a nice and uniform **user interface** (UI).

> In this book, we will use MUI version 5. If you want to use another version, you should follow the official documentation (https://mui.com/material-ui/getting-started/). MUI version 5 supports Material Design version 2.

In this section, we will create a small shopping list app and style the UI using MUI components. In our app, a user can enter shopping items that contain two fields: *product* and *amount*. Entered shopping items are displayed in the application as a list. The final UI looks like the following screenshot. The **ADD ITEM** button opens a modal form, where the user can enter a new shopping item:

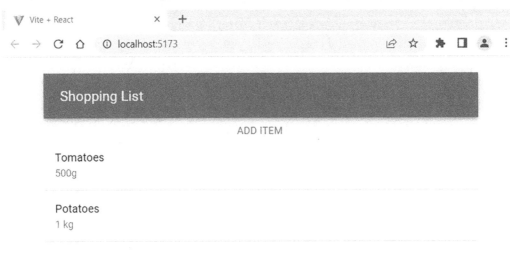

Figure 11.8: Shopping List UI

Now, we are ready to start the implementation:

1. Create a new React app called shoppinglist (select the **React** framework and **TypeScript** variant) and install dependencies by running the following commands:

    ```
    npm create vite@latest
    cd shoppinglist
    npm install
    ```

2. Open the shopping list app with VS Code. Install MUI by typing the following command in the project root folder in PowerShell or any suitable terminal:

    ```
    npm install @mui/material @emotion/react @emotion/styled
    ```

3. MUI uses the *Roboto* font by default, but it is not provided out of the box. The easiest way to install Roboto fonts is by using Google Fonts. To use Roboto fonts, add the following line inside the head element of your index.html file:

    ```
    <link
      rel="stylesheet"
    ```

```
     href="https://fonts.googleapis.com/css?family=\
         Roboto:300,400,500,700&display=swap"
/>
```

4. Open the App.tsx file and remove all the code inside the fragment (<></>). Also, remove unused code and imports. Now, your App.tsx file should look like this:

```
// App.tsx
import './App.css';

function App() {
  return (
    <>
    </>
  );
}

export default App;
```

You should also see an empty page in the browser.

5. MUI provides different layout components, and the basic layout component is the Container. This is used to center your content horizontally. You can specify the maximum width of a container using the maxWidth prop; the default value is lg (large), which is suitable for us. Let's use the Container component in our App.tsx file, as follows:

```
import Container from '@mui/material/Container';
import './App.css';

function App() {
  return (
    <Container>
    </Container>
  );
}

export default App;
```

6. Remove the `index.css` file import from the `main.tsx` file so that we get full screen for our app. We also don't want to use predefined styles from Vite:

```
// main.tsx
import React from 'react'
import ReactDOM from 'react-dom/client'
import App from './App.jsx'
import './index.css' // REMOVE THIS LINE

ReactDOM.createRoot(document.getElementById('root')).render(
  <React.StrictMode>
    <App />
  </React.StrictMode>,
)
```

7. Next, we will use the MUI AppBar component to create the toolbar in our app. Import the AppBar, ToolBar, and Typography components into your App.tsx file. Also, import useState from React, which we will need later. The code is illustrated in the following snippet:

```
import { useState } from 'react';
import Container from '@mui/material/Container';
import AppBar from '@mui/material/AppBar';
import Toolbar from '@mui/material/Toolbar';
import Typography from '@mui/material/Typography';
import './App.css'
```

8. Render the AppBar by adding the following code to your App component's return statement. The Typography component provides predefined text sizes, and we will use this in our toolbar text. variant props can be used to define text size:

```
function App() {
  return (
    <Container>
      <AppBar position="static">
        <Toolbar>
          <Typography variant="h6">
            Shopping List
```

```
            </Typography>
          </Toolbar>
        </AppBar>
      </Container>
    );
  }
```

9. Start your app. It should now look like this:

Figure 11.9: AppBar component

10. In the App component, we need one array state to save the shopping list items. One shopping list item contains two fields: product and amount. We have to create a type for the shopping items, Item, which we will also export because we need it in other components later:

```
// App.tsx
export type Item = {
  product: string;
  amount: string;
}
```

11. Next, we will create the state where we save our shopping items. Create a state called items, whose type is an array of Item types:

```
const [items, setItems] = useState<Item[]>([]);
```

12. Then, create a function that adds a new item to the items state. In the addItem function, we will use spread notation (...) to add a new item at the beginning of an existing array:

```
const addItem = (item: Item) => {
  setItems([item, ...items]);
}
```

13. We need to add a new component for adding shopping items. Create a new file called `AddItem.tsx` in the root folder of the app, and add the following code to your `AddItem.tsx` file. The `AddItem` component function receives props from its parent component. The code is illustrated in the following snippet. We will define the props type later:

```
function AddItem(props) {
  return(
    <></>
  );
}


export default AddItem;
```

The `AddItem` component will use the MUI modal dialog to collect data. In the form, we will add two input fields, `product` and `amount`, and a button that calls the `App` component's `addItem` function. To be able to call the `addItem` function, which is in the `App` component, we have to pass it in props when rendering the `AddItem` component. Outside the modal `Dialog` component, we will add a button that opens the modal form where the user can enter a new shopping item. This button is the only visible element when the component is rendered initially.

The following steps describe the implementation of the modal form.

14. We have to import the following MUI components for the modal form: `Dialog`, `DialogActions`, `DialogContent`, and `DialogTitle`. For the UI of the modal form, we require the following components: `Button` and `TextField`. Add the following imports to your `AddItem.tsx` file:

```
import Button from '@mui/material/Button';
import TextField from '@mui/material/TextField';
import Dialog from '@mui/material/Dialog';
import DialogActions from '@mui/material/DialogActions';
import DialogContent from '@mui/material/DialogContent';
import DialogTitle from '@mui/material/DialogTitle';
```

15. The `Dialog` component has one prop called open, and if the value is `true`, the dialog is visible. The default value of open props is `false`, and the dialog is hidden. We will declare one state called open and two functions to open and close the modal dialog. The default value of the open state is `false`. The `handleOpen` function sets the open state to `true`, and the `handleClose` function sets it to `false`. The code is illustrated in the following snippet:

```
// AddItem.tsx
// Import useState
import { useState } from 'react';

// Add state, handleOpen and handleClose functions
const [open, setOpen] = useState(false);

const handleOpen = () => {
  setOpen(true);
}

const handleClose = () => {
  setOpen(false);
}
```

16. We will add `Dialog` and `Button` components inside the `return` statement. We have one button outside the dialog that will be visible when the component is rendered for the first time. When the button is pressed, it calls the `handleOpen` function, which opens the dialog. Inside the dialog, we have two buttons: one for canceling and one for adding a new item. The **Add** button calls the `addItem` function, which we will implement later. The code is illustrated in the following snippet:

```
return(
    <>
        <Button onClick={handleOpen}>
          Add Item
        </Button>
        <Dialog open={open} onClose={handleClose}>
          <DialogTitle>New Item</DialogTitle>
          <DialogContent>
          </DialogContent>
          <DialogActions>
            <Button onClick={handleClose}>
              Cancel
            </Button>
            <Button onClick={addItem}>
              Add
            </Button>
```

```
          </DialogActions>
        </Dialog>
      </>
  );
```

17. To collect data from a user, we have to declare one more state. This state is used to store a shopping item that the user enters, and its type is Item. We can import the Item type from the App component:

```
// Add the following import to AddItem.tsx
import { Item } from './App';
```

18. Add the following state to the AddItem component. The type of the state is Item, and we initialize it to an empty item object:

```
// item state
const [item, setItem] = useState<Item>({
  product: '',
  amount: '',
});
```

19. Inside the DialogContent component, we will add two inputs to collect data from a user. There, we will use the TextField MUI component that we have already imported. The margin prop is used to set the vertical spacing of text fields, and the fullwidth prop is used to make input take up the full width of its container. You can find all the props in the MUI documentation. The value props of the text fields must be the same as the state where we want to save the typed value. The onChange event listener saves the typed value to the item state when the user types something into the text fields. In the product field, the value is saved to the item.product property, and in the amount field, the value is saved to the item.amount property. The code is illustrated in the following snippet:

```
<DialogContent>
  <TextField value={item.product} margin="dense"
    onChange={ e => setItem({...item,
      product: e.target.value}) }
    label="Product" fullWidth />
  <TextField value={item.amount} margin="dense"
    onChange={ e => setItem({...item,
      amount: e.target.value}) }
    label="Amount" fullWidth />
</DialogContent>
```

20. Finally, we have to create a function that calls the addItem function that we receive in the props. The function takes a new shopping item as an argument. First, we define a type for the props. The addItem function that is passed from the App component accepts one argument of type Item, and the function doesn't return anything. The type definition and prop typing look like the following:

```
// AddItem.tsx
type AddItemProps = {
  addItem: (item: Item) => void;
}

function AddItem(props: AddItemProps) {
  const [open, setOpen] = useState(false);
  // Continues...
```

21. The new shopping item is now stored in the item state and contains the values that the user typed in. Because we get the addItem function from the props, we can call it using the props keyword. We will also call the handleClose function, which closes the modal dialog. The code is illustrated in the following snippet:

```
// Calls addItem function and passes item state into it
const addItem = () => {
  props.addItem(item);
  // Clear text fields and close modal dialog
  setItem({ product: '', amount: '' });
  handleClose();
}
```

22. Our AddItem component is now ready, and we have to import it into our App.tsx file and render it there. Add the following import statement to your App.tsx file:

```
import AddItem from './AddItem';
```

23. Add the AddItem component to the return statement in the App.tsx file. Pass the addItem function in a prop to the AddItem component, as follows:

```
// App.tsx
return (
  <Container>
    <AppBar position="static">
      <Toolbar>
```

```
      <Typography variant="h6">
        Shopping List
      </Typography>
    </Toolbar>
  </AppBar>
  <AddItem addItem={addItem}/>
  </Container>
);
```

24. Now, open your app in the browser and press the **ADD ITEM** button. You will see the modal form opening, and you can type in a new item, as illustrated in the following screenshot. The modal form is closed when you press the **ADD** button:

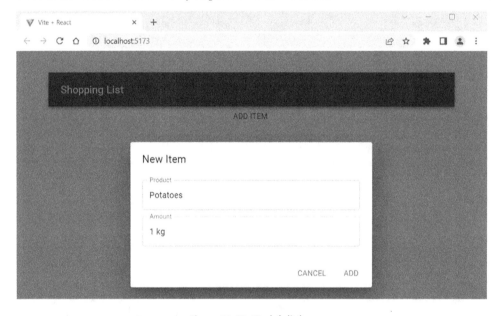

Figure 11.10: Modal dialog

25. Next, we will add a list to the App component that shows our shopping items. For that, we will use the MUI List, ListItem, and ListItemText components. Import the components into the App.tsx file:

```
// App.tsx
import List from '@mui/material/List';
import ListItem from '@mui/material/ListItem';
import ListItemText from '@mui/material/ListItemText';
```

26. Then, we will render the List component. Inside that, we will use the map function to generate ListItem components. Each ListItem component should have a unique key prop, and we use a divider prop to get a divider at the end of each list item. We will display the product in the primary text and the amount in the secondary text of the ListItemText component. The code is illustrated in the following snippet:

```tsx
// App.tsx
return (
    <Container>
        <AppBar position="static">
            <Toolbar>
                <Typography variant="h6">
                    Shopping List
                </Typography>
            </Toolbar>
        </AppBar>
        <AddItem addItem={addItem} />
        <List>
            {
                items.map((item, index) =>
                    <ListItem key={index} divider>
                        <ListItemText
                            primary={item.product}
                            secondary={item.amount}/>
                    </ListItem>
                )
            }
        </List>
    </Container>
);
```

27. Now, the UI looks like this:

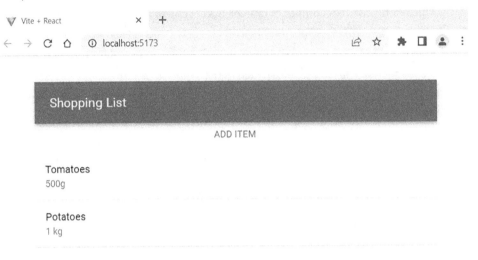

Figure 11.11: Shopping List

The MUI `Button` component has three variants: `text`, `contained`, and `outlined`. The `text` variant is the default, and you can change it using the `variant` prop. For example, if we wanted to have an outlined **ADD ITEM** button, we could change the button's `variant` prop in the `AddItem.ts` file, like this:

```
<Button variant="outlined" onClick={handleOpen}>
    Add Item
</Button>
```

In this section, we learned how to get a consistent design in our React app by using the Material UI library. You can easily get a polished and professional look to your apps with MUI. Next, we will learn how to use React Router, a popular routing library.

Managing routing with React Router

There are a few good libraries available for routing in React. React frameworks such as Next.js and Remix provide built-in routing solutions. The most popular library, which we are using, is **React Router** (`https://github.com/ReactTraining/react-router`). For web applications, React Router provides a package called `react-router-dom`. React Router uses **URL-based routing**, which means that we can define which component is rendered based on the URL.

To start using React Router, we have to install dependencies using the following command. In this book, we will use React Router version 6:

```
npm install react-router-dom@6
```

The `react-router-dom` library provides components that are used to implement routing. `BrowserRouter` is the router for web-based applications. The `Route` component renders the defined component if the given locations match.

The following code snippet provides an example of the `Route` component. The `element` prop defines a rendered component when the user navigates to the `contact` endpoint that is defined in the `path` prop. The path is relative to the current location:

```
<Route path="contact" element={<Contact />} />
```

You can use a * wildcard at the end of the `path` prop, like this:

```
<Route path="/contact/*" element={<Contact />} />
```

Now, it will match all endpoints under the contact – for example, `contact/mike`, `contact/john`, and so on.

The `Routes` component wraps multiple `Route` components. The `Link` component provides navigation to your application. The following example shows the `Contact` link and navigates to the `/contact` endpoint when the link is clicked:

```
<Link to="/contact">Contact</Link>
```

Let's see how we can use these components in practice:

1. Create a new React app called `routerapp` using Vite, selecting the **React** framework and the **TypeScript** variant. Move to your project folder and install dependencies. Also install the `react-router-dom` library:

```
npm create vite@latest
cd routerapp
npm install
npm install react-router-dom@6
```

2. Open the src folder with VS Code and open the App.tsx file in the editor view. Import components from the react-router-dom package and remove extra code from the return statement, along with unused imports. After these modifications, your App.tsx source code should look like this:

```
import { BrowserRouter, Routes, Route, Link } from 'react-
  router-dom';
import './App.css';

function App() {
  return (
    <>
    </>
  );
}

export default App;
```

3. Let's first create two simple components that we can use in routing. Create two new files, Home.tsx and Contact.tsx, in the application src folder. Then, add headers to the return statements to show the name of the component. The code of the components looks like this:

```
// Home.tsx
function Home() {
  return <h3>Home component</h3>;
}

export default Home;

// Contact.tsx
function Contact() {
  return <h3>Contact component</h3>;
}

export default Contact;
```

4. Open the `App.tsx` file, and then add a router that allows us to navigate between the components, as follows:

```tsx
import { BrowserRouter, Routes, Route, Link } from 'react-
  router-dom';
import Home from './Home';
import Contact from './Contact';
import './App.css';

function App() {
  return (
    <>
      <BrowserRouter>
        <nav>
          <Link to="/">Home</Link>{' | '}
          <Link to="/contact">Contact</Link>
        </nav>
        <Routes>
          <Route path="/" element={<Home />} />
          <Route path="contact" element={<Contact />} />
        </Routes>
      </BrowserRouter>
    </>
  );
}

export default App;
```

5. Now, when you start the app, you will see the links and the Home component, which is shown in the root endpoint (localhost:5173), as defined in the first Route component. You can see a representation of this in the following screenshot:

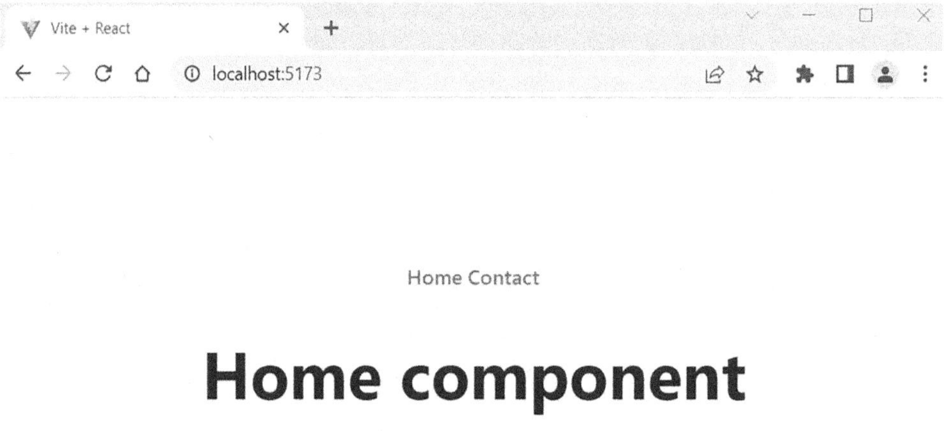

Home Contact

Home component

Figure 11.12: React Router

6. When you click the **Contact** link, the Contact component is rendered, as illustrated here:

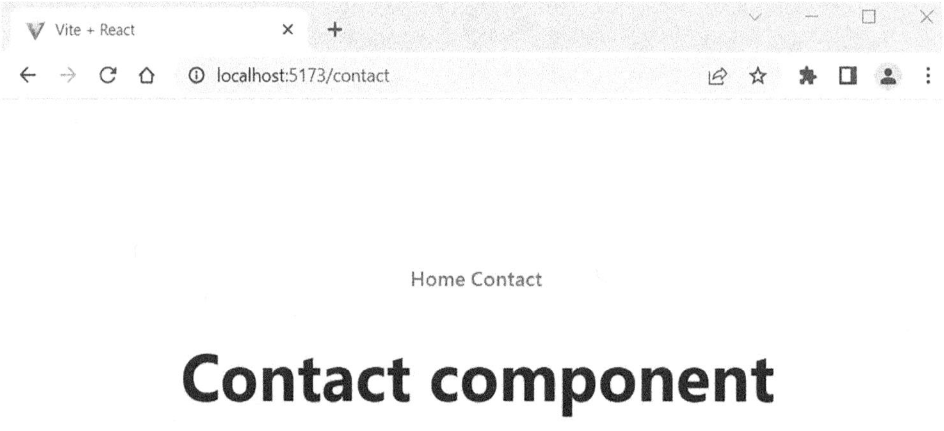

Home Contact

Contact component

Figure 11.13: React Router (continued)

7. You can create a PageNotFound route by using a * wildcard at the path prop. In the following example, if any other route doesn't match, the last one is used. First, create a component to show when a page is not found:

```
// Create PageNotFound component
function PageNotFound() {
  return <h1>Page not found</h1>;
}


export default PageNotFound;
```

8. Then, import the PageNotFound component into the App component, and create a new route:

```
// Import PageNotFound component into App.tsx
import PageNotFound from './PageNotFound';


// Add new page not found route
<Routes>
  <Route path="/" element={<Home />} />
  <Route path="contact" element={<Contact />} />
  <Route path="*" element={<PageNotFound />} />
</Routes>
```

9. You can also have nested routes, such as the ones shown in the next example. Nested routing means that different parts of the app can have their own routing configuration. In the following example, Contact is the parent route, and it has two child routes:

```
<Routes>
  <Route path="contact" element={<Contact />}>
      <Route path="london" element={<ContactLondon />} />
      <Route path="paris" element={<ContactParis />} />
  </Route>
</Routes>
```

 You can use a useRoutes() hook to declare routes using JavaScript objects instead of React elements, but we will not cover that in this book. You can find more information about hooks in the React Router documentation: https://reactrouter.com/en/main/start/overview.

So far, you have learned how to install and use a variety of third-party components with React. These skills will be required in the following chapters when we start to build our frontend.

Summary

In this chapter, we learned how to use third-party React components. We familiarized ourselves with several components that we will use in our frontend. `ag-grid` is a data grid component with built-in features like sorting, paging, and filtering. MUI is a component library that provides multiple UI components that implement Google's Material Design language. We also learned how to use React Router for routing in React applications.

In the next chapter, we will create an environment to develop the frontend for our existing car backend.

Questions

1. How can you find components for React?

2. How should you install components?

3. How can you use the `ag-grid` component?

4. How can you use the MUI component library?

5. How can you implement routing in a React application?

Further reading

Here are some resources for learning about React:

- *Awesome React*, a great resource for finding React libraries and components (`https://github.com/enaqx/awesome-react`)

- *The Top React Component Libraries that are Worth Trying*, by Technostacks (`https://technostacks.com/blog/react-component-libraries/`)

Learn more on Discord

To join the Discord community for this book – where you can share feedback, ask the author questions, and learn about new releases – follow the QR code below:

`https://packt.link/FullStackSpringBootReact4e`

Part III

Full Stack Development

12

Setting Up the Frontend for Our Spring Boot RESTful Web Service

This chapter explains the steps that are required to start the development of the frontend part of our car database application. We will first define the functionalities that we are developing. Then, we will do a mock-up of the UI. As a backend, we will use our Spring Boot application from *Chapter 5, Securing Your Backend*. We will begin development using the unsecured version of the backend. Finally, we will create the React app that we will use in our frontend development.

In this chapter, we will cover the following topics:

- Mocking up the UI
- Preparing the Spring Boot backend
- Creating the React project for the frontend

Technical requirements

The Spring Boot application that we created in *Chapter 5, Securing Your Backend*, is required.

Node.js also has to be installed, and the code available at the following GitHub link will be required to follow along with the examples in this chapter: https://github.com/PacktPublishing/Full-Stack-Development-with-Spring-Boot-3-and-React-Fourth-Edition/tree/main/Chapter12.

Mocking up the UI

In the first few chapters of this book, we created a car database backend that provides the RESTful API. Now, it is time to start building the frontend for our application.

We will create a frontend with the following specifications:

- It lists cars from the database in a table and provides **paging**, **sorting**, and **filtering**.
- There is a button that opens a **modal form** to add new cars to the database.
- In each row of the car table, there is a button to **edit** the car or **delete** it from the database.
- There is a link or button to **export** data from the table to a **CSV** file.

UI mock-ups are often created at the beginning of frontend development to provide customers with a visual representation of what the user interface will look like. Mock-ups are quite often done by designers and then provided to developers. There are lots of different applications for creating mock-ups, such as Figma, Balsamiq, and Adobe XD, or you can even use a pencil and paper. You can also create interactive mock-ups to demonstrate a number of functionalities.

If you have done a mock-up, it is much easier to discuss requirements with the client before you start to write any actual code. With the mock-up, it is also easier for the client to understand the idea of the frontend and suggest corrections for it. Changes to mock-ups are really easy and fast to implement, compared to modifications involving actual frontend source code.

The following screenshot shows the example mock-up of our car list frontend:

Brand	Model	Color	Year	Price		
Tesla	Model X	White	2022	87900	✏	🗑
Toyota	Prius	Black	2019	29000	✏	🗑
Ford	Mustang	Black	2021	65000	✏	🗑

Figure 12.1: The frontend mock-up

The modal form that is opened when the user presses the **+ CREATE** button looks like the following:

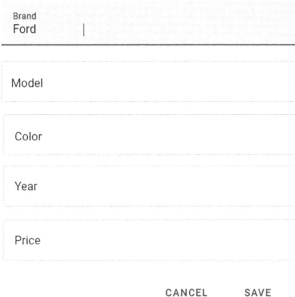

Figure 12.2: The modal form mock-up

Now that we have a mock-up of our UI ready, let's look at how we can prepare our Spring Boot backend.

Preparing the Spring Boot backend

We will begin frontend development in this chapter with the unsecured version of our backend. Then:

- In *Chapter 13, Adding CRUD Functionalities*, we will implement all the CRUD functionalities.
- In *Chapter 14, Styling the Frontend with MUI*, we will continue to polish our UI using Material UI components.
- Finally, in *Chapter 16, Securing Your Application*, we will enable security in our backend, make some modifications that are required, and implement authentication.

In Eclipse, open the Spring Boot application that we created in *Chapter 5, Securing Your Backend*. Open the SecurityConfig.java file that defines the Spring Security configuration. Temporarily comment out the current configuration and give everyone access to all endpoints. Refer to the following modifications:

```java
@Bean
public SecurityFilterChain filterChain(HttpSecurity http) throws Exception
  {
    // Add this one
    http.csrf((csrf) -> csrf.disable()).cors(withDefaults())
        .authorizeHttpRequests((authorizeHttpRequests) ->
            authorizeHttpRequests.anyRequest().permitAll());

    /* COMMENT THIS OUT
    http.csrf((csrf) -> csrf.disable())
        .cors(withDefaults())
        .sessionManagement((sessionManagement) ->
            sessionManagement.sessionCreationPolicy(\
                SessionCreationPolicy.STATELESS))
        .authorizeHttpRequests( (authorizeHttpRequests) ->
            authorizeHttpRequests
        .requestMatchers(HttpMethod.POST, "/login").permitALL()
        .anyRequest().authenticated())
        .addFilterBefore(authenticationFilter,
            UsernamePasswordAuthenticationFilter.class)
        .exceptionHandling((exceptionHandling) ->
            exceptionHandling.authenticationEntryPoint(
                exceptionHandler));
    */

    return http.build();
  }
}
```

Now, if you start the MariaDB database, run the backend, and send the GET request to the http:/ localhost:8080/api/cars endpoint, you should get all the cars in the response, as shown in the following screenshot:

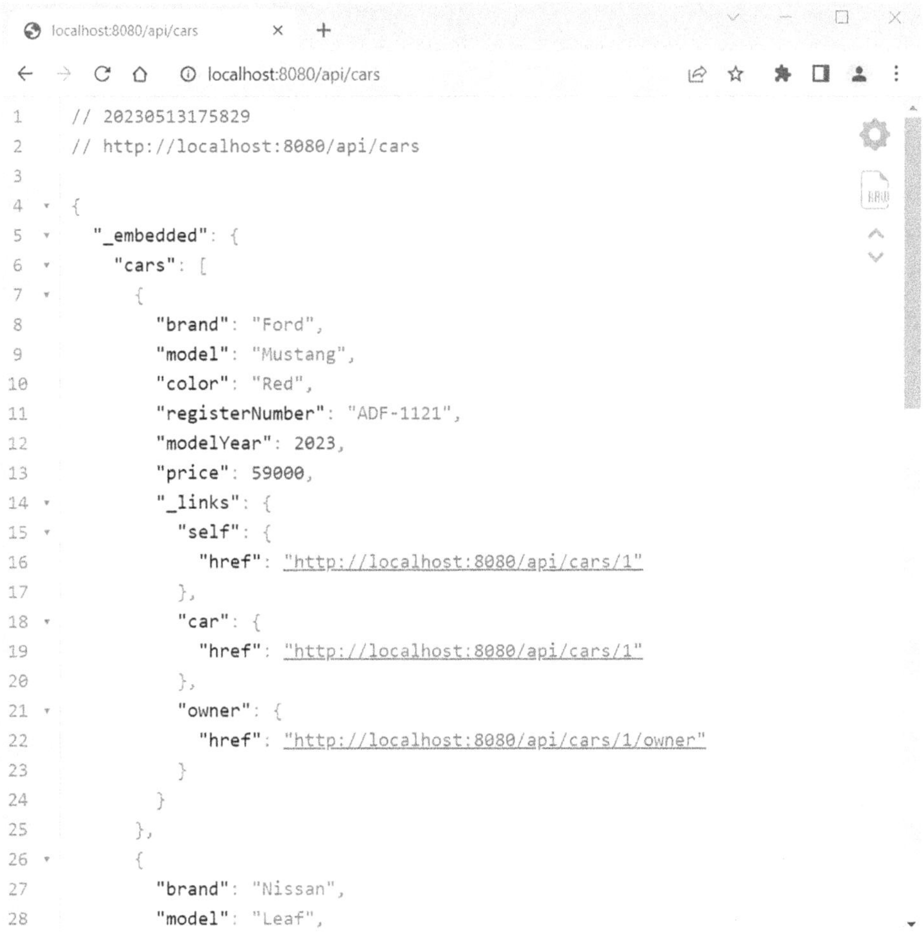

Figure 12.3: The GET request

Now, we are ready to create our React project for the frontend.

Creating the React project for the frontend

Before we start coding the frontend, we have to create a new React app. We will use TypeScript in our React frontend:

1. Open PowerShell, or any other suitable terminal. Create a new React app by typing the following command:

```
npm create vite@4
```

In this book, we are using Vite version 4.4. You can also use the latest version, but then you have to check for changes in the Vite documentation.

2. Name your project carfront, and select the **React** framework and **TypeScript** variant:

```
PS C:\> npm create vite@4
√ Project name: ... carfront
√ Select a framework: » React
√ Select a variant: » TypeScript

Scaffolding project in C:\carfront ...

Done. Now run:

  cd carfront
  npm install
  npm run dev
```

Figure 12.4: Frontend project

3. Move to the project folder and install dependencies by typing the following commands:

```
cd carfront
npm install
```

4. Install the MUI component library by typing the following command, which installs the Material UI core library and two Emotion libraries. **Emotion** is a library designed for writing CSS with JavaScript (https://emotion.sh/docs/introduction):

```
npm install @mui/material @emotion/react @emotion/styled
```

5. Also, install React Query v4 and Axios, which we will use for networking in our frontend:

```
npm install @tanstack/react-query@4
npm install axios
```

6. Run the app by typing the following command in the project's root folder:

```
npm run dev
```

7. Open the src folder with Visual Studio Code and remove any superfluous code from the App.tsx file. The file extension is now .tsx because we are using TypeScript. Also, re-move the App.css style sheet file import. We will use the MUI AppBar component in the App.tsx file to create the toolbar for our app.

We have already looked at the MUI AppBar in *Chapter 11, Useful Third-Party Components for React*, if you would like a reminder.

As shown in the code below, wrap the AppBar component inside the MUI Container component, which is a basic layout component that centers your app content horizontally. We can use the position prop to define the positioning behavior of the app bar. The value static means that the app bar is not fixed to the top when the user scrolls. If you use position= "fixed", it will fix the app bar at the top of the page. You also have to import all the MUI components that we are using:

```
import AppBar from '@mui/material/AppBar';
import Toolbar from '@mui/material/Toolbar';
import Typography from '@mui/material/Typography';
import Container from '@mui/material/Container';
import CssBaseline from '@mui/material/CssBaseline';

function App() {
  return (
    <Container maxWidth="xl">
    <CssBaseline />
      <AppBar position="static">
        <Toolbar>
          <Typography variant="h6">
            Car Shop
          </Typography>
        </Toolbar>
      </AppBar>
    </Container>
  );
}

export default App;
```

The maxWidth prop defines the maximum width of our app, and we have used the largest value. We have also used the MUI CssBaseline component, which is used to fix inconsistencies across browsers, ensuring that the React app's appearance is uniform across different browsers. It is typically included at the top level of your application to ensure that its styles are applied globally.

8. We will remove all predefined styling. Therefore, remove the index.css style sheet import from the main.tsx file. The code should look like the following:

```
import React from 'react'
import ReactDOM from 'react-dom/client'
import App from './App.tsx'

ReactDOM.createRoot(document.getElementById('root') as HTMLElement).
  render(
  <React.StrictMode>
    <App />
  </React.StrictMode>,
)
```

Now, your frontend starting point should look like this:

Figure 12.5: Car Shop

We have now created the React project for our frontend and can continue with further development.

Summary

In this chapter, we started the development of our frontend using the backend that we created in *Chapter 5*, *Securing Your Backend*. We defined the functionalities of the frontend and created a mock-up of the UI. We started frontend development with an unsecured version of the backend and, therefore, made some modifications to our Spring Security configuration class. We also created the React app that we will use during development.

In the next chapter, we will add **create**, **read**, **update**, and **delete** (**CRUD**) functionalities to our frontend.

Questions

1. Why should you do a mock-up of the UI?

2. How do you disable Spring Security from the backend?

Further reading

There are many other good resources available for learning about UI design and MUI. A few are listed here:

*   *Don't Make Me Think, Revisited: A Common Sense Approach to Web Usability (3rd Edition)*, by Steve Krug (`https://sensible.com/dont-make-me-think/`)

*   MUI blog – the latest about MUI (`https://mui.com/blog/`)

*   Material UI GitHub repository (`https://github.com/mui/material-ui`)

Learn more on Discord

To join the Discord community for this book – where you can share feedback, ask the author questions, and learn about new releases – follow the QR code below:

`https://packt.link/FullStackSpringBootReact4e`

13

Adding CRUD Functionalities

This chapter describes how we can implement **Create**, **Read**, **Update**, and **Delete** (**CRUD**) functionalities in our frontend. We are going to use the components that we learned about in *Chapter
11, Useful Third-Party Components for React*. We will fetch data from our backend and present the
data in a table. Then, we will implement the delete, edit, and create functionalities. In the final
part of this chapter, we will add features so that we can export our data to a CSV file.

In this chapter, we will cover the following topics:

- Creating the list page
- Adding the delete functionality
- Adding the add functionality
- Adding the edit functionality
- Exporting the data to CSV

Technical requirements

The Spring Boot cardatabase application that we created in *Chapter 12, Setting Up the Frontend
for Our Spring Boot RESTful Web Service*, (the unsecured backend) is required, as is the React app
that we created in the same chapter, carfront.

The following GitHub link will also be required: https://github.com/PacktPublishing/Full-
Stack-Development-with-Spring-Boot-3-and-React-Fourth-Edition/tree/main/Chapter13.

Creating the list page

In this first section, we will create the list page to show cars with paging, filtering, and sorting features:

1. Run your unsecured Spring Boot backend. The cars can be fetched by sending the GET request to the http://localhost:8080/api/cars URL, as shown in *Chapter 4, Creating a RESTful Web Service with Spring Boot*. Now, let's inspect the JSON data from the response. The array of cars can be found in the _embedded.cars node of the JSON response data:

```
GET    ∨    http://localhost:8080/api/cars

Params   Authorization   Headers (6)   Body   Pre-request Script   Tests   Settings

Body   Cookies   Headers (14)   Test Results                    ⊕  200 OK  10 ms  2.11 KB  🖫 Save

Pretty    Raw    Preview    Visualize    JSON ∨   ⇌

 1  {
 2      "_embedded": {
 3          "cars": [
 4              {
 5                  "brand": "Ford",
 6                  "model": "Mustang",
 7                  "color": "Red",
 8                  "registrationNumber": "ADF-1121",
 9                  "modelYear": 2023,
10                  "price": 23000,
11                  "_links": {
12                      "self": {
13                          "href": "http://localhost:8080/api/cars/1"
14                      },
15                      "car": {
16                          "href": "http://localhost:8080/api/cars/1"
17                      },
18                      "owner": {
19                          "href": "http://localhost:8080/api/cars/1/owner"
20                      }
21              }
```

Figure 13.1: Fetching cars

2. Open the carfront React app with Visual Studio Code (the React app we created in the previous chapter).

3. We are using React Query for networking, so we have to initialize the query provider first.

 You learned the basics of React Query in *Chapter 10, Consuming the REST API with React.*

The QueryClientProvider component is used to connect and provide QueryClient to your application. Open your App.tsx file and add the highlighted imports and components to your App component:

```
import AppBar from '@mui/material/AppBar';
import Toolbar from '@mui/material/Toolbar';
import Typography from '@mui/material/Typography';
import Container from '@mui/material/Container';
import CssBaseline from '@mui/material/CssBaseline';
import { QueryClient, QueryClientProvider } from '@tanstack/react-
  query';

const queryClient = new QueryClient();

function App() {
  return (
    <Container maxWidth="xl">
      <CssBaseline />
      <AppBar position="static">
        <Toolbar>
        <Typography variant="h6">
        Car Shop
        </Typography>
        </Toolbar>
      </AppBar>
      <QueryClientProvider client={queryClient}>
      </QueryClientProvider>
    </Container>
  )
}

export default App;
```

Now, let's fetch some cars.

Fetching data from the backend

Once we know how to fetch cars from the backend, we will be ready to implement the list page to show the cars. The following steps describe this in practice:

1.   When your app has multiple components, it is recommended that you create a folder for them. Create a new folder called components in the src folder. With Visual Studio Code, you can create a folder by right-clicking the folder in the sidebar file explorer and selecting **New Folder...** from the menu:

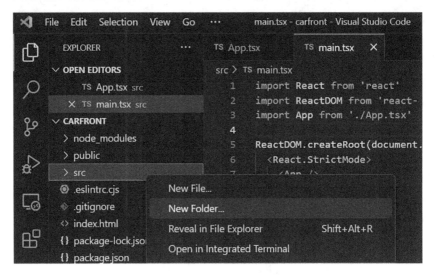

Figure 13.2: New folder

2.   Create a new file called Carlist.tsx in the components folder. Your project structure should look like the following:

Figure 13.3: Project structure

3. Open the `Carlist.tsx` file in the editor view and write the base code of the component, as follows:

```
function Carlist() {
  return(
    <></>
  );
}


export default Carlist;
```

4. Now, when we are using TypeScript, we have to define the type for our car data. Let's create a new file where we define our types. Create a file called `types.ts` in the `src` folder of your project. From the response, you can see that the car object looks like the following, and it contains all the car properties and also links:

```
{
    "brand": "Ford",
    "model": "Mustang",
    "color": "Red",
    "registrationNumber": "ADF-1121",
    "modelYear": 2023,
    "price": 59000,
    "_links": {
      "self": {
         "href": "http://localhost:8080/api/cars/1"
      },
      "car": {
         "href": "http://localhost:8080/api/cars/1"
      },
      "owner": {
         "href": "http://localhost:8080/api/cars/1/owner"
      }
    }
}
```

5. Create the following CarResponse type in the types.ts file and export it so that we can use it in files where it is needed:

```
export type CarResponse = {
  brand: string;
  model: string;
  color: string;
  registrationNumber: string;
  modelYear: number;
  price: number;
  _links: {
    self: {
      href: string;
    },
    car: {
      href: string;
    },
    owner: {
      href: string;
    }
  };
}
```

6. Next, we will create a function that fetches cars from our backend by sending a GET request to the http://localhost:8080/api/cars endpoint. The function returns a **promise** that contains an array of CarResponse objects that we defined in our types.ts file. We can use the Promise<Type> generic, where Type indicates the resolved value type of the promise. Open the Carlist.tsx file and add the following imports and function:

```
import { CarResponse } from '../types';
import axios from 'axios';

function Carlist() {
  const getCars = async (): Promise<CarResponse[]> => {
    const response = await axios.get("http://localhost:8080/api/
                                     cars");
    return response.data._embedded.cars;
  }
```

```
      return(
        <></>
      );
  }


  export default Carlist;
```

7. Next, we will use the useQuery hook to fetch cars:

```
import { useQuery } from '@tanstack/react-query';
import { CarResponse } from '../types';
import axios from 'axios';

function Carlist() {
  const getCars = async (): Promise<CarResponse[]> => {
    const response = await axios.get("http://localhost:8080/api/
                                     cars");
    return response.data._embedded.cars;
  }

  const { data, error, isSuccess } = useQuery({
    queryKey: ["cars"],
    queryFn: getCars
  });

  return (
    <></>
  );
}

export default Carlist;
```

The useQuery hook uses TypeScript generics because it doesn't fetch data and doesn't know the type of your data. However, React Query can infer the type of the data, so we don't have to do it manually here using generics. If you explicitly set generics, the code looks like this:

```
useQuery<CarResponse[], Error>
```

8. We will use **conditional rendering** to check if the fetch is successful and if there are any
    errors. If isSuccess is false, it means the data fetching is still in progress and, in this case,
    a loading message is returned. We also check if error is true, which indicates there's an
    error, and an error message is returned. When data is available, we use the map function to
    transform car objects into table rows in the return statement and add the table element:

```tsx
// CarList.tsx
if (!isSuccess) {
  return <span>Loading...</span>
}
else if (error) {
  return <span>Error when fetching cars...</span>
}
else {
  return (
    <table>
      <tbody>
      {
        data.map((car: CarResponse) =>
          <tr key={car._links.self.href}>
            <td>{car.brand}</td>
            <td>{car.model}</td>
            <td>{car.color}</td>
            <td>{car.registrationNumber}</td>
            <td>{car.modelYear}</td>
            <td>{car.price}</td>
          </tr>)
      }
      </tbody>
    </table>
  );
}
```

9. Finally, we have to import and render the `Carlist` component in our `App.tsx` file. In the
`App.tsx` file, add the `import` statement, and then render the `Carlist` component inside
the `QueryClientProvider` component, as highlighted. `QueryClientProvider` is a component that provides the React Query context to your components, and it should wrap
the components where you are making REST API requests from:

```
import AppBar from '@mui/material/AppBar';
import Toolbar from '@mui/material/Toolbar';
import Typography from '@mui/material/Typography';
import Container from '@mui/material/Container';
import CssBaseline from '@mui/material/CssBaseline';
import { QueryClient, QueryClientProvider } from '@tanstack/react-
  query';
import Carlist from './components/Carlist';

const queryClient = new QueryClient();

function App() {
  return (
    <Container maxWidth="xl">
      <CssBaseline />
      <AppBar position="static">
        <Toolbar>
          <Typography variant="h6">
          Car shop
          </Typography>
        </Toolbar>
      </AppBar>
      <QueryClientProvider client={queryClient}>
        <Carlist />
      </QueryClientProvider>
    </Container>
  )
}

export default App;
```

10. Now, if you start the React app using the `npm run dev` command, you should see the following list page. Note that your backend should also be running:

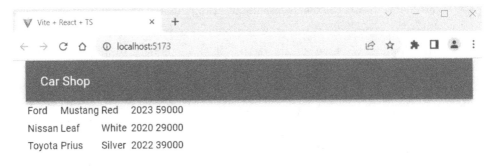

Figure 13.4: Car frontend

Using environment variables

Let's do some code refactoring before we move on. The server URL can be repeated multiple times in the source code when we create more CRUD functionalities, and it will change when the backend is deployed to a server other than the local host; therefore, it is better to define it as an **environment variable**. Then, when the URL value changes, we only have to modify it in one place.

When using Vite, environment variable names should start with the text `VITE_`. Only variables prefixed with `VITE_` are exposed to your source code:

1. Create a new `.env` file in the root folder of our app. Open the file in the editor and add the following line to the file:

    ```
    VITE_API_URL=http://localhost:8080
    ```

2. We will also separate all API call functions into their own module. Create a new folder named api in the src folder of your project. Create a new file called carapi.ts in the api folder, and now your project structure should look like the following:

Figure 13.5: Project structure

3. Copy the getCars function from the Carlist.tsx file to the carapi.ts file. Add export at the beginning of the function so that we can use it in other components. In Vite, the environment variables are exposed to your app source code via import.meta.env as strings. Then, we can import the server URL environment variable to our getCars function and use it there. We also need to import axios and the CarResponse type into the carapi.ts file:

```ts
// carapi.ts
import { CarResponse } from '../types';
import axios from 'axios';

export const getCars = async (): Promise<CarResponse[]> => {
  const response = await axios.get(`${import.meta.env.VITE_API_URL}/
                                    api/cars`);
  return response.data._embedded.cars;
}
```

4. Now, we can remove the `getCars` function and unused `axios` import from the `Carlist.tsx` file and import it from the `carapi.ts` file. The source code should appear as follows:

```
// Carlist.tsx
// Remove getCars function and import it from carapi.ts
import { useQuery } from '@tanstack/react-query';
import { getCars } from '../api/carapi';

function Carlist() {
  const { data, error, isSuccess } = useQuery({
    queryKey: ["cars"],
    queryFn: getCars
  });

  if (!isSuccess) {
    return <span>Loading...</span>
  }
  else if (error) {
    return <span>Error when fetching cars...</span>
  }
  else {
    return (
      <table>
        <tbody>
        {
        data.map((car: CarResponse) =>
          <tr key={car._links.self.href}>
            <td>{car.brand}</td>
            <td>{car.model}</td>
            <td>{car.color}</td>
            <td>{car.registrationNumber}</td>
            <td>{car.modelYear}</td>
            <td>{car.price}</td>
          </tr>)
        }
        </tbody>
      </table>
```

```
      );
     }
    }

  export default Carlist;
```

After these refactoring steps, you should see the car list page like previously.

Adding paging, filtering, and sorting

We have already used the ag-grid component to implement a data grid in *Chapter 11*, *Useful Third-Party Components for React*, and it could be used here as well. Instead, we will use the new MUI DataGrid component to get paging, filtering, and sorting features out of the box:

1. Stop the development server by pressing *Ctrl* + *C* in the terminal.

2. We will install the MUI data grid community version. The following is the installation command at the time of writing, but you should check the latest installation command and usage from the MUI documentation:

    ```
    npm install @mui/x-data-grid
    ```

3. After installation, restart the app.

4. Import the DataGrid component into your Carlist.tsx file. We will also import GridColDef, which is a type for the column definitions in the MUI data grid:

    ```
    import { DataGrid, GridColDef } from '@mui/x-data-grid';
    ```

5. The grid columns are defined in the columns variable, which has the type GridColDef[]. The column field property defines where data in the columns is coming from; we are using our car object properties. The headerName prop can be used to set the title of the columns. We will also set the width of the columns. Add the following column definition code inside the Carlist component:

    ```
    const columns: GridColDef[] = [
      {field: 'brand', headerName: 'Brand', width: 200},
      {field: 'model', headerName: 'Model', width: 200},
      {field: 'color', headerName: 'Color', width: 200},
      {field: 'registrationNumber', headerName: 'Reg.nr.', width: 150},
      {field: 'modelYear', headerName: 'Model Year', width: 150},
      {field: 'price', headerName: 'Price', width: 150},
    ];
    ```

6. Then, remove the `table` and all its child elements from the component's return statement
    and add the `DataGrid` component. Also remove the unused `CarResponse` import that we
    used in the map function. The data source of the data grid is the data, which contains
    fetched cars and is defined using the `rows` prop. The `DataGrid` component requires all
    rows to have a unique ID property that is defined using the `getRowId` prop. We can use
    the `link` field of the car object because that contains the unique car ID (`_links.self.`
    `href`). Refer to the source code of the following return statement:

```
if (!isSuccess) {
  return <span>Loading...</span>
}
else if (error) {
  return <span>Error when fetching cars...</span>
}
else {
  return (
    <DataGrid
      rows={data}
      columns={columns}
      getRowId={row => row._links.self.href}
    />
  );
}
```

With the MUI DataGrid component, we implemented all the necessary features for our table with only a small amount of coding. Now, the list page looks like the following:

Figure 13.6: Car frontend

Data grid columns can be filtered using the column menu and clicking the **Filter** menu item. You can also set the visibility of the columns from the column menu:

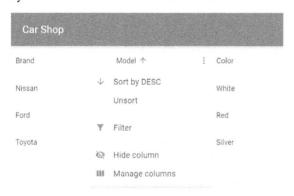

Figure 13.7: Column menu

Next, we will implement the delete functionality.

Adding the delete functionality

Items can be deleted from the database by sending the DELETE method request to the `http://localhost:8080/api/cars/{carId}` endpoint. If we look at the JSON response data, we can see that each car contains a link to itself, which can be accessed from the `_links.self.href` node, as shown in the following screenshot:

Figure 13.8: Car link

We already used the link field in the previous section to set a unique ID for every row in the grid. That row ID can be used in deletion, as we will see later.

The following steps demonstrate how to implement the delete functionality:

1. First, we will create a button for each row in the MUI DataGrid. When we need more complex cell content, we can use the renderCell column property to define how a cell's contents are rendered.

Let's add a new column to the table using renderCell to render the button element. The params argument that is passed to the function is a row object that contains all values from a row. The type of params is GridCellParams, which is provided by MUI. In our case, it contains a link to a car in each row, and that is needed in the deletion. The link is in the row's _links.self.href property, and we will pass this value to a delete function. Let's first show an alert with the ID when a button is pressed to test that the button is working properly. Refer to the following source code:

```
// Import GridCellParams
import { DataGrid, GridColDef, GridCellParams } from '@mui/x-data-
  grid';

// Add delete button column to columns
const columns: GridColDef[] = [
  {field: 'brand', headerName: 'Brand', width: 200},
  {field: 'model', headerName: 'Model', width: 200},
  {field: 'color', headerName: 'Color', width: 200},
  {field: 'registrationNumber', headerName: 'Reg.nr.', width: 150},
  {field: 'modelYear', headerName: 'Model Year', width: 150},
  {field: 'price', headerName: 'Price', width: 150},
  {
    field: 'delete',
    headerName: '',
    width: 90,
    sortable: false,
    filterable: false,
    disableColumnMenu: true,
    renderCell: (params: GridCellParams) => (
      <button
        onClick={() => alert(params.row._links.car.href)}
      >
        Delete
      </button>
    ),
  },
];
```

We don't want to enable sorting and filtering for the button column, so the `filterable` and `sortable` props are set to `false`. We also disable the column menu in this column by setting the `disableColumnMenu` prop to `true`. The button invokes the `onDelClick` function when pressed and passes a link (`row.id`) to the function as an argument, and the link value is shown in an alert.

2. Now, you should see a **delete** button in each row. If you press any of the buttons, you can see an alert that shows the link for the car. To delete a car, we should send a `DELETE` request to its link:

Figure 13.9: Delete button

3. Next, we will implement the `deleteCar` function, which sends the `DELETE` request to a car link using the Axios delete method. A `DELETE` request to the backend returns a deleted car object. We will implement the `deleteCar` function in the `carapi.ts` file and export it. Open the `carapi.ts` file and add the following function there:

```
// carapi.ts
export const deleteCar = async (link: string): Promise<CarResponse> =>
{
    const response = await axios.delete(link);
    return response.data
}
```

4. We use the React Query `useMutation` hook to handle deletion. We saw an example in *Chapter 10*. First, we have to add the `useMutation` import to the `Carlist.tsx` file. We will also import the `deleteCar` function from the `carapi.ts` file:

```
// Carlist.tsx
import { useQuery, useMutation } from '@tanstack/react-query';
import { getCars, deleteCar } from '../api/carapi';
```

5. Add the useMutation hook, which calls our deleteCar function:

```
// CarList.tsx
const { mutate } = useMutation(deleteCar, {
    onSuccess: () => {
        // Car deleted
    },
    onError: (err) => {
        console.error(err);
    },
});
```

6. Then, call mutate in our delete button and pass the car link as an argument:

```
// CarList.tsx columns
{
    field: 'delete',
    headerName: '',
    width: 90,
    sortable: false,
        filterable: false,
    disableColumnMenu: true,
    renderCell: (params: GridCellParams) => (
        <button
        onClick={() => mutate(params.row._links.car.href)}
        >
        Delete
        </button>
    ),
    },
});
```

7. Now, if you start the app and press the **delete** button, the car is deleted from the database, but it still exists in the frontend. You can manually refresh the browser, after which the car disappears from the table.

8. We can also refresh the frontend automatically when a car is deleted. In React Query, the fetched data is saved to a cache that the query client handles. The QueryClient has a **query invalidation** feature that we can use to fetch data again. First, we have to import and call the useQueryClient hook function, which returns the current query client:

```
// Carlist.tsx
import { useQuery, useMutation, useQueryClient } from '@tanstack/
  react-query';
import { deleteCar } from '../api/carapi';
import { DataGrid, GridColDef, GridCellParams } from '@mui/x-data-
  grid';

function Carlist() {
  const queryClient = useQueryClient();

  // continue...
```

9. The queryClient has an invalidateQueries method that we can call to re-fetch our data after successful deletion. You can pass the key of the query that you want to re-fetch. Our query key for fetching cars is cars, which we defined in our useQuery hook:

```
// Carlist.tsx
const { mutate } = useMutation(deleteCar, {
    onSuccess: () => {
      queryClient.invalidateQueries({ queryKey: ['cars'] });
    },
    onError: (err) => {
      console.error(err);
    },
  });
```

Now, every time a car is deleted, all the cars are fetched again. The car disappears from the list when the **Delete** button is pressed. After a deletion, you can restart the backend to re-populate the database.

You can also see that when you click any row in the grid, the row is selected. You can disable that by setting the `disableRowSelectionOnClick` prop in the grid to `true`:

```
<DataGrid
  rows={cars}
  columns={columns}
  disableRowSelectionOnClick={true}
  getRowId={row => row._links.self.href}
/>
```

Displaying a toast message

It would be nice to show the user some feedback in the case of a successful deletion, or if there are any errors. Let's implement a **toast message** to show the status of the deletion. For this, we are going to use the MUI `Snackbar` component:

1. First, we have to import the `Snackbar` component by adding the following `import` statement to our `Carlist.tsx` file:

   ```
   import Snackbar from '@mui/material/Snackbar';
   ```

2. The `Snackbar` component's open prop value is a boolean, and if it is `true`, the component is shown; otherwise, it is hidden. Let's import the `useState` hook and define a state called `open` to handle the visibility of our `Snackbar` component. The initial value is `false` because the message is shown only after the deletion:

   ```
   //Carlist.tsx
   import { useState } from 'react';
   import { useQuery, useMutation, useQueryClient } from '@tanstack/
     react-query';
   import { deleteCar } from '../api/carapi';
   import { DataGrid, GridColDef, GridCellParams } from '@mui/x-data-
     grid';
   import Snackbar from '@mui/material/Snackbar';

   function Carlist() {
     const [open, setOpen] = useState(false);

     const queryClient = useQueryClient();
     // continue...
   ```

3. Next, we add the Snackbar component in the return statement after the MUI DataGrid component. The autoHideDuration prop defines the time in milliseconds after which the onClose function is called automatically and the message disappears. The message prop defines the message to display. We also have to wrap the DataGrid and Snackbar components inside the fragment (<></>):

```tsx
// Carlist.tsx
if (!isSuccess) {
  return <span>Loading...</span>
}
else if (error) {
  return <span>Error when fetching cars...</span>
}
else {
  return (
    <>
      <DataGrid
        rows={data}
        columns={columns}
        disableRowSelectionOnClick={true}
        getRowId={row => row._links.self.href} />
      <Snackbar
        open={open}
        autoHideDuration={2000}
        onClose={() => setOpen(false)}
        message="Car deleted" />
    </>
  );
```

4. Finally, we set the open state to true after the successful deletion in our useMutation hook:

```tsx
// Carlist.tsx
const { mutate } = useMutation(deleteCar, {
  onSuccess: () => {
    setOpen(true);
    queryClient.invalidateQueries(["cars"]);
  },
  onError: (err) => {
    console.error(err);
```

```
        },
    });
```

Now, you will see the toast message when the car is deleted, as shown in the following screenshot:

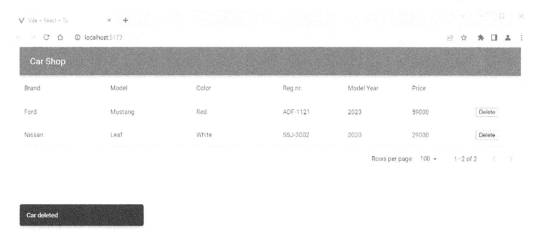

Figure 13.10: Toast message

Adding a confirmation dialog window

To avoid accidental deletion of a car, it would be useful to have a confirmation dialog after the **Delete** button has been pressed. We will implement this using the window object's confirm method. It opens a dialog with an optional message and returns true if you press the **OK** button. Add confirm to the delete button's onClick event handler:

```
// Carlist.tsx columns
{
  field: 'delete',
  headerName: '',
  width: 90,
  sortable: false,
  filterable: false,
  disableColumnMenu: true,
  renderCell: (params: GridCellParams) => (
    <button
      onClick={() => {
        if (window.confirm(`Are you sure you want to delete ${params.row.
                          brand} ${params.row.model}?`)) {
          mutate(params.row._links.car.href);
```

```
        }
      }}
    >
      Delete
    </button>
  ),
}
```

In the confirmation message, we have used ES6 string interpolation to display the car's brand and model. (Note! Remember to use backticks.)

If you press the **Delete** button now, the confirmation dialog will open and the car will only be deleted if you press the **OK** button:

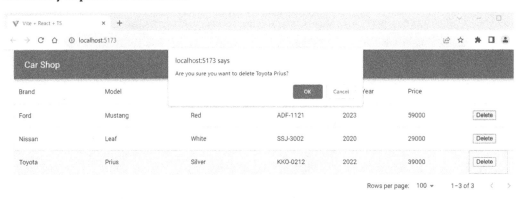

Figure 13.11: Confirmation dialog

Next, we will begin the implementation of the functionality to add a new car.

Adding the add functionality

The next step is to add an add functionality to the frontend. We will implement this using the MUI modal dialog.

We went through the MUI modal form in *Chapter 11, Useful Third-Party Components for React.*

We will add the **New Car** button to the user interface, which opens the modal form when it is pressed. The modal form contains all the fields that are required to add a new car, as well as the buttons for saving and canceling.

The following steps show you how to create the add functionality using the modal dialog component:

1. Create a new file called AddCar.tsx in the components folder and write some functional component base code to the file, as shown here. Add the imports for the MUI Dialog component:

    ```
    import Dialog from '@mui/material/Dialog';
    import DialogActions from '@mui/material/DialogActions';
    import DialogContent from '@mui/material/DialogContent';
    import DialogTitle from '@mui/material/DialogTitle';

    function AddCar() {
      return(
        <></>
      );
    }

    export default AddCar;
    ```

2. We have already defined the type for our Car response data (a car object with links). Let's also create a type for the car object that doesn't contain links, because the user doesn't enter links in the form. We need this for the state where we will save a new car. Add the following Car type to your types.ts file:

    ```
    export type Car = {
      brand: string;
      model: string;
      color: string;
      registrationNumber: string;
      modelYear: number;
      price: number;
    }
    ```

3. Declare a state of type Car that contains all car fields using the useState hook. For the dialog, we also need a boolean state to define the visibility of the dialog form:

```tsx
import { useState } from 'react';
import Dialog from '@mui/material/Dialog';
import DialogActions from '@mui/material/DialogActions';
import DialogContent from '@mui/material/DialogContent';
import DialogTitle from '@mui/material/DialogTitle';
import { Car } from '../types';

function AddCar() {
  const [open, setOpen] = useState(false);
  const [car, setCar] = useState<Car>({
    brand: '',
    model: '',
    color: '',
    registrationNumber: '',
    modelYear: 0,
    price: 0
  });

  return(
    <></>
  );
}
export default AddCar;
```

4. Next, we add two functions to close and open the dialog form. The handleClose and handleOpen functions set the value of the open state, which affects the visibility of the modal form:

```tsx
// AddCar.tsx
// Open the modal form
const handleClickOpen = () => {
  setOpen(true);
};

// Close the modal form
const handleClose = () => {
```

```
    setOpen(false);
  };
```

5. Add the Dialog component inside the AddCar component's return statement. The form
    contains the MUI Dialog component with buttons and the input fields that are required
    to collect the car data. The button that opens the modal window, which will be shown on
    the car list page, must be outside of the Dialog component. All input fields should have
    a name attribute with a value that is the same as the name of the state the value will be
    saved to. Input fields also have the onChange prop, which saves the value to the car state
    by invoking the handleChange function. The handleChange function dynamically updates
    the car state by creating a new object with the existing state properties and updating a
    property based on the input element's name and the new value entered by the user:

```tsx
// AddCar.tsx
const handleChange = (event : React.ChangeEvent<HTMLInputElement>) =>
{
  setCar({...car, [event.target.name]:
      event.target.value});
}

return(
  <>
    <button onClick={handleClickOpen}>New Car</button>
    <Dialog open={open} onClose={handleClose}>
      <DialogTitle>New car</DialogTitle>
      <DialogContent>
        <input placeholder="Brand" name="brand"
          value={car.brand} onChange={handleChange}/><br/>
        <input placeholder="Model" name="model"
          value={car.model} onChange={handleChange}/><br/>
        <input placeholder="Color" name="color"
          value={car.color} onChange={handleChange}/><br/>
        <input placeholder="Year" name="modelYear"
          value={car.modelYear} onChange={handleChange}/><br/>
        <input placeholder="Reg.nr" name="registrationNumber"
          value={car.registrationNumber} onChange={handleChange}/><br/>
```

```
        <input placeholder="Price" name="price"
          value={car.price} onChange={handleChange}/><br/>
      </DialogContent>
      <DialogActions>
        <button onClick={handleClose}>Cancel</button>
        <button onClick={handleClose}>Save</button>
      </DialogActions>
    </Dialog>
  </>
);
```

6. Implement the addCar function in the carapi.ts file, which will send the POST request
    to the backend api/cars endpoint. We are using the Axios post method to send POST
    requests. The request will include the new car object inside the body and the 'Content-
    Type':'application/json' header. We also need to import the Car type because we are
    passing a new car object as an argument to the function:

```
// carapi.ts
import { CarResponse, Car} from '../types';

// Add a new car
export const addCar = async (car: Car): Promise<CarResponse> => {
  const response = await axios.post(`${import.meta.env.VITE_API_
                  URL}/api/cars`, car, {
    headers: {
      'Content-Type': 'application/json',
    },
  });

  return response.data;
}
```

7. Next, we use the React Query useMutation hook, like we did in the delete functionality.
    We also invalidate the cars query after the car has been added successfully. The addCar
    function that we use in the useMutation hook is imported from the carapi.ts file. Add the
    following imports and the useMutation hook to your AddCar.tsx file. We also need to get
    the query client from the context using the useQueryClient hook. Remember that context
    is used to provide access to the query client to components deep in the component tree:

```
// AddCar.tsx
// Add the following imports
import { useMutation, useQueryClient } from '@tanstack/react-query';
import { addCar } from '../api/carapi';

// Add inside the AddCar component function
const queryClient = useQueryClient();

// Add inside the AddCar component function
const { mutate } = useMutation(addCar, {
  onSuccess: () => {
    queryClient.invalidateQueries(["cars"]);
  },
  onError: (err) => {
    console.error(err);
  },
});
```

8. Import the AddCar component into the Carlist.tsx file:

```
// Carlist.tsx
import AddCar from './AddCar';
```

9. Add the AddCar component to the Carlist.tsx file's return statement. You also have to import the AddCar component. Now, the return statement of the Carlist.tsx file should appear as follows:

```
// Carlist.tsx
// Add the following import
import AddCar from './AddCar';

// Render the AddCar component
return (
  <>
    <AddCar />
    <DataGrid
      rows={data}
      columns={columns}
      disableRowSelectionOnClick={true}
```

```
        getRowId={row => row._links.self.href}/>
      <Snackbar
        open={open}
        autoHideDuration={2000}
        onClose={() => setOpen(false)}
        message="Car deleted"
      />
    </>
  );
```

10. If you start the car shop app, it should now look like the following:

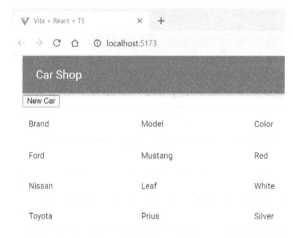

Figure 13.12: Car Shop

If you press the **New Car** button, it should open the modal form.

11. To save a new car, create a function called `handleSave` in the `AddCar.tsx` file. The `handleSave` function calls `mutate`. Then, we set the `car` state back to its initial state, and the modal form is closed:

```
// AddCar.tsx
// Save car and close modal form
const handleSave = () => {
  mutate(car);
  setCar({ brand: '', model: '', color: '',  registrationNumber:'',
          modelYear: 0, price: 0 });
  handleClose();
}
```

12. Finally, we have to change the `AddCar` component's `onClick` save button to call the `handleSave` function:

```
// AddCar.tsx
<DialogActions>
  <button onClick={handleClose}>Cancel</button>
  <button onClick={handleSave}>Save</button>
</DialogActions>
```

13. Now, you can open the modal form by pressing the **New Car** button. You will see that there is placeholder text in each field when it is empty. You can fill out the form with data and press the **Save** button. At this point, the form doesn't have a nice appearance, but we are going to style it in the next chapter:

Figure 13.13: Add new car

14. After saving, the list page is refreshed, and the new car can be seen in the list:

Figure 13.14: Car Shop

15. Now, we can do some code refactoring. When we start to implement the edit functionality, we will actually need the same fields in the **Edit** form as in the **New Car** form. Let's create a new component that renders the text fields in our **New Car** form. The idea is that we are splitting the text fields into their own component, which can then be used in both the **New Car** and **Edit** forms. Create a new file called CarDialogContent.tsx in the components folder. We have to pass the car object and the handleChange function to the component using props. To do that, we create a new type called DialogFormProps. We can define this type in the same file because we don't need it in any other file:

```tsx
// CarDialogContent.tsx
import { Car } from '../types';

type DialogFormProps = {
  car: Car;
  handleChange: (event: React.ChangeEvent<HTMLInputElement>) =>
    void;
}

function CarDialogContent({ car, handleChange }: DialogFormProps) {
  return (
    <></>
  );
}

export default CarDialogContent;
```

16. Then, we can move our DialogContent component from the AddCar component to the CarDialogContent component. Your code should look like the following:

```tsx
// CarDialogContent.tsx
import DialogContent from '@mui/material/DialogContent';
import { Car } from '../types';

type DialogFormProps = {
  car: Car;
  handleChange: (event: React.ChangeEvent<HTMLInputElement>) =>
    void;
}
```

```
function CarDialogContent({ car, handleChange}: DialogFormProps) {
  return (
    <DialogContent>
      <input placeholder="Brand" name="brand"
        value={car.brand} onChange={handleChange}/><br/>
      <input placeholder="Model" name="model"
        value={car.model} onChange={handleChange}/><br/>
      <input placeholder="Color" name="color"
        value={car.color} onChange={handleChange}/><br/>
      <input placeholder="Year" name="modelYear"
        value={car.modelYear} onChange={handleChange}/><br/>
      <input placeholder="Reg.nr." name="registrationNumber"
        value={car.registrationNumber} onChange={handleChange}/><br/>
      <input placeholder="Price" name="price"
        value={car.price} onChange={handleChange}/><br/>
    </DialogContent>
  );
}


export default CarDialogContent;
```

17. Now, we can import the `CarDialogContent` to the `AddCar` component and render it in-side the `Dialog` component. Pass the `car` state and the `handleChange` function to the component using props. Also, remove the unused MUI `DialogContent` import from the `AddCar` component:

```
// AddCar.tsx
// Add the following import
// and remove unused imports: DialogContent
import CarDialogContent from './CarDialogContent';

// render CarDialogContent and pass props
return(
  <div>
    <Button onClick={handleClickOpen}>New Car</Button>
    <Dialog open={open} onClose={handleClose}>
      <DialogTitle>New car</DialogTitle>
```

```
        <CarDialogContent car={car} handleChange={handleChange}/>
      <DialogActions>
        <Button onClick={handleClose}>Cancel</Button>
        <Button onClick={handleSave}>Save</Button>
      </DialogActions>
    </Dialog>
  </div>
);
```

18. Try to add a new car, and it should work like it did before the refactoring.

Next, we will begin to implement the edit functionality.

Adding the edit functionality

We will implement the edit functionality by adding the **Edit** button to each table row. When the row **Edit** button is pressed, it opens a modal form where the user can edit the existing car and save their changes. The idea is that we pass car data from the grid row to the edit form, and the form fields are populated when the form is opened:

1. First, create a file called EditCar.tsx in the components folder. We have to define a FormProps type for our props, and this can be defined inside our component because we don't need this type anywhere else. The type of data that will be passed to the EditCar component is the CarResponse type. We will also create a state for car data like we did in the add functionality section. The code for the EditCar.tsx file looks like the following:

```
// EditCar.tsx
import { useState } from 'react';
import { Car, CarResponse } from '../types';

type FormProps = {
  cardata: CarResponse;
}

function EditCar({ cardata }: FormProps) {
  const [car, setCar] = useState<Car>({
    brand: '',
    model: '',
    color: '',
    registrationNumber: '',
```

```
      modelYear: 0,
      price: 0
    });

    return(
      <></>
    );
  }


export default EditCar;
```

2. We will create a dialog that will be opened when the **Edit** button is pressed. We need the open state to define if the dialog is visible or hidden. Add the functions that open and close the `Dialog` component and save updates:

```tsx
// EditCar.tsx
import { useState } from 'react';
import Dialog from '@mui/material/Dialog';
import DialogActions from '@mui/material/DialogActions';
import DialogTitle from '@mui/material/DialogTitle';
import { Car, CarResponse } from '../types';

type FormProps = {
  cardata: CarResponse;
}

function EditCar({ cardata }: FormProps) {
  const [open, setOpen] = useState(false);
  const [car, setCar] = useState<Car>({
    brand: '',
    model: '',
    color: '',
    registrationNumber: '',
    modelYear: 0,
    price: 0
  });

  const handleClickOpen = () => {
```

```
    setOpen(true);
  };

  const handleClose = () => {
    setOpen(false);
  };

  const handleSave = () => {
    setOpen(false);
  }

  return(
    <>
      <button onClick={handleClickOpen}>
        Edit
      </button>
      <Dialog open={open} onClose={handleClose}>
        <DialogTitle>Edit car</DialogTitle>
        <DialogActions>
          <button onClick={handleClose}>Cancel</button>
          <button onClick={handleSave}>Save</button>
        </DialogActions>
      </Dialog>
    </>
  );
}

export default EditCar;
```

3. Next, we will import the `CarDialogContent` component and render it inside the `Dialog` component. We also need to add the `handleChange` function, which saves edited values to the car state. We pass in the `car` state and the `handleChange` function using the props, as we did earlier with the add functionality:

```
// EditCar.tsx
// Add the following import
import CarDialogContent from './CarDialogContent';

// Add handleChange function
```

```
const handleChange = (event : React.ChangeEvent<HTMLInputElement>) =>
{
  setCar({...car, [event.target.name]: event.target.value});
}

// render CarDialogContent inside the Dialog
return(
  <>
    <button onClick={handleClickOpen}>
      Edit
    </button>
    <Dialog open={open} onClose={handleClose}>
      <DialogTitle>Edit car</DialogTitle>
      <CarDialogContent car={car} handleChange={handleChange}/>
      <DialogActions>
        <button onClick={handleClose}>Cancel</button>
        <button onClick={handleSave}>Save</button>
      </DialogActions>
    </Dialog>
  </>
);
```

4. Now, we will set the values of the car state using the props in the `handleClickOpen` function:

```
// EditCar.tsx
const handleClickOpen = () => {
  setCar({
    brand: cardata.brand,
    model: cardata.model,
    color: cardata.color,
    registrationNumber: cardata.registrationNumber,
    modelYear: cardata.modelYear,
    price: cardata.price
  });

  setOpen(true);
};
```

Our form will be populated with the values from the car object that is passed to the component in props.

5. In this step, we will add the edit functionality to our data grid in the `Carlist` component. Open the `Carlist.tsx` file and import the `EditCar` component. Create a new column that renders the `EditCar` component using the `renderCell` column property, as we did in the delete functionality section. We pass the row object to the `EditCar` component, and that object contains the car object:

```tsx
// Carlist.tsx
// Add the following import
import EditCar from './EditCar';

// Add a new column
const columns: GridColDef[] = [
  {field: 'brand', headerName: 'Brand', width: 200},
  {field: 'model', headerName: 'Model', width: 200},
  {field: 'color', headerName: 'Color', width: 200},
  {field: 'registrationNumber', headerName: 'Reg.nr.', width: 150},
  {field: 'modelYear', headerName: 'Model Year', width: 150},
  {field: 'price', headerName: 'Price', width: 150},
  {
    field: 'edit',
    headerName: '',
    width: 90,
    sortable: false,
    filterable: false,
    disableColumnMenu: true,
    renderCell: (params: GridCellParams) =>
      <EditCar cardata={params.row} />
  },
  {
    field: 'delete',
    headerName: '',
    width: 90,
    sortable: false,
    filterable: false,
    disableColumnMenu: true,
```

```
    renderCell: (params: GridCellParams) => (
      <button
        onClick={() => {
          if (window.confirm(`Are you sure you want to delete
            ${params.row.brand} ${params.row.model}?`))
            mutate(params.row._links.car.href)
        }}>
        Delete
      </button>
    ),
  },
];
```

6. Now, you should see the **Edit** button in each table row in your car list. When you press the **Edit** button, it should open the car form and populate fields using the car from the row where you pressed the button:

Figure 13.15: Edit button

7. Next, we have to implement the update request that sends an updated car to the backend. To update the car data, we have to send a PUT request to the http://localhost:8080/api/ cars/[carid] URL. The link will be the same as it is for the delete functionality. The request contains the updated car object inside the body, and the 'Content-Type':'application/ json' header that we also set for the add functionality. For the update functionality, we need a new type. In React Query, the mutation function can only take one parameter, but in our case, we have to send the car object (Car type) and its link.

We can solve that by passing an object that contains both values. Open the `types.ts` file and create the following type, called `CarEntry`:

```
export type CarEntry = {
  car: Car;
  url: string;
}
```

8. Then, open the `carapi.ts` file, create the following function, and export it. The function gets the `CarEntry` type object as an argument and it has `car` and `url` properties, where we get the values that are needed in the request:

```
// carapi.ts
// Add CarEntry to import
import { CarResponse, Car, CarEntry } from '../types';


// Add updateCar function
export const updateCar = async (carEntry: CarEntry):
  Promise<CarResponse> => {
  const response = await axios.put(carEntry.url, carEntry.car, {
    headers: {
      'Content-Type': 'application/json'
    },
  });
  return response.data;
}
```

9. Next, we import the `updateCar` function into the `EditCar` component and use the `useMutation` hook to send a request. We invalidate the cars query to re-fetch the list after a successful edit; therefore, we also have to get the query client:

```
// EditCar.tsx
// Add the following imports
import { updateCar } from '../api/carapi';
import { useMutation, useQueryClient } from '@tanstack/react-query';
```

```
// Get query client
const queryClient = useQueryClient();

// Use useMutation hook
const { mutate } = useMutation(updateCar, {
  onSuccess: () => {
    queryClient.invalidateQueries(["cars"]);
  },
  onError: (err) => {
    console.error(err);
  }
});
```

10. Then, we call `mutate` in the `handleSave` function. As was already mentioned, `mutate` only accepts one parameter, and we have to pass the car object and URL; therefore, we create an object that contains both values and pass that one. We also need to import the `CarEntry` type:

```
// EditCar.tsx
// Add CarEntry import
import { Car, CarResponse, CarEntry } from '../types';

// Modify handleSave function
const handleSave = () => {
  const url = cardata._links.self.href;
  const carEntry: CarEntry = {car, url}
  mutate(carEntry);
  setCar({ brand: '', model: '', color: '',  registrationNumber:'',
           modelYear: 0, price: 0 });
  setOpen(false);
}
```

11. Finally, if you press the **Edit** button in the table, it opens the modal form and displays the car from that row. The updated values are saved to the database when you press the **Save** button:

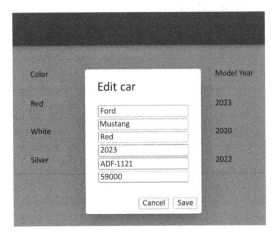

Figure 13.16: Edit car

Similarly, if you press the **New Car** button, it will open an empty form and save the new car to the database when the form is filled and the **Save** button is pressed. We used one component to handle both use cases by using the component props.

12. You can also see what happens in the backend when you edit a car. If you look at the Eclipse console after a successful edit, you can see that there is an update SQL statement that updates the database:

```
Console ×  Ju JUnit
CardatabaseApplication [Java Application] C:\Program Files\Java\jdk-17.0.2\bin\javaw.exe  (28.9.2023 klo 8.24.28) [pid: 21388]
Hibernate: select c1_0.id,c1_0.brand,c1_0.color,c1_0.model,c1_0.model_year,c1_0.owner,c1_0.price,c1_0.registrati
Hibernate: select c1_0.id,c1_0.brand,c1_0.color,c1_0.model,c1_0.model_year,c1_0.owner,c1_0.price,c1_0.registrati
Hibernate: update car set brand=?,color=?,model=?,model_year=?,owner=?,price=?,registration_number=? where id=?
```

Figure 13.17: Update car statement

Now, we have implemented all the CRUD functionalities.

Exporting the data to CSV

One feature that we will also implement is a **comma-separated values (CSV)** export of the data. We don't need any extra libraries for the export because the MUI data grid provides this feature. We will activate the data grid toolbar, which contains a lot of nice features:

1. Add the following import to the `Carlist.tsx` file. The `GridToolbar` component is a toolbar for the MUI data grid that contains nice functionalities, such as export:

```
import {
  DataGrid,
  GridColDef,
  GridCellParams,
  GridToolbar
} from '@mui/x-data-grid';
```

2. We need to enable our toolbar, which contains the **Export** button and other buttons. To enable the toolbar in the MUI data grid, you have to use the `slots` prop and set the value to `toolbar: GridToolbar`. The `slots` prop can be used to override the data grid's internal components:

```
return(
  <>
    <AddCar />
    <DataGrid
      rows={cars}
      columns={columns}
      disableRowSelectionOnClick={true}
      getRowId={row => row._links.self.href}
      slots={{ toolbar: GridToolbar }}
    />
    <Snackbar
      open={open}
      autoHideDuration={2000}
      onClose={() => setOpen(false)}
      message="Car deleted"
    />
  </>
);
```

3. Now, you will see the **EXPORT** button in the grid. If you press the button and select **Download as CSV**, the grid data is exported to a CSV file. You can **Print** your grid using the **EXPORT** button, and you will get a printer-friendly version of your page (you can also hide and filter columns and set row density using the toolbar):

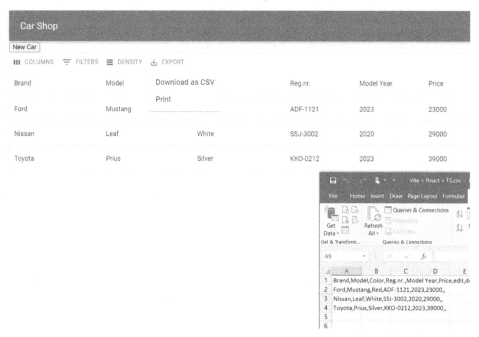

Figure 13.18: Export CSV

4. You can change the page title and icon by editing the index.html page, as shown in the following code. The icon can be found in your project's public folder, and you can use your own icon instead of Vite's default one:

```html
<!DOCTYPE html>
<html lang="en">
  <head>
    <meta charset="UTF-8" />
    <link rel="icon" type="image/svg+xml" href="/vite.svg" />
    <meta name="viewport" content="width=device-width, initial-
                                   scale=1.0" />
    <title>Car Shop</title>
  </head>
  <body>
    <div id="root"></div>
```

```
            <script type="module" src="/src/main.tsx"></script>
        </body>
    </html>
```

Now, all the functionalities have been implemented. In *Chapter 14*, *Styling the Frontend with React MUI*, we will focus on styling the frontend.

Summary

In this chapter, we implemented all the functionalities for our app. We started with fetching the cars from the backend and showing these in the MUI `DataGrid`, which provides paging, sorting, and filtering features. Then, we implemented the delete functionality and used the `SnackBar` component to give feedback to the user.

The add and edit functionalities were implemented using the MUI modal `dialog` component. Finally, we implemented the ability to export data to a CSV file.

In the next chapter, we are going to style the rest of our frontend using the React Material UI component library.

Questions

1. How do you fetch and present data using the REST API with React?
2. How do you delete data using the REST API with React?
3. How do you show toast messages with React and MUI?
4. How do you add data using the REST API with React?
5. How do you update data using the REST API with React?
6. How do you export data to a CSV file with React?

Further reading

There are other good resources available for learning about React and React Query. For example:

- *Practical React Query – TkDoDo's blog*, by Dominik Dorfmeister (`https://tkdodo.eu/blog/practical-react-query`)
- *Material Design Blog*, by Google (`https://material.io/blog/`)

Learn more on Discord

To join the Discord community for this book – where you can share feedback, ask the author
questions, and learn about new releases – follow the QR code below:

`https://packt.link/FullStackSpringBootReact4e`

14

Styling the Frontend with MUI

This chapter explains how to use **Material UI (MUI)** components in our frontend. We will use the `Button` component to show styled buttons. We will also use MUI icons and the `IconButton` component. The input fields in our modal forms will be replaced by `TextField` components.

In this chapter, we will cover the following topics:

- Using the MUI `Button` component
- Using the MUI `Icon` and `IconButton` components
- Using the MUI `TextField` component

At the end of the chapter, we will have a professional and polished user interface with minimal code changes in our React frontend.

Technical requirements

The Spring Boot application that we created in *Chapter 5, Securing Your Backend*, is required, together with the modification from *Chapter 12, Setting Up the Frontend for Our Spring Boot RESTful Web Service* (the unsecured backend).

We also need the React app that we used in *Chapter 13, Adding CRUD Functionalities*.

The code samples available at the following GitHub link will also be required: https://github.com/PacktPublishing/Full-Stack-Development-with-Spring-Boot-3-and-React-Fourth-Edition/tree/main/Chapter14.

Using the MUI Button component

Our frontend already uses some Material UI components, such as AppBar and Dialog, but we are still using a lot of HTML elements without any styling. First, we will replace HTML button elements with the Material UI Button component.

Execute the following steps to implement the Button component in our **New car** and **Edit car** modal forms:

1. Import the MUI Button component into the AddCar.tsx and EditCar.tsx files:

    ```
    // AddCar.tsx & EditCar.tsx
    import Button from '@mui/material/Button';
    ```

2. Change the buttons to use the Button component in the AddCar component. We are using 'text' buttons, which is the default Button type.

     If you want to use some other button type, such as 'outlined', you can change it by using the variant prop (https://mui.com/material-ui/ api/button/#Button-prop-variant).

    The following code shows the AddCar component's return statements with the changes:

    ```
    // AddCar.tsx
    return(
      <>
        <Button onClick={handleClickOpen}>New Car</Button>
        <Dialog open={open} onClose={handleClose}>
          <DialogTitle>New car</DialogTitle>
          <CarDialogContent car={car} handleChange={handleChange}/>
          <DialogActions>
            <Button onClick={handleClose}>Cancel</Button>
            <Button onClick={handleSave}>Save</Button>
          </DialogActions>
        </Dialog>
      </>
    );
    ```

3. Change the buttons in the EditCar component to the Button component. We will set the **Edit** button's size to "small" because the button is shown within the car grid. The following code shows the EditCar component's return statements with the changes:

```
// EditCar.tsx
return(
  <>
    <Button size="small" onClick={handleClickOpen}>
      Edit
    </Button>
    <Dialog open={open} onClose={handleClose}>
      <DialogTitle>Edit car</DialogTitle>
      <CarDialogContent car={car} handleChange={handleChange}/>
      <DialogActions>
        <Button onClick={handleClose}>Cancel</Button>
        <Button onClick={handleSave}>Save</Button>
      </DialogActions>
    </Dialog>
  </>
);
```

4. Now, the car list looks like the following screenshot:

Figure 14.1: The Carlist buttons

The modal form buttons should look like the following:

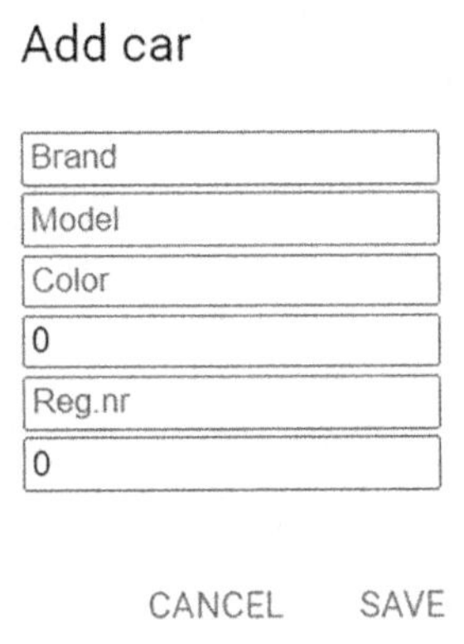

Add car

Figure 14.2: The form buttons

Now, the buttons in the add and edit form have been implemented using the MUI `Button` component.

Using the MUI Icon and IconButton components

In this section, we will use the `IconButton` component for the **EDIT** and **DELETE** buttons in the grid. MUI provides pre-built SVG icons that we have to install by using the following command in the terminal:

```
npm install @mui/icons-material
```

Let's first implement the **DELETE** button in the grid. The MUI `IconButton` component can be used to render icon buttons. The `@mui/icons-material` package, which we just installed, contains lots of icons that can be used with MUI.

You can find a list of icons available in the MUI documentation (`https://mui.com/material-ui/material-icons/`). There is a search functionality, and if you click any of the icons in the list, you can find the correct import statement for a specific icon:

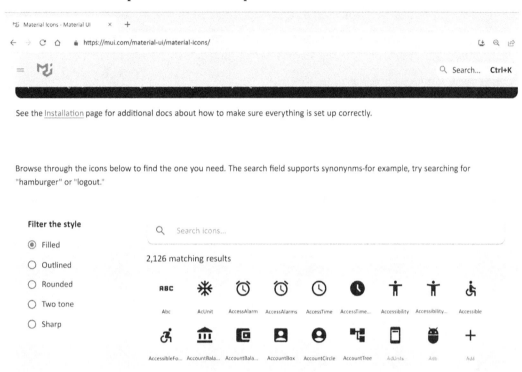

Figure 14.3: Material Icons

We need an icon for our **DELETE** button, so we will use an icon called `DeleteIcon`:

1. Open the `Carlist.tsx` file and add the following imports:

    ```
    // Carlist.tsx
    import IconButton from '@mui/material/IconButton';
    import DeleteIcon from '@mui/icons-material/Delete';
    ```

2. Next, we will render the IconButton component in our grid. We will modify the **DELETE** button in the code where we define the grid columns. Change the button element to the IconButton component and render the DeleteIcon inside the IconButton component. Set both the button and icon size to small. The icon buttons don't have an accessible name, so we will use aria-label to define a string that labels our delete icon button. The aria-label attribute is only visible to assistive technologies such as screen readers:

```
// CarList.tsx
const columns: GridColDef[] = [
  {field: 'brand', headerName: 'Brand', width: 200},
  {field: 'model', headerName: 'Model', width: 200},
  {field: 'color', headerName: 'Color', width: 200},
  {field: 'registrationNumber', headerName: 'Reg.nr.', width: 150},
  {field: 'modelYear', headerName: 'Model Year', width: 150},
  {field: 'price', headerName: 'Price', width: 150},
  {
    field: 'edit',
    headerName: '',
    width: 90,
    sortable: false,
    filterable: false,
    disableColumnMenu: true,
    renderCell: (params: GridCellParams) =>
      <CarForm mode="Edit" cardata={params.row} />
  },
  {
    field: 'delete',
    headerName: '',
    width: 90,
    sortable: false,
    filterable: false,
    disableColumnMenu: true,
    renderCell: (params: GridCellParams) => (
      <IconButton aria-label="delete" size="small"
        onClick={() => {
          if (window.confirm(`Are you sure you want to delete
              ${params.row.brand} ${params.row.model}?`))
            mutate(params.row._links.car.href)
        }}>
```

```
            <DeleteIcon fontSize="small" />
          </IconButton>
        ),
      },
    ];
```

3. Now, the **DELETE** button in the grid should look like the following screenshot:

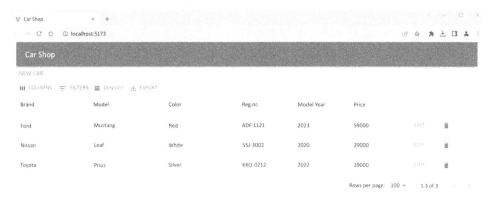

Figure 14.4: The Delete icon button

4. Next, we will implement the **EDIT** button using the `IconButton` component. Open the `EditCar.tsx` file and import the `IconButton` component and the `EditIcon` icon:

```
// EditCar.tsx
import IconButton from '@mui/material/IconButton';
import EditIcon from '@mui/icons-material/Edit';
```

5. Then, render the `IconButton` and `EditIcon` in the return statement. The button and icon size are set to small, as with the delete buttons:

```
// EditCar.tsx
return(
  <>
    <IconButton aria-label="edit" size="small"
      onClick={handleClickOpen}>
      <EditIcon fontSize= "small" />
    </IconButton>
    <Dialog open={open} onClose={handleClose}>
      <DialogTitle>Edit car</DialogTitle>
      <CarDialogContent car={car} handleChange={handleChange}/>
      <DialogActions>
```

```
        <Button onClick={handleClose}>Cancel</Button>
        <Button onClick={handleSave}>Save</Button>
      </DialogActions>
    </Dialog>
  </>
);
```

6. Finally, you will see both buttons are rendered as icons, as shown in the following screenshot:

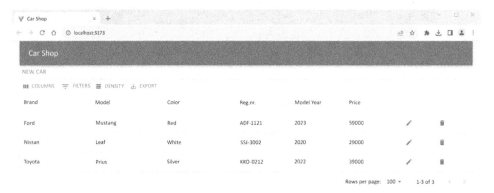

Figure 14.5: Icon buttons

We can also add **tooltips** to our edit and delete icon buttons using the Tooltip component. The Tooltip component wraps the component to which you want to attach the tooltip. The following example shows how to add a tooltip to the edit button:

1. First, import the Tooltip component by adding the following import to your EditCar component:

```
import Tooltip from '@mui/material/Tooltip';
```

2. Then, use the Tooltip component to wrap the IconButton component. The title prop is used to define the text that is shown in the tooltip:

```
// EditCar.tsx
<Tooltip title="Edit car">
  <IconButton aria-label="edit" size="small"
    onClick={handleClickOpen}>
    <EditIcon fontSize= "small" />
  </IconButton>
</Tooltip>
```

3. Now, if you hover your mouse over the edit button, you will see a tooltip, as shown in the following screenshot:

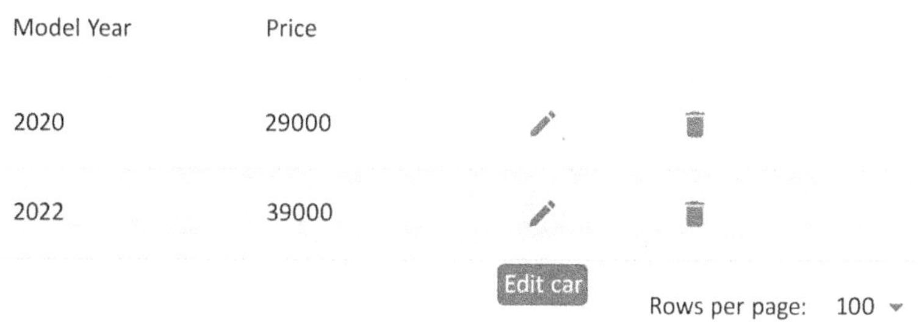

Model Year	Price			
2020	29000	✏		🗑
2022	39000	✏		🗑
		Edit car	Rows per page:	100 ▾

Figure 14.6: Tooltip

Next, we will implement text fields using the MUI TextField component.

Using the MUI TextField component

In this section, we'll change the text input fields in the modal forms to the MUI TextField and Stack components:

1. Add the following import statements to the CarDialogContent.tsx file. Stack is a one-dimensional MUI layout component that we can use to set spaces between text fields:

```
import TextField from '@mui/material/TextField';
import Stack from '@mui/material/Stack';
```

2. Then, change the input elements to the TextField components in the add and edit forms. We are using the label prop to set the labels of the TextField components. There are three different variants (visual styles) of text input available, and we are using the outlined one, which is the default variant. The other variants are standard and filled. You can use the variant prop to change the value. The text fields are wrapped inside the Stack component to get some spacing between the components and to set the top margin:

```
// CarDialogContent.tsx
return (
  <DialogContent>
    <Stack spacing={2} mt={1}>
      <TextField label="Brand" name="brand"
        value={car.brand} onChange={handleChange}/>
      <TextField label="Model" name="model"
        value={car.model} onChange={handleChange}/>
```

```
    <TextField label="Color" name="color"
      value={car.color} onChange={handleChange}/>
    <TextField label="Year" name="modelYear"
      value={car.modelYear} onChange={handleChange}/>
    <TextField label="Reg.nr." name="registrationNumber"
      value={car.registrationNumber} onChange={handleChange}/>
    <TextField label="Price" name="price"
      value={car.price} onChange={handleChange}/>
  </Stack>
 </DialogContent>
);
```

 You can read more about spacing and the units that are used at https://
mui.com/system/spacing/.

3. After the modifications, both the add and edit modal forms should look like the following because we are using the CarDialogContent component in both forms:

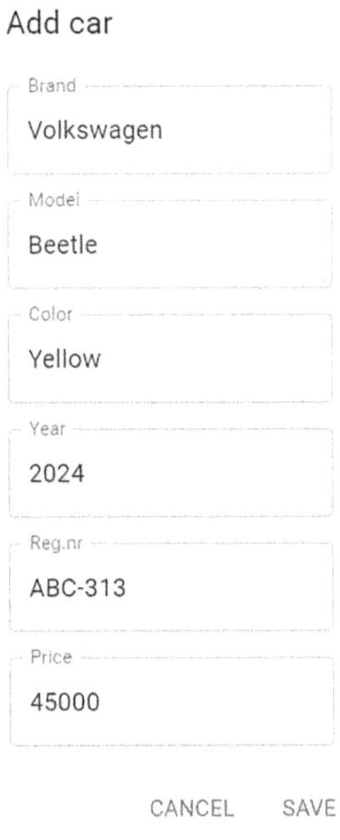

Add car

Brand
Volkswagen

Model
Beetle

Color
Yellow

Year
2024

Reg.nr
ABC-313

Price
45000

CANCEL   SAVE

Figure 14.7: Text fields

Now, we have completed the styling of our frontend using MUI components.

Summary

In this chapter, we finalized our frontend using MUI, which is the React component library that implements Google's Material Design. We replaced the buttons with the MUI `Button` and `IconButton` components. Our modal form got a new look with the MUI `TextField` component. After these modifications, our frontend looks more professional and uniform.

In the next chapter, we will focus on frontend testing.

Questions

1. What is MUI?

2. How can you use different Material UI components?

3. How do you use MUI icons?

Further reading

- Another good resource for learning about Material UI is the *MUI Design Resources* (`https://mui.com/material-ui/getting-started/design-resources/`.)

Learn more on Discord

To join the Discord community for this book – where you can share feedback, ask the author questions, and learn about new releases – follow the QR code below:

`https://packt.link/FullStackSpringBootReact4e`

15

Testing React Apps

This chapter explains the basics of testing React apps. It will give us an overview of using Jest, which is a JavaScript testing framework. We will look at how you can create and run new test suites and tests. To test our React Vite project, we will also learn how to use the React Testing Library together with Vitest.

In this chapter, we will cover the following topics:

- Using Jest
- Using the React Testing Library
- Using Vitest
- Firing events in tests
- End-to-end testing

Technical requirements

The Spring Boot application that we created in *Chapter 5, Securing Your Backend*, is required, as is the React app that we used in *Chapter 14, Styling the Frontend with React MUI*.

The code samples available at the following GitHub link will also be required to follow along with this chapter: `https://github.com/PacktPublishing/Full-Stack-Development-with-Spring-Boot-3-and-React-Fourth-Edition/tree/main/Chapter15`.

Using Jest

Jest is a testing framework for JavaScript, developed by Meta Inc. (https://jestjs.io/). It is widely used with React and provides lots of useful features for testing. For example, you can create a **snapshot** test, whereby you can take snapshots from React trees and investigate how states are changing. Jest has mocking functionalities that you can use to test, for example, your asynchronous REST API calls. It also provides functions that are required for assertions in your test cases.

To demonstrate the syntax, we will see how to create a test case for a basic TypeScript function that performs some simple calculations. The following function takes two numbers as arguments and returns the product of the numbers:

```typescript
// multi.ts
export const calcMulti = (x: number, y: number): number => {
  return x * y;
}
```

The following code snippet shows a Jest test for the preceding function:

```typescript
// multi.test.ts
import { calcMulti } from './multi';

test("2 * 3 equals 6", ()  => {
  expect(calcMulti(2, 3)).toBe(6);
});
```

The test case starts with a test() method that runs the test case. The test() method takes two required arguments: the test name (a descriptive string) and the anonymous function that contains the test code. The expect() function is used when you want to test values, and it gives you access to multiple **matchers**. The toBe() function is one matcher that checks whether the result from the function equals the value in the matcher.

 There are many different matchers available in Jest, and you can find them in the documentation: https://jestjs.io/docs/using-matchers.

describe() is a function that's used in test suites to group related test cases together. It helps you to organize tests based on their functionality, or in React, based on the component being tested. In the following example, we have a test suite that contains two test cases for the App component:

```
describe("App component", () => {
  test("App component renders", () => {
    // 1st test case
  })

  test("Header text", () => {
    // 2nd test case
  })
});
```

Using the React Testing Library

The **React Testing Library** (https://testing-library.com/) is a set of tools and APIs for testing React components. It can be used for DOM testing and queries. The React Testing Library provides a set of query functions that help you search elements based on their text content, label, and so on. It also provides tools to simulate user actions such as clicking a button and typing into input fields.

Let's go through some important concepts in the React Testing Library. The Testing Library provides a render() method that renders a React element into the DOM and makes it available for testing:

```
import { render } from '@testing-library/react'

render(<MyComponent />);
```

Queries can be used to find elements on the page. The screen object is a utility for querying the rendered components. It provides a set of query methods that can be used to find elements on the page. There are different types of queries that start with various keywords: getBy, findBy, or queryBy. The getBy and findBy queries throw an error if no element is found. The queryBy queries return null if no element is found.

 The right query to use depends on the situation, and you can read more about the differences at https://testing-library.com/docs/dom-testing-library/ cheatsheet/.

For example, the getByText() method queries the document for an element that contains the specified text:

```
import { render, screen } from '@testing-library/react'

render(<MyComponent />);
// Find text Hello World (case-insensitive)
screen.getByText(/Hello World/i);
```

The forward slash (/) in /Hello World/i is used to define a regular expression pattern, and the i-flag at the end stands for case-insensitive. This means it is looking for rendered content that contains the "Hello World" text in a case-insensitive matter. You can also use a full string match that is case-sensitive by passing a string as an argument:

```
screen.getByText("Hello World");
```

Then, we can use expect to make an assertion. jest-dom is a companion library for the React Testing Library, and it provides custom matchers that are useful when testing React components. For example, its toBeInTheDocument() matcher checks if the element is present in the document. If the following assertion passes, the test case will pass; otherwise, it will fail:

```
import { render, screen } from '@testing-library/react'
import matchers from '@testing-library/jest-dom/matchers ';

render(<MyComponent />);
expect(screen.getByText(/Hello World/i)).toBeInTheDocument();
```

 You can find all the matchers in the jest-dom documentation: https://github. com/testing-library/jest-dom.

We have now learned the basics of Jest and the React Testing Library. Both libraries are needed to test React applications. Jest is a testing framework that provides a testing environment and assertion library. The React Testing Library is a utility library designed for testing React components. Next, we will learn how to start testing in a Vite project.

Using Vitest

Vitest (`https://vitest.dev/`) is the testing framework for Vite projects. It is also possible to use Jest in Vite projects, and there are libraries that provide Vite integration for Jest (for example, `https://github.com/sodatea/vite-jest`). In this book, we will use Vitest because it is easier to start using it with Vite. Vitest is similar to Jest, and it provides `test`, `describe`, and `expect`, which we learned about in the Jest section.

In this section, we will create tests with Vitest and the React Testing Library for the frontend project that we used in *Chapter 14, Styling the Frontend with MUI*.

Installing and configuring

The first step is installing Vitest and the React Testing Library to our project:

1. Open the project in Visual Studio Code. Move to your project folder in the terminal and execute the following npm command inside your project folder:

    ```
    npm install -D vitest @testing-library/react @testing-library/jest-
        dom jsdom
    ```

    The `-D` flag in the npm command means that a package should be saved as a development dependency in the devDependencies section of the package.json file. These packages are necessary for development and testing but are not required for the production runtime of the application.

2. Next, we have to configure Vitest by using a Vite configuration file, `vite.config.ts`. Open the file and add a new `test` property with the following changes:

    ```
    import { defineConfig } from 'vite/config'
    import react from '@vitejs/plugin-react'

    // https://vitejs.dev/config/
    export default defineConfig({
      plugins: [react()],
      test: {
        globals: true,
        environment: 'jsdom',
      },
    })
    ```

By default, Vitest does not provide a global API. The `globals: true` setting allows us to reference APIs globally (`test`, `expect`, and so on), like Jest. The `environment: 'jsdom'` setting defines that we are using the browser environment instead of Node.js.

3. Now, you can see a TypeScript type error in the `test` property because the test type doesn't exist in Vite's configuration. You can import extended Vite configuration from Vitest to get rid of the error. Modify the `defineConfig` import as shown in the following code:

```
// Modify defineConfig import
import { defineConfig } from 'vitest/config'
```

4. Next, we will add the test script to our `package.json` file:

```
"scripts": {
    "dev": "vite",
    "build": "tsc && vite build",
    "lint": "eslint src --ext ts,tsx --report-unused-disable-
            directives --max-warnings 0",
    "preview": "vite preview",
    "test":"vitest"
},
```

5. We can now run our tests using the following `npm` command. In this phase, you will get an error because we don't have any tests yet:

```
npm run test
```

 You can also find a Visual Studio Code extension for Vitest if you want to run your tests from the VS Code IDE: https://marketplace.visualstudio. com/items?itemName=ZixuanChen.vitest-explorer.

By default, files to include in the test run are defined using the following glob pattern (https:// vitest.dev/config/#include):

```
['**/*.{test,spec}.?(c|m)[jt]s?(x)']
```

We will name our test files using the `component.test.tsx` naming convention.

Running our first test

Now, we will create our first test case to verify that our App component is rendered and that the app header text can be found:

1. Create a new file called App.test.tsx in the src folder of your React app and create a new test case. We are using Vitest, so we import describe and test from vitest:

```
import { describe, test } from 'vitest';

describe("App tests", () => {
  test("component renders", () => {
  // Test case code
  })
});
```

2. Then, we can use the render method from the React Testing Library to render our App component:

```
import { describe, test } from 'vitest';
import { render } from '@testing-library/react';
import App from './App';

describe("App tests", () => {
  test("component renders", () => {
    render(<App />);
  })
});
```

3. Next, we use the screen object and its query API to verify that the app header text has been rendered:

```
import { describe, test, expect } from 'vitest';
import { render, screen } from '@testing-library/react';
import App from './App';

describe("App tests", () => {
  test("component renders", () => {
    render(<App />);
    expect(screen.getByText(/Car Shop/i)).toBeDefined();
  })
});
```

4. If you want to use `jest-dom` library matchers such as `toBeInTheDocument()`, which we used earlier, you should import the `jest-dom/vitest` package, which extends matchers:

```
import { describe, test, expect } from 'vitest';
import { render, screen } from '@testing-library/react';
import App from './App';
import '@testing-library/jest-dom/vitest';

describe("App tests", () => {
  test("component renders", () => {
    render(<App />);
    expect(screen.getByText(/Car Shop/i
        )).toBeInTheDocument();
  })
});
```

5. Finally, we can run our test by typing the following command in the terminal:

```
npm run test
```

We should see that the test passes:

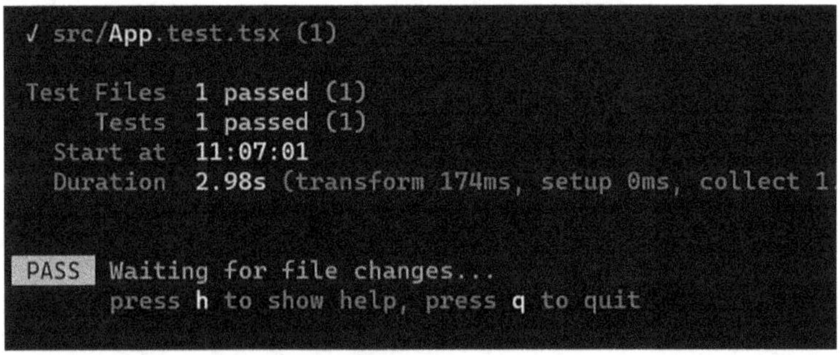

```
✓ src/App.test.tsx (1)

Test Files  1 passed (1)
     Tests  1 passed (1)
  Start at  11:07:01
  Duration  2.98s (transform 174ms, setup 0ms, collect 1

PASS  Waiting for file changes...
      press h to show help, press q to quit
```

Figure 15.1: Test run

Tests are run in **watch mode,** meaning each time you make changes to your source code, the tests that are related to the code changes are rerun. You can quit watch mode by pressing *q*, as shown in the figure. You can also invoke test reruns manually by pressing *r*.

If you need, you can create a test setup file that can be used to set up the environment and configuration required for running tests. The setup file will be run before each test file.

You have to specify the path to the test setup file in the `vite.config.ts` file, inside the `test` node:

```
// vite.config.ts
test: {
  setupFiles: ['./src/testSetup.ts'],
  globals: true,
  environment: 'jsdom',
},
```

You can also perform tasks that are required before or after test cases. Vitest provides the `beforeEach` and `afterEach` functions that you can use to invoke code before or after your test cases. For example, you can run the React Testing Library's `cleanup` function after each test case to unmount React components that were mounted. If you only want to invoke some code once before or after *all* test cases, you can use the `beforeAll` or `afterAll` functions.

Testing our Carlist component

Let's now make a test for our `Carlist` component. We will use our backend REST API, and in this section, you should run the backend that we used in the previous chapter. Using a real API in your tests is closer to a real-world scenario and allows end-to-end integration testing. However, real APIs always have some latency and make your tests slower to run.

You can alternatively use a **mock API**. This is common if the developer doesn't have access to the real API. Using a mock API requires creating and maintaining the mock API implementation. There are several libraries that you can use for this with React, such as **msw** (**Mock Service Worker**) and **nock**.

Let's begin:

1. Create a new file called `Carlist.test.tsx` in your `src` folder. We will import the `Carlist` component and render it. The component renders the `'Loading...'` text when data from the backend is not available yet. The starter code looks like the following:

    ```
    import { describe, expect, test } from 'vitest';
    import { render, screen } from '@testing-library/react';
    import '@testing-library/jest-dom/vitest';
    import Carlist from './components/Carlist';

    describe("Carlist tests", () => {
      test("component renders", () => {
        render(<Carlist />);
        expect(screen.getByText(/Loading/i)).toBeInTheDocument();
      })
    });
    ```

2. Now, if you run your test cases, you will get the following error: **No QueryClient set, use QueryClientProvider to set one**. We used React Query for networking in our `Carlist` component; therefore, we need `QueryClientProvider` in our component. The source code below shows how we can do that. We have to create a new `QueryClient` and set retries to `false`. By default, React Query retries queries three times, which might cause timeouts in your test case if you want to test error cases:

    ```
    import { QueryClient, QueryClientProvider } from
      '@tanstack/react-query';
    import { describe, test } from 'vitest';
    import { render, screen } from '@testing-library/react';
    import '@testing-library/jest-dom/vitest';
    import Carlist from './components/Carlist';

    const queryClient = new QueryClient({
      defaultOptions: {
        queries: {
          retry: false,
        },
      },
    });
    ```

```
const wrapper = ({
  children } : { children: React.ReactNode }) => (
    <QueryClientProvider client = {
      queryClient}>{children}
    </QueryClientProvider>);

describe("Carlist tests", () => {
  test("component renders", () => {
    render(<Carlist />, { wrapper });
  expect(screen.getByText(/Loading/i)).toBeInTheDocument();
  })
});
```

We also created a wrapper that returns a QueryClientProvider component. Then, we used the render function's second argument and passed our wrapper, which is a React component, so that the wrapper wraps the Carlist component. This is useful function-ality when you want to wrap your component with additional wrappers. The final result is that the Carlist component is wrapped inside the QueryClientProvider.

3. Now, if you rerun your tests, you won't get an error and your new test case will pass. The test run now includes two test files and two tests:

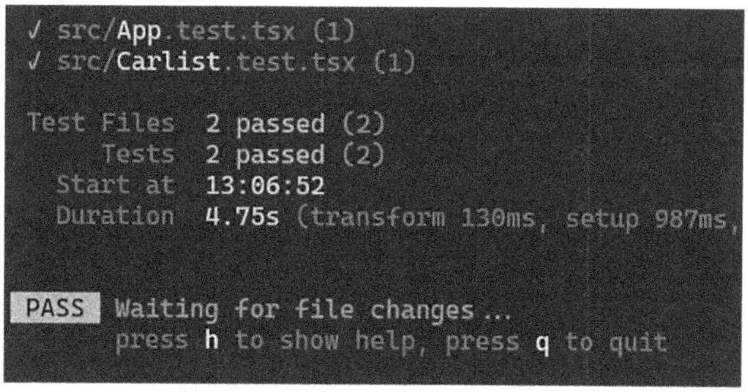

Figure 15.2: Test run

4. Next, we will test that our getCars fetch is invoked and the cars are rendered in the data grid. The network calls are asynchronous, and we don't know when the response will arrive. We will use the React Testing Library's waitFor function to wait until the **NEW CAR** button is rendered because then we know that the network request has succeeded. The test will proceed after the condition is met.

Finally, we will use a matcher to check that the Ford text can be found in the document. Add the following highlighted import to the Carlist.test.tsx file:

```
import { render, screen, waitFor } from '@testing-library/
   react';
```

5. The test looks like the following:

```
describe("Carlist tests", () => {
  test("component renders", () => {
    render(<Carlist />, { wrapper });
    expect(screen.getByText(/Loading/i)
      ).toBeInTheDocument();
  })

  test("Cars are fetched", async () => {
    render(<Carlist />, { wrapper });

    await waitFor(() => screen.getByText(/New Car/i));
    expect(screen.getByText(/Ford/i)).toBeInTheDocument();
  })
});
```

6. If you rerun the tests, you can see that three tests pass now:

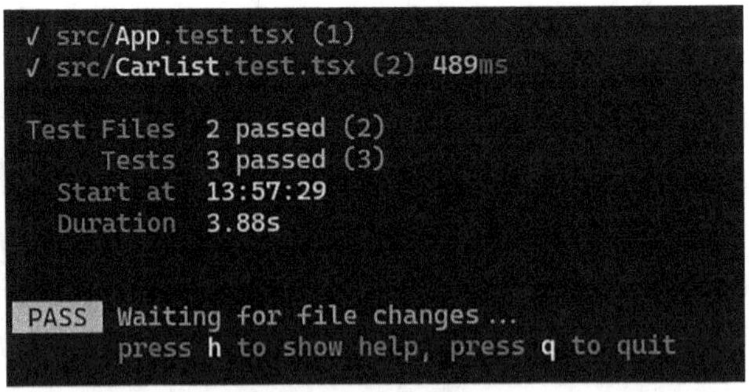

```
√ src/App.test.tsx (1)
√ src/Carlist.test.tsx (2) 489ms

Test Files  2 passed (2)
     Tests  3 passed (3)
  Start at  13:57:29
  Duration  3.88s


PASS  Waiting for file changes ...
      press h to show help, press q to quit
```

Figure 15.3: Test run

We have now learned the basics of Vitest and how to create and run test cases in a Vite React app. Next, we will learn how to simulate user actions in our test cases.

Firing events in tests

The React Testing Library provides a `fireEvent()` method that can be used to fire DOM events in your test cases. The `fireEvent()` method is used in the following way. First, we have to import it from the React Testing Library:

```
import { render, screen, fireEvent } from '@testing-library/react';
```

Next, we have to find the element and trigger its event. The following example shows how to trigger an input element's change event and a button's click event:

```
// Find input element by placeholder text
const input = screen.getByPlaceholderText('Name');

// Set input element's value
fireEvent.change(input, {target: {value: 'John'}});

// Find button element by text
const btn = screen.getByText('Submit');

// Click button
fireEvent.click(btn);
```

After the events are triggered, we can assert the expected behavior.

There is also a companion library for the Testing Library that is called `user-event`. The `fireEvent` function triggers element events, but browsers do more than only triggering one event. For example, if a user types some text into an input element, it is first focused, and then keyboard and input events are fired. `user-event` simulates the full user interaction.

To use the `user-event` library, we have to install it in our project with the following *npm* command:

```
npm install -D @testing-library/user-event
```

Next, we have to import `userEvent` in the test file:

```
import userEvent from '@testing-library/user-event';
```

Then, we can create an instance of userEvent using the userEvent.setup() function. We can also call the API directly, which will call userEvent.setup() internally, and this is how we will use it in the following examples. The userEvent provides multiple functions to interact with the UI, such as click() and type():

```
// Click a button
await userEvent.click(element);

// Type a value into an input element
await userEvent.type(element, value);
```

As an example, we will create a new test case that simulates a **NEW CAR** button press in our Carlist component and then checks that the modal form is opened:

1. Open the Carlist.test.tsx file and import userEvent:

    ```
    import userEvent from '@testing-library/user-event';
    ```

2. Create a new test inside the describe() function where we have our Carlist component tests. In the test, we will render the Carlist component and wait until the **NEW CAR** button is rendered:

    ```
    test("Open new car modal", async () => {
      render(<Carlist />, { wrapper });

      await waitFor(() => screen.getByText(/New Car/i));
    })
    ```

3. Then, find the button using the getByText query and use the userEvent.click() function to press the button. Use a matcher to verify that the **SAVE** button can be found in the document:

    ```
    test("Open new car modal", async () => {
      render(<Carlist />, { wrapper });

      await waitFor(() => screen.getByText(/New Car/i));
      await userEvent.click(screen.getByText(/New Car/i));
      expect(screen.getByText(/Save/i)).toBeInTheDocument();
    })
    ```

4. Now, rerun your tests and see that four test cases pass:

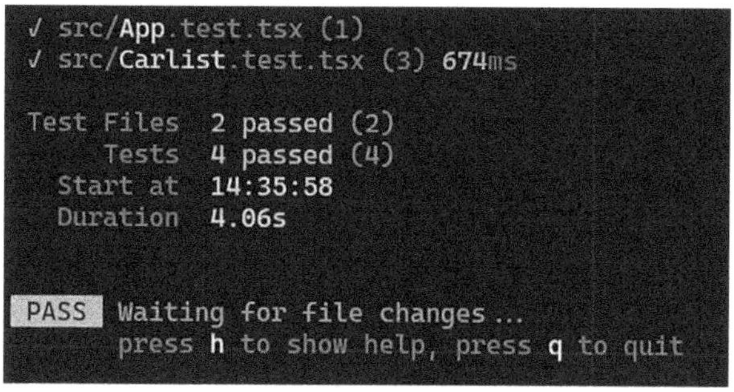

```
√ src/App.test.tsx (1)
√ src/Carlist.test.tsx (3) 674ms

Test Files  2 passed (2)
      Tests  4 passed (4)
   Start at  14:35:58
   Duration  4.06s


 PASS  Waiting for file changes ...
       press h to show help, press q to quit
```

Figure 15.4: Test run

We can use the getByRole query to find elements based on their roles, such as buttons, links, and so on. Below is an example of how to find a button that contains the text Save by using the getByRole query. The first argument defines the role, and the second argument's name option defines the button text:

```
screen.getByRole('button', { name: 'Save' });
```

5. We can also test how a failed test looks by changing the text in the test matcher, for example:

```
expect(screen.getByText(/Saving/i)).toBeInTheDocument();
```

Now, if we rerun the tests, we can see that one test fails, along with the reason for the failure:

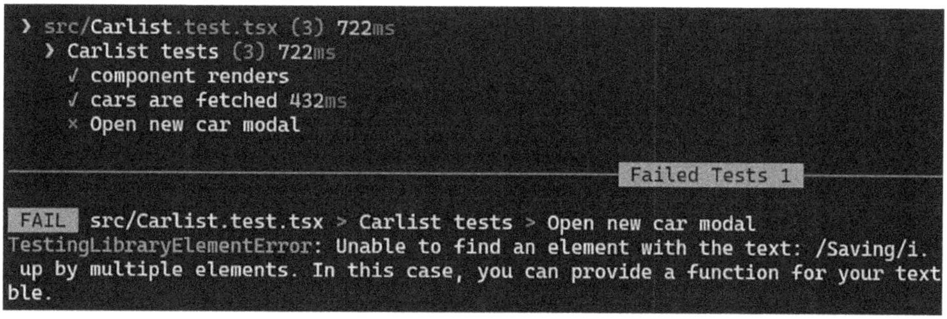

```
❯ src/Carlist.test.tsx (3) 722ms
  ❯ Carlist tests (3) 722ms
    √ component renders
    √ cars are fetched 432ms
    × Open new car modal

────────────────────────────────────── Failed Tests 1 ──────

 FAIL  src/Carlist.test.tsx > Carlist tests > Open new car modal
TestingLibraryElementError: Unable to find an element with the text: /Saving/i.
 up by multiple elements. In this case, you can provide a function for your text
ble.
```

Figure 15.5: Failed test

Now, you know the basics of testing user interactions in your React components.

End-to-end testing

End-to-end (E2E) testing is a methodology that focuses on testing an entire application's workflow. We will not cover it in detail in this book, but we will give you an idea about it and cover some tools that we can use.

The goal is to simulate user scenarios and interactions with the application to make sure that all components work together correctly. E2E testing covers frontend, backend, and all interfaces or external dependencies of the software that is being tested. The E2E testing scope can also be *cross-browser* or *cross-platform*, where an application is tested using multiple different web browsers or mobile devices.

There are several tools available for end-to-end testing, such as:

- **Cypress** (`https://www.cypress.io/`): This is a tool that can be used to create E2E tests for web applications. Cypress tests are simple to write and read. You can see your application's behavior during the test execution in the browser and it also helps you to debug if there are any failures. You can use Cypress for free, with some limitations.

- **Playwright** (`https://playwright.dev/`): This is a test automation framework designed for E2E testing, and it is developed by Microsoft. You can get a Visual Studio Code extension for Playwright and start to use it in your project. The default language for writing tests with Playwright is TypeScript, but you can also use JavaScript.

E2E testing helps to verify that your application meets its functional requirements.

Summary

In this chapter, we provided a basic overview of how to test React apps. We introduced Jest, a JavaScript testing framework, and the React Testing Library, which can be used to test React components. We also learned how to create and run tests in our Vite React app using Vitest, and finished off with a brief discussion on E2E testing.

In the next chapter, we will secure our application and add the login functionality to the frontend.

Questions

1. What is Jest?
2. What is the React Testing Library?
3. What is Vitest?
4. How can you fire events in test cases?

5. What is the purpose of E2E testing?

Further reading

Here are some other resources for learning about React and testing:

- *Simplify Testing with React Testing Library*, by Scottie Crump (`https://www.packtpub.com/product/simplify-testing-with-react-testing-library/9781800564459`)

- *React Testing Library Tutorial*, by Robin Wieruch (`https://www.robinwieruch.de/react-testing-library/`)

Learn more on Discord

To join the Discord community for this book – where you can share feedback, ask the author questions, and learn about new releases – follow the QR code below:

`https://packt.link/FullStackSpringBootReact4e`

16

Securing Your Application

We will learn how to secure our application in this chapter. This chapter will explain how to implement authentication in our frontend when we are using **JSON Web Token (JWT)** authentication in the backend. First, we will switch on security in our backend to enable JWT authentication. Then, we will create a component for the login functionality. Finally, we will modify our CRUD functionalities to send the token in the request's authorization header to the backend, and implement the logout functionality.

In this chapter, we will cover the following topics:

- Securing the backend
- Securing the frontend

Technical requirements

The Spring Boot application that we created in *Chapter 5, Securing Your Backend*, is required (https://github.com/PacktPublishing/Full-Stack-Development-with-Spring-Boot-3-and-React-Fourth-Edition/tree/main/Chapter05), as is the React app that we used in *Chapter 14, Styling the Frontend with React MUI* (https://github.com/PacktPublishing/Full-Stack-Development-with-Spring-Boot-3-and-React-Fourth-Edition/tree/main/Chapter14).

The following GitHub link for this chapter will also be useful: https://github.com/PacktPublishing/Full-Stack-Development-with-Spring-Boot-3-and-React-Fourth-Edition/tree/main/Chapter16.

Securing the backend

In *Chapter 13*, we implemented CRUD functionalities in our frontend using an unsecured backend. Now, it is time to switch on security for our backend and go back to the version that we created in *Chapter 5*, *Securing Your Backend*:

1. Open your backend project with the Eclipse IDE and open the SecurityConfig.java file in the editor view. We have commented the security out and allowed everyone access to all endpoints. Now, we can remove that line and also remove the comments from the original version. Now, the filterChain() method of your SecurityConfig.java file should look like the following:

```
@Bean
public SecurityFilterChain filterChain(HttpSecurity http) throws
Exception {
  http.csrf((csrf) -> csrf.disable()) .cors(withDefaults())
    .sessionManagement((sessionManagement) ->
      sessionManagement.sessionCreationPolicy(
      SessionCreationPolicy.STATELESS))
    .authorizeHttpRequests( (authorizeHttpRequests) ->
      authorizeHttpRequests.requestMatchers(HttpMethod.POST, "/
      login").permitAll().anyRequest().authenticated())
    .addFilterBefore(authenticationFilter,
      UsernamePasswordAuthenticationFilter.class)
    .exceptionHandling((exceptionHandling) ->
      exceptionHandling.authenticationEntryPoint(exceptionHandler));

  return http.build();
}
```

2. Let's test what happens when the backend is secured again. Run the backend by pressing the **Run** button in Eclipse, and check from the console view that the application started correctly. Run the frontend by typing the npm run dev command into your terminal, and the browser should be opened to the address localhost:5173.

3. You should now see that the list page and the car list are loading. If you open the developer tools and the **Network** tab, you will notice that the response status is **401 Unauthorized**. This is actually what we want because we haven't yet executed authentication in relation to our frontend:

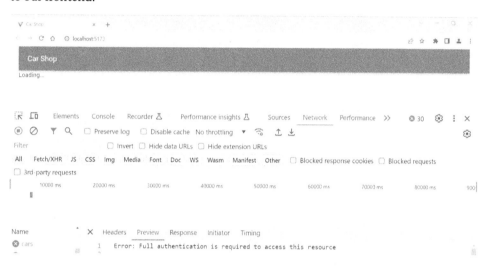

Figure 16.1: 401 Unauthorized

Now, we are ready to work with the frontend.

Securing the frontend

In *Chapter 5, Securing Your Backend*, we created JWT authentication and allowed everyone access to the /login endpoint without authentication. Now, on the frontend login page, we have to send a POST request to the /login endpoint using user credentials to get a token. After that, the token will be included in all requests that we send to the backend, as demonstrated in the following figure:

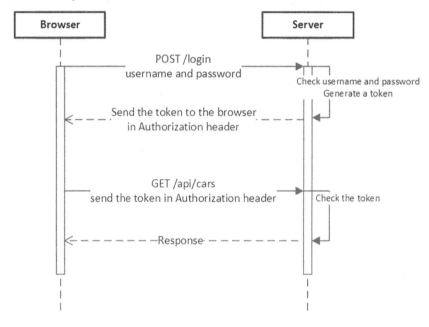

Figure 16.2: Secured application

With this knowledge, we will start to implement login functionality on our frontend. We will implement the login page where the user enters credentials, and then we will send a login request to get a token from the server. We will use the stored token in the requests that we send to the server.

Creating a login component

Let's first create a login component that asks for credentials from the user to get a token from the backend:

1. Create a new file called Login.tsx in the components folder. Now, the file structure of the frontend should be the following:

Figure 16.3: Project structure

2. Open the file in the VS Code editor view and add the following base code to the Login component. We need axios to send POST requests to the /login endpoint:

```
import { useState } from 'react';
import axios from 'axios';

function Login() {
  return(
    <></>
  );
}

export default Login;
```

3. We need two states for the authentication: one for the credentials (username and password), and one boolean value to indicate the status of the authentication. We also create a type for the user state. The initial value of the authentication status state is `false`:

```
import { useState } from 'react';
import axios from 'axios';

type User = {
  username: string;
  password: string;
}

function Login() {
  const [user, setUser] = useState<User>({
    username: '',
    password: ''
  });
  const [isAuthenticated, setAuth] = useState(false);

  return(
    <></>
  );
}

export default Login;
```

4. In the user interface, we are going to use the **Material UI (MUI)** component library, as we did with the rest of the user interface. We need `TextField` components for the credentials, the `Button` component to call a login function, and the `Stack` component for layout. Add imports for the components to the `Login.tsx` file:

```
import Button from '@mui/material/Button';
import TextField from '@mui/material/TextField';
import Stack from '@mui/material/Stack';
```

 We have already used all three of these component types in *Chapter 14, Styling the Frontend with MUI*, to style our UI.

5. Add the imported components to the `return` statement. We need two `TextField` components: one for the username and one for the password. One `Button` component is needed
   to call the login function that we are going to implement later in this section. We use the
   `Stack` component to align our `TextField` components to the center and to get spacing
   between them:

```
return(
    <Stack spacing={2} alignItems="center" mt={2}>
      <TextField
        name="username"
        label="Username"
        onChange={handleChange} />
      <TextField
        type="password"
        name="password"
        label="Password"
        onChange={handleChange}/>
      <Button
        variant="outlined"
        color="primary"
        onClick={handleLogin}>
          Login
      </Button>
    </Stack>
);
```

6. Implement the change handler function for the `TextField` components, in order to save
   typed values to the states. You have to use the spread syntax because it ensures that you
   retain all the other properties of the `user` object that are not modified in this update:

```
const handleChange = (event: React.ChangeEvent<HTMLInputElement>) =>
  {
  setUser({...user,
      [event.target.name] : event.target.value
  });
}
```

7. As shown in *Chapter 5, Securing Your Backend*, the login is done by calling the /login end-
    point using the POST method and sending the user object inside the body. If authentication
    succeeds, we get a token in a response Authorization header. We will then save the token
    to session storage and set the isAuthenticated state value to true.

 Session storage is similar to local storage, but it is cleared when a page session ends (when the page is closed). localStorage and sessionStorage
are properties of the Window interface.

When the isAuthenticated state value is changed, the user interface is re-rendered:

```
const handleLogin = () => {
  axios.post(import.meta.env.VITE_API_URL + "/login", user, {
    headers: { 'Content-Type': 'application/json' }
  })
  .then(res => {
    const jwtToken = res.headers.authorization;

    if (jwtToken !== null) {
      sessionStorage.setItem("jwt", jwtToken);
      setAuth(true);
    }
  })
  .catch(err => console.error(err));
}
```

8. We will implement some conditional rendering that renders the Login component if the
    isAuthenticated state is false, or the Carlist component if the isAuthenticated state
    is true. First, import the Carlist component into the Login.tsx file:

```
import Carlist from './Carlist';
```

Then, implement the following changes to the return statement:

```
if (isAuthenticated) {
  return <Carlist />;
}
else {
  return(
    <Stack spacing={2} alignItems="center" mt={2} >
```

```
        <TextField
          name="username"
          label="Username"
          onChange={handleChange} />
        <TextField
          type="password"
          name="password"
          label="Password"
          onChange={handleChange}/>
        <Button
          variant="outlined"
          color="primary"
          onClick={handleLogin}>
            Login
        </Button>
      </Stack>
    );
  }
```

9. To show the login form, we have to render the `Login` component instead of the `Carlist` component in the `App.tsx` file. Import and render the `Login` component and remove the unused `Carlist` import:

```
// App.tsx
import AppBar from '@mui/material/AppBar';
import Toolbar from '@mui/material/Toolbar';
import Typography from '@mui/material/Typography';
import Container from '@mui/material/Container';
import CssBaseline from '@mui/material/CssBaseline';
import Login from './components/Login';
import { QueryClient, QueryClientProvider } from '@tanstack/react-
  query';

const queryClient = new QueryClient();

function App() {
  return (
    <Container maxWidth="xl">
```

```
      <CssBaseline />
      <AppBar position="static">
        <Toolbar>
          <Typography variant="h6">
            Carshop
          </Typography>
        </Toolbar>
      </AppBar>
      <QueryClientProvider client={queryClient}>
        <Login />
      </QueryClientProvider>
    </Container>
  )
}

export default App;
```

Now, when your frontend and backend are running, your frontend should look like the following screenshot:

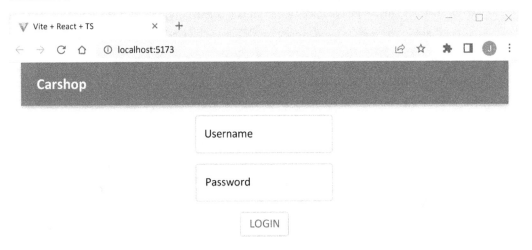

Figure 16.4: Login page

If you log in using the *user/user* or *admin/admin* credentials that we have inserted into the database, you should see the car list page. If you open the developer tools' **Application** tab, you can see that the token is now saved to session storage:

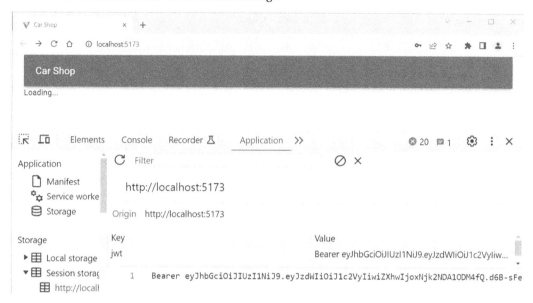

Figure 16.5: Session storage

Implementing REST API calls

At the end of the previous section, the car list is still loading and we can't fetch cars. This is the correct behavior because we haven't included the token in any requests yet. That is required for JWT authentication, which we will implement in the next phase:

1. Open the carapi.ts file in the VS Code editor view. To fetch the cars, we first have to read the token from session storage and then add the Authorization header with the token value to the GET request. You can see the source code for the getCars function here:

    ```
    // carapi.ts
    export const getCars = async (): Promise<CarResponse[]> => {
      const token = sessionStorage.getItem("jwt");
      const response = await axios.get(`${import.meta.env.VITE_API_URL}/
                        api/cars`, {
        headers: { 'Authorization' : token }
      });
      return response.data._embedded.cars;
    }
    ```

2. If you log in to your frontend, you should see the car list populated with cars from the database.

3. Check the request content from the developer tools; you can see that it contains the `Authorization` header with the token value:

```
✕   Headers   Preview   Response   Initiator   Timing
▼ Request Headers      View source
   Accept: */*
   Accept-Encoding: gzip, deflate, br
   Accept-Language: en-US,en;q=0.9
   Authorization: Bearer eyJhbGciOiJIUzI1NiJ9.eyJzdWIiOiJhZG1pbiIsImV4cCI6MTY0MDI1ODY1MH0.cPNb-Fz4JZCmbRXM_TwrTR7eKuy
   JrfaqjqM7BK6atU4
   Connection: keep-alive
   Host: localhost:8080
```

Figure 16.6: Request headers

4. Modify the other CRUD functionalities in the same way so they work correctly. The source code for the `deleteCar` function appears as follows, after the modifications:

```
// carapi.ts
export const deleteCar = async (link: string): Promise<CarResponse> =>
{
  const token = sessionStorage.getItem("jwt");
  const response = await axios.delete(link, {
    headers: { 'Authorization': token }
  })
  return response.data
}
```

The source code for the `addCar` and `editCar` functions appears as follows, after the modifications:

```
// carapi.ts
export const addCar = async (car: Car): Promise<CarResponse> => {
  const token = sessionStorage.getItem("jwt");
  const response = await axios.post(`${import.meta.env.VITE_API_
                   URL}/api/cars`, car, {
    headers: {
      'Content-Type': 'application/json',
      'Authorization': token
    },
```

```
    });

    return response.data;
}


export const updateCar = async (carEntry: CarEntry):
Promise<CarResponse> => {
  const token = sessionStorage.getItem("jwt");
  const response = await axios.put(carEntry.url, carEntry.car, {
    headers: {
      'Content-Type': 'application/json',
      'Authorization': token
    },
  });

  return response.data;
}
```

Refactoring duplicate code

Now, all the CRUD functionalities will work after you have logged in to the application. But, as you can see, we have quite a lot of duplicate code, such as the lines where we retrieve our token from session storage. We can do some refactoring to avoid repeating the same code and make our code easier to maintain:

1. First, we will create a function that retrieves the token from session storage and creates a configuration object for Axios requests that contains headers with the token. Axios provides the AxiosRequestConfig interface, which can be used to configure requests we send using Axios. We also set the content-type header value to application/json:

```
// carapi.ts
import axios, { AxiosRequestConfig } from 'axios';
import { CarResponse, Car, CarEntry } from '../types';

const getAxiosConfig = (): AxiosRequestConfig => {
  const token = sessionStorage.getItem("jwt");

  return {
    headers: {
```

```
        'Authorization': token,
        'Content-Type': 'application/json',
      },
   };
};
```

2. Then, we can use the getAxiosConfig() function without retrieving a token in each function, by removing the configuration object and calling the getAxiosConfig() function instead, as shown in the following code:

```
// carapi.ts
export const getCars = async (): Promise<CarResponse[]> => {
  const response = await axios.get(`${import.meta.env.VITE_API_URL}/
                    api/cars`, getAxiosConfig());
  return response.data._embedded.cars;
}


export const deleteCar = async (link: string): Promise<CarResponse> =>
{
  const response = await axios.delete(link, getAxiosConfig())
  return response.data
}


export const addCar = async (car: Car): Promise<CarResponse> => {
  const response = await axios.post(`${import.meta.env.VITE_API_
                    URL}/api/cars`, car, getAxiosConfig());

  return response.data;
}


export const updateCar = async (carEntry: CarEntry):
  Promise<CarResponse> => {
  const response = await axios.put(carEntry.url, carEntry.car,
                                   getAxiosConfig());

return response.data;
}
```

Axios also provides **interceptors** that can be used to intercept and modify requests and responses before they are handled by then or catch. You can read more about interceptors in the Axios documentation: `https://axios-http.com/docs/interceptors`.

Displaying an error message

In this phase, we are going to implement an error message that is shown to a user if authentication fails. We will use the Snackbar MUI component to show the message:

1. Add the following import to the Login.tsx file:

```
import Snackbar from '@mui/material/Snackbar';
```

2. Add a new state called open to control the visibility of the Snackbar:

```
const [open, setOpen] = useState(false);
```

3. Add the Snackbar component to the return statement, inside the stack just under the Button component. The Snackbar component is used to show toast messages. The component is shown if the open prop value is true. The autoHideDuration defines the number of milliseconds to wait before the onClose function is called:

```
<Snackbar
  open={open}
  autoHideDuration={3000}
  onClose={() => setOpen(false)}
  message="Login failed: Check your username and password"
/>
```

4. Open the Snackbar component if authentication fails by setting the open state value to true:

```
const login = () => {
  axios.post(import.meta.env.VITE_API_URL + "/login", user, {
    headers: { 'Content-Type': 'application/json' }
  })
  .then(res => {
    const jwtToken = res.headers.authorization;
```

```
      if (jwtToken !== null) {
        sessionStorage.setItem("jwt", jwtToken);
        setAuth(true);
      }
    })
    .catch(() => setOpen(true));
}
```

5. If you now try to log in with the wrong credentials, you will see the following message in the bottom-left corner of the screen:

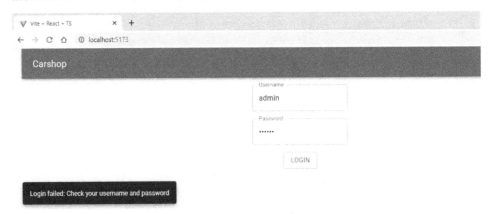

Figure 16.7: Login failed

Logging out

In this last section, we will implement the logout functionality in the Login component. The logout button is rendered on the car list page. The Carlist component is a child component of the Login component; therefore, we can pass the logout function to the car list using the props. Let's do this:

1. First, we create a handleLogout() function for the Login component, which updates the isAuthenticated state to false and clears the token from session storage:

    ```
    // Login.tsx
    const handleLogout = () => {
      setAuth(false);
      sessionStorage.setItem("jwt", "");
    }
    ```

2. Next, we pass the handleLogout function to the Carlist component using the props, as shown in the highlighted code:

```
// Login.tsx
if (isAuthenticated) {
  return <Carlist logOut={handleLogout}/>;
}
else {
  return(
    ...
```

3. We have to create a new type for the props that we receive in the Carlist component. The prop name is logOut, which is a function that takes no arguments, and we mark this prop as optional. Add the following type to the Carlist component and receive the logOut prop in the function arguments:

```
//Carlist.tsx
type CarlistProps = {
  logOut?: () => void;
}

function Carlist({ logOut }: CarlistProps) {
  const [open, setOpen] = useState(false);
  ...
```

4. Now, we can call the logout function and add the logout button. We use the Material UI Stack component to align the buttons so that the **NEW CAR** button is on the left and the **LOG OUT** button is on the right side of the screen:

```
// Carlist.tsx
// Add the following imports
import Button from '@mui/material/Button';
import Stack from '@mui/material/Stack';

// Render the Stack and Button
if (!isSuccess) {
    return <span>Loading...</span>
}
```

```
else if (error) {
  return <span>Error when fetching cars...</span>
}
else {
  return (
    <>
      <Stack direction="row" alignItems="center"
       justifyContent="space-between">
        <AddCar />
        <Button onClick={logOut}>Log out</Button>
      </Stack>
      <DataGrid
        rows={data}
        columns={columns}
        disableRowSelectionOnClick={true}
        slots={{ toolbar: GridToolbar }}
        getRowId={row => row._links.self.href} />
      <Snackbar
        open={open}
        autoHideDuration={2000}
        onClose={() => setOpen(false)}
        message="Car deleted" />
    </>
  );
}
```

5. Now, if you log in to your frontend, you can see the **LOG OUT** button on the car list page, as shown in the following screenshot. When you click the button, the login page is rendered because the isAuthenticated state is set to false and the token is cleared from session storage:

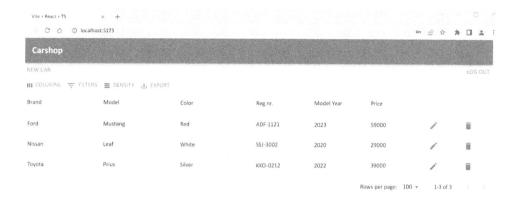

Figure 16.8: Log out

If you have a more complicated frontend with multiple pages, it would be wise to render the logout button in the app bar so that it is shown on each page. Then, you can use a state management technique to share a state with the whole component tree in your app. One solution would be to use the **React Context API** that we introduced in *Chapter 8, Getting Started with React*. In this scenario, you could use context to share the isAuthenticated state in your application's component tree.

As your application grows in complexity, managing state becomes crucial to ensuring that your components can access and update data efficiently. There are also other alternatives to the React Context API to manage states that you can study. The most common state management libraries are **React Redux** (https://react-redux.js.org) and MobX (https://github.com/mobxjs/mobx).

In the previous chapter, we created test cases for the CarList component, and at that point the app was unsecured. At this stage, our CarList component test cases will fail, and you should refactor them. To create a React test that simulates a login process and then tests whether data is fetched from a backend REST API, you can also use libraries like axios-mock-adapter (https://github.com/ctimmerm/axios-mock-adapter). Mocking Axios allows you to simulate the login process and data fetching without making actual network requests. We are not going into the details here, but we recommend you explore this further.

Now, we are ready with our car application.

Summary

In this chapter, we learned how to implement a login and logout functionality for our frontend when we are using JWT authentication. Following successful authentication, we used session storage to save the token that we received from the backend. The token was then used in all requests that we sent to the backend; therefore, we had to modify our CRUD functionalities to work with authentication properly.

In the next and final chapter, we will deploy our backend and frontend and also demonstrate how to create Docker containers.

Questions

1. How should you create a login form?
2. How should you log in to the backend using JWT?
3. What is session storage?
4. How should you send a token to the backend in CRUD functions?

Further reading

Here are some other resources for learning about React and state management:

- *State Management with React Query*, by Daniel Afonso (`https://www.packtpub.com/product/state-management-with-react-query/9781803231341`)
- *MobX Quick Start Guide*, by Pavan Podila and Michel Weststrate (`https://www.packtpub.com/product/mobx-quick-start-guide/9781789344837`)

Learn more on Discord

To join the Discord community for this book – where you can share feedback, ask the author questions, and learn about new releases – follow the QR code below:

`https://packt.link/FullStackSpringBootReact4e`

17

Deploying Your Application

This chapter will explain how to deploy your backend and frontend to a server. Successful deployment is a key part of the software development process, and it is important to learn how a modern deployment process works. There are a variety of cloud servers or **PaaS** (short for **Platform-as-a-Service**) providers available, such as **Amazon Web Services (AWS)**, DigitalOcean, Microsoft Azure, Railway, and Heroku.

In this book, we are using AWS and Netlify, which support multiple programming languages that are used in web development. We will also show you how to use Docker containers in deployments.

In this chapter, we will cover the following topics:

- Deploying the backend with AWS
- Deploying the frontend with Netlify
- Using Docker containers

Technical requirements

The Spring Boot application that we created in *Chapter 5, Securing Your Backend*, is required (https://github.com/PacktPublishing/Full-Stack-Development-with-Spring-Boot-3-and-React-Fourth-Edition/tree/main/Chapter05), as is the React app that we used in *Chapter 16, Securing Your Application* (https://github.com/PacktPublishing/Full-Stack-Development-with-Spring-Boot-3-and-React-Fourth-Edition/tree/main/Chapter16).

A Docker installation is necessary for the final section of the chapter.

Deploying the backend with AWS

If you are going to use your own server, the easiest way to deploy a Spring Boot application is to use an executable **Java ARchive (JAR)** file. With Gradle, an executable JAR file can be created using the Spring Boot Gradle wrapper. You can build your project using the following Gradle wrapper command in your project folder:

```
./gradlew build
```

Alternatively, you can run a Gradle task in Eclipse by right-clicking **Project** in the Project Explorer, navigating to **Window | Show View | Other**, and selecting **Gradle | Gradle Tasks** from the list. This opens a list of Gradle tasks, and you can start the build process by double clicking the **build** task, as illustrated in the following screenshot. If the Gradle tasks window is empty, click the root folder of the project in Eclipse:

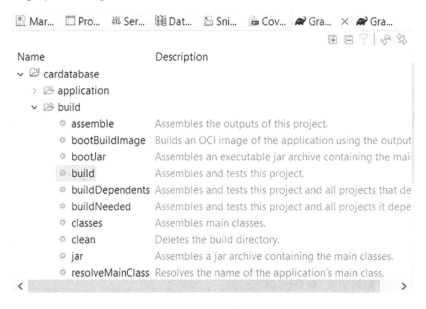

Figure 17.1: Gradle tasks

This creates a new build/libs folder to your project, where you will find JAR files. By default, two JAR files are created:

- The file with extension .plain.jar contains Java bytecode and other resources, but it doesn't contain any application framework or dependencies.
- The other .jar file is a fully executable archive that you can run using the java -jar your_appfile.jar Java command, as illustrated in the following screenshot:

```
PS C:\work\tmp\Chapter05\build\libs> java -jar .\cardatabase-0.0.1-SNAPSHOT.jar

  /\\ / ___'_ __ _ _(_)_ __  __ _ \ \ \ \
 ( ( )\___ | '_ | '_| | '_ \/ _` | \ \ \ \
  \\/  ___)| |_)| | | | | || (_| |  ) ) ) )
   '  |____| .__|_| |_|_| |_\__, | / / / /
 =========|_|==============|___/=/_/_/_/
 :: Spring Boot ::                (v3.1.0)

2023-06-07T09:49:29.482+03:00  INFO 22456 --- [           main] c.p.cardatabase.CardatabaseApplication   : Starting Card
atabaseApplication v0.0.1-SNAPSHOT using Java 17.0.2 with PID 22456 (C:\work\tmp\Chapter05\build\libs\cardatabase-0.0.1-
SNAPSHOT.jar started by h01270 in C:\work\tmp\Chapter05\build\libs)
2023-06-07T09:49:29.485+03:00  INFO 22456 --- [           main] c.p.cardatabase.CardatabaseApplication   : No active pro
file set, falling back to 1 default profile: "default"
2023-06-07T09:49:30.179+03:00  INFO 22456 --- [           main] .s.d.r.c.RepositoryConfigurationDelegate : Bootstrapping
```

Figure 17.2: Running the executable JAR file

Nowadays, cloud servers are the principal means of providing your application to end users. We are going to deploy our backend to **Amazon Web Services (AWS)** (https://aws.amazon.com/). The AWS Free Tier offers users an opportunity to explore products for free.

Create a Free Tier account and log in to AWS. You have to enter your contact information, including a functioning mobile phone number. AWS will send you an SMS confirmation message to verify your account. You must add a valid credit card, debit card, or another payment method for your accounts covered under the AWS Free Tier.

 You can read about the reasons why a payment method is needed at https://repost.aws/knowledge-center/free-tier-payment-method.

Deploying our MariaDB database

In this first section, we will deploy our MariaDB database to AWS. **Amazon Relational Database Service (RDS)** can be used to set up and operate relational databases. Amazon RDS supports several popular databases, including MariaDB. The following steps will take you through the process that creates a database in RDS:

1. After you have created a Free Tier account with AWS, log in to the AWS website. The AWS dashboard contains a search bar that you can use to find different services. Type RDS into the search bar and find RDS, as illustrated in the following screenshot. Click on **RDS** in the **Services** list:

Figure 17.3: RDS

2. Click the **Create database** button to begin the database creation process:

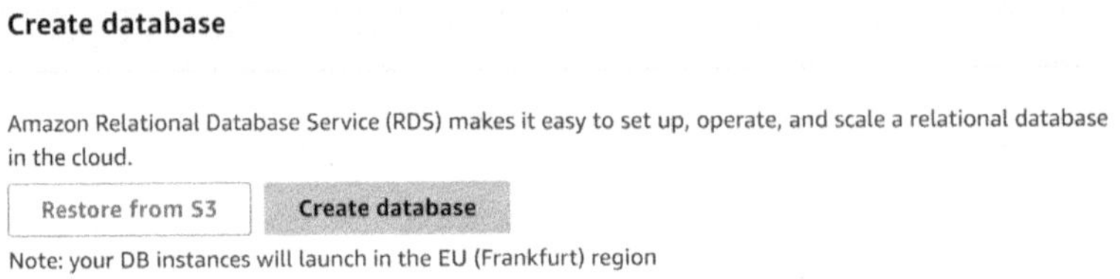

Create database

Amazon Relational Database Service (RDS) makes it easy to set up, operate, and scale a relational database in the cloud.

> Restore from S3   **Create database**

Note: your DB instances will launch in the EU (Frankfurt) region

Figure 17.4: Create database

3. Select **MariaDB** from the database engine options:

Engine options

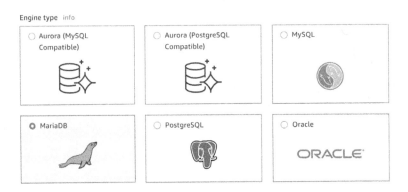

Figure 17.5: Engine options

4. Select **Free tier** from the templates.

5. Type a name for your database instance and the password for the database master user. You can use the default username (*admin*):

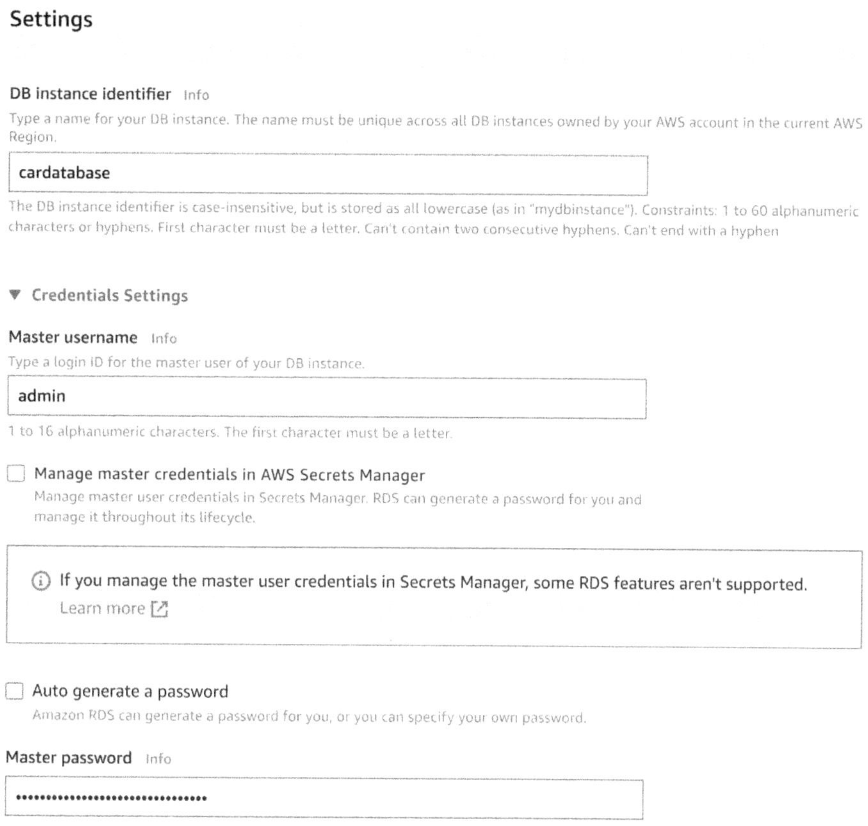

Settings

DB instance identifier Info

Type a name for your DB instance. The name must be unique across all DB instances owned by your AWS account in the current AWS Region.

cardatabase

The DB instance identifier is case-insensitive, but is stored as all lowercase (as in "mydbinstance"). Constraints: 1 to 60 alphanumeric characters or hyphens. First character must be a letter. Can't contain two consecutive hyphens. Can't end with a hyphen

▼ **Credentials Settings**

Master username Info

Type a login ID for the master user of your DB instance.

admin

1 to 16 alphanumeric characters. The first character must be a letter.

☐ Manage master credentials in AWS Secrets Manager

Manage master user credentials in Secrets Manager. RDS can generate a password for you and manage it throughout its lifecycle.

ⓘ If you manage the master user credentials in Secrets Manager, some RDS features aren't supported. Learn more ⧉

☐ Auto generate a password

Amazon RDS can generate a password for you, or you can specify your own password.

Master password Info

••••••••••••••••••••••••••••••

Figure 17.6: Database instance name

6. Select **Yes** under the **Public access** section to allow public access to your database:

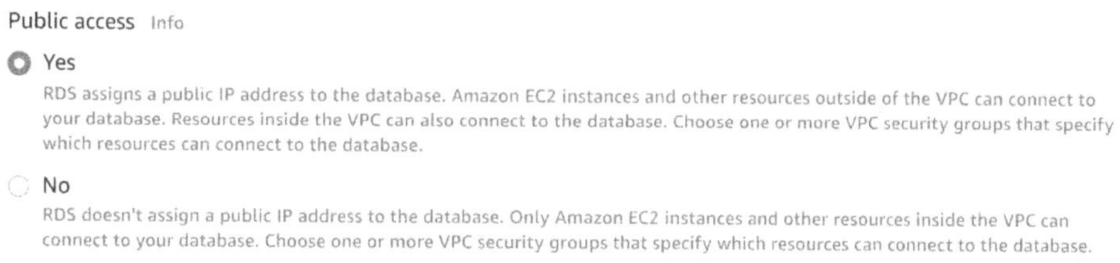

Public access Info

🔘 Yes

RDS assigns a public IP address to the database. Amazon EC2 instances and other resources outside of the VPC can connect to your database. Resources inside the VPC can also connect to the database. Choose one or more VPC security groups that specify which resources can connect to the database.

⚪ No

RDS doesn't assign a public IP address to the database. Only Amazon EC2 instances and other resources inside the VPC can connect to your database. Choose one or more VPC security groups that specify which resources can connect to the database.

Figure 17.7: Public access

7.   In the **Additional configuration** section at the bottom of the page, name your database
     `cardb`:

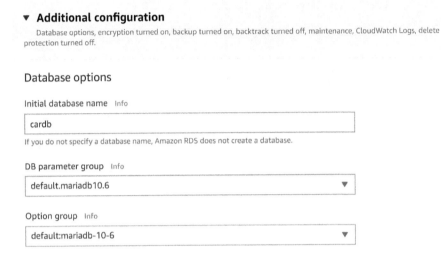

Figure 17.8: Additional configuration

 Note! The database will not be created if the name is left empty.

8.   Finally, click the **Create database** button. RDS will start to create your database instance,
     which might take a few minutes.

9. After your database is successfully created, you can press the **View connection details** button to open a window that shows the connection details to your database. The **Endpoint** is the address of your database. Copy the connection details for later use:

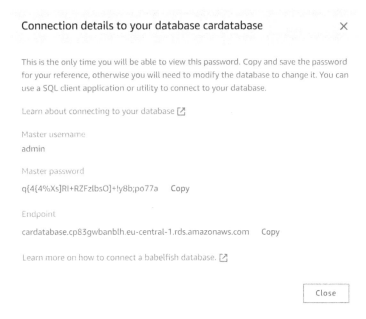

Figure 17.9: Connection details

10. Now, we are ready to test our database. In this phase, we will use our local Spring Boot application. For this, we have to allow access to our database from outside. To change this, click on your database in the RDS database list. Then, click **VPC security groups**, as shown in the next screenshot:

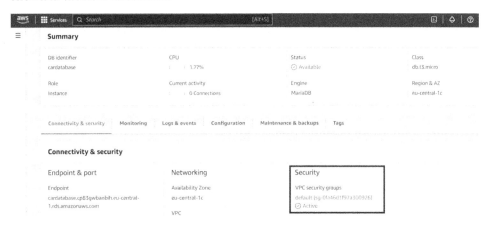

Figure 17.10: Connectivity & security

11. On the opening page, click the **Edit inbound rules** button from the **Inbound rules** tab. Click the **Add rule** button to add a new rule. For the new rule, select the **MySQL/Aurora** type and the **My IP** destination under the **Source** column. The **My IP** destination automatically adds the current IP address of your local computer as an allowed destination:

Figure 17.11: Inbound rules

12. After you have added a new rule, press the **Save rules** button.

13. Open the Spring Boot application that we created in *Chapter 5, Securing Your Backend*. Change the url, username, and password database settings in the application.properties file to match your Amazon RDS database. The format of the spring.datasource.url property value is jdbc:mariadb://your_rds_db_domain:3306/your_db_name, as shown in the following screenshot:

```
application.properties ×
1 spring.jpa.show-sql=true
2 spring.datasource.url=jdbc:mariadb://cardatabase.cp83gwbanblh.eu-central-1.rds.amazonaws.com:3306/cardb
3 spring.datasource.username=admin
4 spring.datasource.password=q{4{4%Xs]RI+RZhzIbs0}+!y6b;po77s
5 spring.datasource.driver-class-name=org.mariadb.jdbc.Driver
6 spring.jpa.generate-ddl=true
7 spring.jpa.hibernate.ddl-auto=create-drop
8 spring.data.rest.basePath=/api
```

Figure 17.12: The application.properties file

14. Now, if you run your application, you can see from the console that database tables are created and demo data is inserted into our Amazon RDS database:

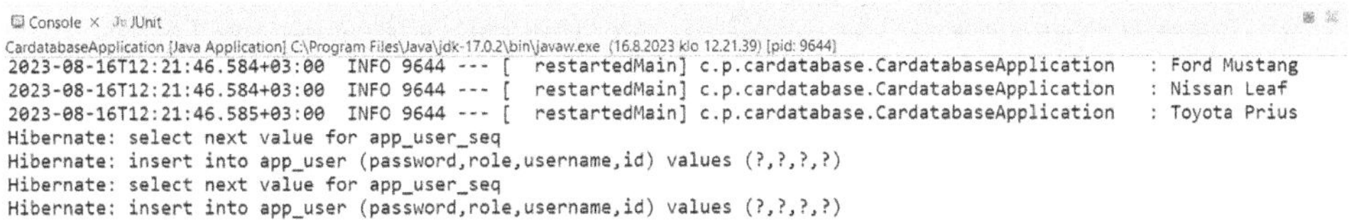

```
Console × Ju JUnit
CardatabaseApplication [Java Application] C:\Program Files\Java\jdk-17.0.2\bin\javaw.exe (16.8.2023 klo 12.21.39) [pid: 9644]
2023-08-16T12:21:46.584+03:00  INFO 9644 --- [  restartedMain] c.p.cardatabase.CardatabaseApplication    : Ford Mustang
2023-08-16T12:21:46.584+03:00  INFO 9644 --- [  restartedMain] c.p.cardatabase.CardatabaseApplication    : Nissan Leaf
2023-08-16T12:21:46.585+03:00  INFO 9644 --- [  restartedMain] c.p.cardatabase.CardatabaseApplication    : Toyota Prius
Hibernate: select next value for app_user_seq
Hibernate: insert into app_user (password,role,username,id) values (?,?,?,?)
Hibernate: select next value for app_user_seq
Hibernate: insert into app_user (password,role,username,id) values (?,?,?,?)
```

Figure 17.13: Console

15. In this phase, you should build your Spring Boot application. Run a Gradle build task in Eclipse by right-clicking **Project** in the Project Explorer, navigating to **Window | Show View | Other**, and selecting **Gradle | Gradle Tasks** from the list. This opens a list of Gradle tasks, and you can start the build process by double-clicking the **build** task. It will create a new JAR file in the build/libs folder.

We now have proper database settings, and we can use our newly built application when we deploy our application to AWS.

Deploying our Spring Boot application

After we have deployed our database to Amazon RDS, we can start to deploy our Spring Boot application. The Amazon service that we are using is **Elastic Beanstalk**, which can be used to run and manage web apps in AWS. There are other alternatives, such as AWS Amplify, that can be used as well. Elastic Beanstalk is available for the Free Tier, and it also supports a wide range of programming languages (for example, Java, Python, Node.js, and PHP).

The following steps will take you through the process of deploying our Spring Boot application to Elastic Beanstalk:

1. First, we have to create a new **role** for our application deployment. The role is needed to allow Elastic Beanstalk to create and manage your environment. You can create a role using the Amazon **IAM (Identity and Access Management)** service. Use the AWS search bar to navigate to the IAM service. In the IAM service, select **Roles** and press the **Create role** button. Select **AWS Service** and **EC2**, as shown in the following screenshot, and press the **Next** button:

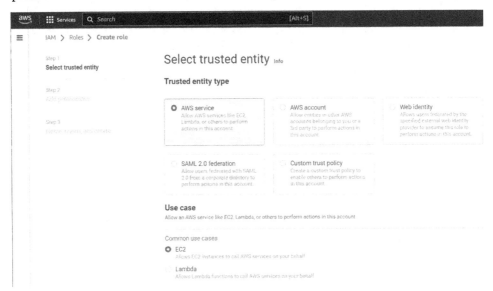

Figure 17.14: Create role

2. In the **Add Permissions** step, select the following permission policies: **AWSElasticBean-stalkWorkerTier**, **AWSElasticBeanstalkWebTier**, and **AWSElasticBeanstalkMulticon-tainerDocker**, then press the **Next** button. You can use the search bar to find the correct policies:

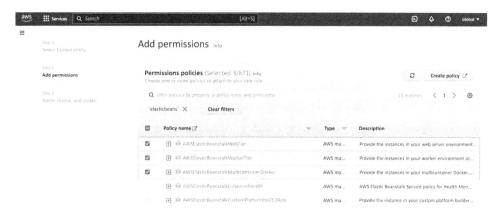

Figure 17.15: Add permissions

 You can read more about managing Elastic Beanstalk instance profiles and policies at https://docs.aws.amazon.com/elasticbeanstalk/latest/dg/iam-instanceprofile.html.

3. Type a name for your role, as illustrated in the next screenshot, and finally press the **Create role** button:

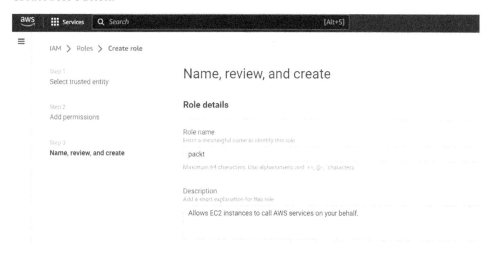

Figure 17.16: Role name

The new role that we just created allows Elastic Beanstalk to create and manage our environment. Now, we can start to deploy our Spring Boot application.

4. Use the AWS dashboard search bar to find the **Elastic Beanstalk** service. Click the service to navigate to the Elastic Beanstalk page:

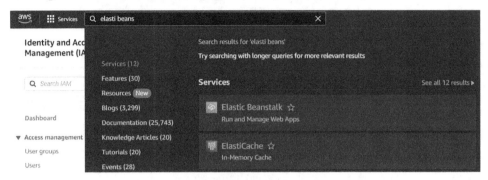

Figure 17.17: Elastic Beanstalk service

5. Click **Applications** in the left side menu, and press the **Create application** button to create a new application. Type a name for your application, as shown in the following screenshot, and press the **Create** button:

Figure 17.18: Create application

6. Next, we have to create an **environment** for our application. An environment is a collection of AWS resources running an application version. You can have multiple environments for one application: for example, development, production, and testing environments. Click the **Create new environment** button to configure a new environment:

Figure 17.19: Create new environment

7. In the environment configuration, you first have to set the platform. In the **Platform type** section, select **Java** and the first version **17** for the branch, as shown in the following screenshot. The **Platform version** is a combination of specific versions of an operating system, runtime, web server, application server, and Elastic Beanstalk components. You can use the recommended **Platform version**:

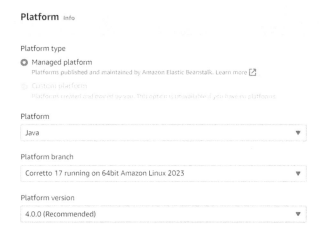

Figure 17.20: Platform type

8. Next, go to the **Application code** section in the configuration page. Select **Upload your code** and **Local file**. Click the **Choose file** button and select the Spring Boot .jar file that we built earlier. You also have to type in a unique **Version label**. Finally, press the **Next** button:

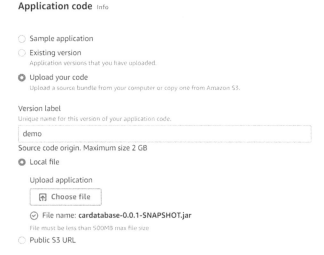

Figure 17.21: Create new environment

9. In the **Configuration service access** step, select the role that you created earlier from the **EC2 instance profile** dropdown list, as shown in the following screenshot. Then, press the **Next** button:

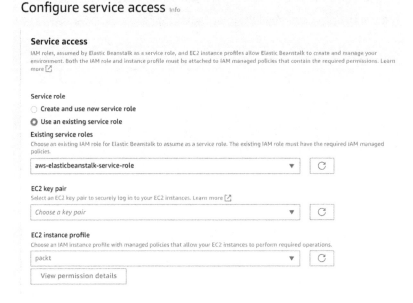

Figure 17.22: Service access

10. You can skip the optional **Set up networking, database, and tags** and **Configure instance traffic and scaling** steps.

11. Next, move to the **Configure updates, monitoring, and logging** step. In the **Environment properties** section, we have to add the following environment properties. You can add new properties by pressing the **Add environment property** button at the bottom of the page. There are already some predefined properties that you don't have to modify (GRADLE_HOME, M2 and M2_HOME):

    *   SERVER_PORT: 5000 (Elastic beans have a Nginx reverse proxy that will forward incoming requests to internal port 5000).

    *   SPRING_DATASOURCE_URL: The database URL you need to use here is identical to the database URL value we previously configured in the 'application.properties' file when we initially tested the AWS database integration.

    *   SPRING_DATASOURCE_USERNAME: The username of your database.

    *   SPRING_DATASOURCE_PASSWORD: The password of your database.

The following screenshot shows the new properties:

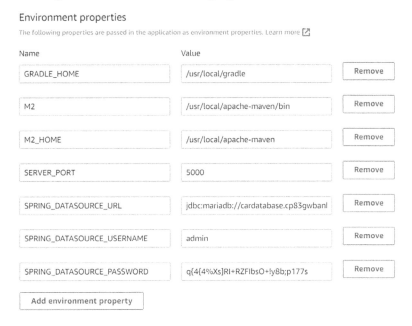

Figure 17.23: Environment properties

12. Finally, in the **Review** step, press the **Submit** button, and your deployment will start. You have to wait until your environment is successfully launched, as illustrated in the next screenshot. The **Domain** in the **Environment overview** is the URL of your deployed REST API:

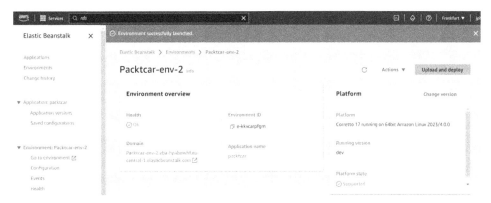

Figure 17.24: Environment successfully launched

13. Now, we have deployed our Spring Boot application, but the application can't access the AWS database yet. For this, we have to allow access from the deployed application to our database. To do this, navigate to Amazon RDS and select your database from the RDS database list. Then, click **VPC security groups** and click the **Edit inbound rules** button, like we did earlier. Delete the rule that allows access from your local IP address.

14. Add a new rule whose **Type** is **MySQL/Aurora**. In the **Destination** field, type in sg. This will open a list of environments, as shown in the following screenshot. Select the environment where your Spring Boot application is running (it begins with the "awseb" text and has a subtitle that shows the name of your environment) and press the **Save rules** button:

Figure 17.25: Inbound rules

15. Now, your application is properly deployed, and you can log in to your deployed REST API using Postman and the URL that you got from the domain in *step 12*. The following screenshot shows the POST request that is sent to the aws_domain_url/login endpoint:

Figure 17.26: Postman authentication

You can also configure a custom domain name for your Elastic Beanstalk environment, and then you can use HTTPS to allow users to connect to your website securely. If you don't own a domain name, you can still use HTTPS with a self-signed certificate for development and testing purposes. You can find the configuration instructions in the AWS documentation: `https://docs.aws.amazon.com/elasticbeanstalk/latest/dg/configuring-https.html`.

 Note! You should delete AWS resources that you have created to avoid being charged unexpectedly. You will get a reminder email from AWS to delete resources before the end of your Free Tier period.

Now, we are ready to deploy our frontend.

Deploying the frontend with Netlify

Before we deploy with Netlify, we will learn how you can build your React project locally. Move to your frontend project folder and execute the following npm command:

```
npm run build
```

By default, your project is built in the /dist folder. You can change the folder by using the `build.outDir` property in your Vite configuration file.

First, the build process compiles your TypeScript code; therefore, you have to fix all TypeScript errors or warnings, if there are any. A commonly encountered error occurs when you forget to remove unused imports, as illustrated in the example error below:

```
src/components/AddCar.tsx:10:1 - error TS6133: 'Snackbar' is declared but
its value is never read.
10 import Snackbar from '@mui/material/Snackbar';
```

This indicates that the `AddCar.tsx` file imports the `Snackbar` component, but the component isn't actually utilized. Therefore, you should remove this unused import. Once all errors have been resolved, you can proceed to rebuilding your project.

Vite uses **Rollup** (`https://rollupjs.org/`) to bundle your code. Test files and development tools are *not* included in the production build. After you have built your app, you can test your local build using the following npm command:

```
npm run preview
```

The command starts a local static web server that serves your built app. You can test your app in a browser by using the URL that is shown in the terminal.

You could deploy your frontend to AWS as well, but we will use **Netlify** (https://www.netlify.com/) for our frontend deployment. Netlify is a modern web development platform that is easy to use. You can use the Netlify **command-line interface** (**CLI**) or GitHub to deploy your project. In this section, we will use Netlify's GitHub integration to deploy our frontend:

1. First, we have to change our REST API URL. Open your frontend project with VS Code and open the .env file in the editor. Change the VITE_API_URL variable to match your backend's URL, as follows, and save the changes:

    ```
    VITE_API_URL=https:// carpackt-env.eba-whufxac5.eu-central-2.
      elasticbeanstalk.com
    ```

2. Create a GitHub repository for your frontend project. Execute the following Git commands in your project folder using the command line. These Git commands create a new Git repository, make an initial commit, set up a remote repository on GitHub, and push the code to your remote repository:

    ```
    git init
    git add .
    git commit -m "first commit"
    git branch -M main
    git remote add origin <YOUR_GITHUB_REPO_URL>
    git push -u origin main
    ```

3. Sign up and log in to Netlify. We will use a free **Starter** account that has limited features. With this account, you can build one concurrent build for free, and there is some limitation in bandwidth.

 You can read more about the Netlify free account features at https://www.netlify.com/pricing/.

4. Open the **Sites** from the left side menu and you should see the **Import an existing project** panel, as shown in the following screenshot:

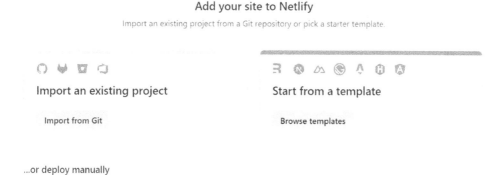

Figure 17.27: Import an existing project

5. Click the **Import from Git** button and select **Deploy with GitHub**. In this phase, you have to authorize your GitHub to get access to your repositories. After you have authorized successfully, you should see your GitHub username and repository search field, as shown in the following screenshot:

Figure 17.28: GitHub repository

6. Search for your frontend repository and click it.

7. Next, you will see the deployment settings. Continue with the default settings by pressing the **Deploy <your_repository_name>** button:

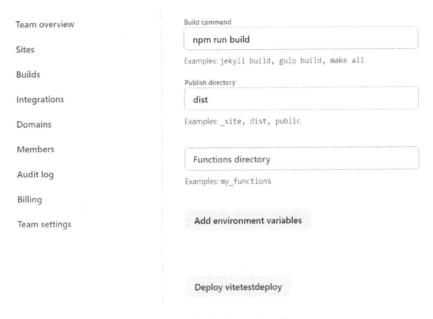

Figure 17.29: Deployment settings

8. After the deployment has finished, you will see the following dialog. Press the **View site deploy** button, as shown in the following figure, and you will be redirected to the **Deploys** page. Netlify generates a random site name for you, but you can use your own domain as well:

Figure 17.30: Deploy success

9. On the **Deploys** page, you will see your deployed site, and you can access your frontend by clicking the **Open production deploy** button:

Figure 17.31: Deploys

10. Now, you should see the login form, as follows:

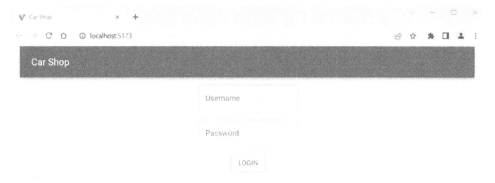

Figure 17.32: Login screen

 You can delete your Netlify deployment from the **Site configuration** in the left side menu.

We have now deployed our frontend, and we can move on to learning about containers.

Using Docker containers

Docker (https://www.docker.com/) is a container platform that makes software development, deployment, and shipping easier. Containers are lightweight and executable software packages that include everything that is needed to run software. Containers can be deployed to cloud services, such as AWS, Azure, and Netlify, and they offer many benefits for deploying applications:

- Containers are isolated, which means each container runs independently of the host system and other containers.

- Containers are portable because they contain everything an application needs to run.

- Containers can also be used to ensure consistency between development and production environments.

 Note! To run Docker containers on Windows, you need the Windows 10 or 11 Professional or Enterprise versions. You read more about this in the Docker installation documentation: https://docs.docker.com/desktop/install/windows-install/.

In this section, we will create a container for our MariaDB database and Spring Boot application, as follows:

1. Install Docker on your workstation. You can find installation packages for multiple platforms at https://www.docker.com/get-docker. If you have a Windows operating system, you can go through the installation wizard using the default settings.

    If you are having problems with the installation, you can read the Docker troubleshooting documentation at https://docs.docker.com/desktop/troubleshoot/topics.

   After the installation, you can check the current version by typing the following command in the terminal. Note! When you run Docker commands, you should start Docker Engine if it is not running (on Windows and macOS, you start Docker Desktop):

   ```
   docker --version
   ```

2. First, we create a container for our MariaDB database. You can pull the latest MariaDB database image version from Docker Hub using the following command:

   ```
   docker pull mariadb:latest
   ```

3. After the `pull` command has finished, you can check that a new `mariadb` image exists by typing the `docker image ls` command, and the output should look as follows. A **Docker image** is a template that contains instructions for creating a container:

```
PS C:\work\tmp\PacktTestCode\cardatabase_05c\build\libs> docker image ls
REPOSITORY      TAG       IMAGE ID        CREATED       SIZE
mariadb         latest    1a580bde192c    4 days ago    404MB
```

Figure 17.33: Docker images

4. Next, we will run the `mariadb` container. The `docker run` command creates and runs a container based on the given image. The following command sets the root user password and creates a new database, called `cardb`, that we need for our Spring Boot application (Note! Use your own MariaDB root user password that you are using in your Spring Boot application):

```
docker run --name cardb -e MYSQL_ROOT_PASSWORD=your_pwd -e MYSQL_
    DATABASE=cardb mariadb
```

5. Now, we have created our database container, and we can start to create a container for the Spring Boot application. First, we have to change the data source URL of our Spring Boot application. Open the `application.properties` file of your application and change the `spring.datasource.url` value to the following:

```
spring.datasource.url=jdbc:mariadb://mariadb:3306/cardb
```

This is because our database is now running in the `cardb` container and the port is 3306.

6. Then, we have to create an executable JAR file from our Spring Boot application, just as we did at the beginning of this chapter. You can also run a Gradle task in the Eclipse by right-clicking **Project** in the Project Explorer, selecting **Window | Show View | Gradle** and then **Gradle Tasks** from the list. This opens a list of Gradle tasks, and you can start the build process by double clicking the **build** task. Once the build is finished, you can find the executable JAR file from the `build/libs` folder inside your project folder.

7. Containers are defined by using **Dockerfiles**. Create a new Dockerfile using Eclipse in the root folder of your project (`cardatabase`) and name it `Dockerfile`. The following lines of code show the contents of the Dockerfile:

```
FROM eclipse-temurin:17-jdk-alpine
VOLUME /tmp
EXPOSE 8080
COPY build/libs/cardatabase-0.0.1-SNAPSHOT.jar app.jar
ENTRYPOINT ["java","-jar","/app.jar"]
```

Let's examine each line:

- FROM defines the **Java Development Kit (JDK)** version, and you should use the same version that you used to build your JAR file. We are using Eclipse Temurin, which is an open-source JDK, and version 17, which we used when we developed our Spring Boot application.

- Volumes are used for persistent data generated by and used by Docker containers.

- EXPOSE defines the port that should be published outside of the container.

- COPY copies the JAR file to the container's filesystem and renames it app.jar.

- Lastly, ENTRYPOINT defines the command-line arguments that the Docker container runs.

 You can read more about the Dockerfile syntax at https://docs.docker.com/engine/reference/builder/.

8. Build an image with the following command in the folder where your Dockerfile is located. With the -t argument, we can give a friendly name to our container:

```
docker build -t carbackend .
```

9. At the end of the build, you should see a **Building [...] FINISHED** message, as illustrated in the following screenshot:

Figure 17.34: Docker build

10. Check the list of images using the `docker image ls` command. You should see two images now, as shown in the following screenshot:

```
PS C:\work\tmp\PacktTestCode\cardatabase_05c> docker image ls
REPOSITORY    TAG       IMAGE ID       CREATED         SIZE
carbackend    latest    f550cb07c922   5 minutes ago   356MB
mariadb       latest    1a580bde192c   4 days ago      404MB
```

Figure 17.35: Docker images

11. Now, we can run our Spring Boot container and link the MariaDB container to it using the following command. This command specifies that our Spring Boot container can access the MariaDB container using the `mariadb` name:

```
docker run -p 8080:8080 --name carapp --link cardb:mariadb -d
    carbackend
```

12. When our application and database are running, we can access the Spring Boot application logs using the following command:

```
docker logs carapp
```

We can see here that our application is up and running:

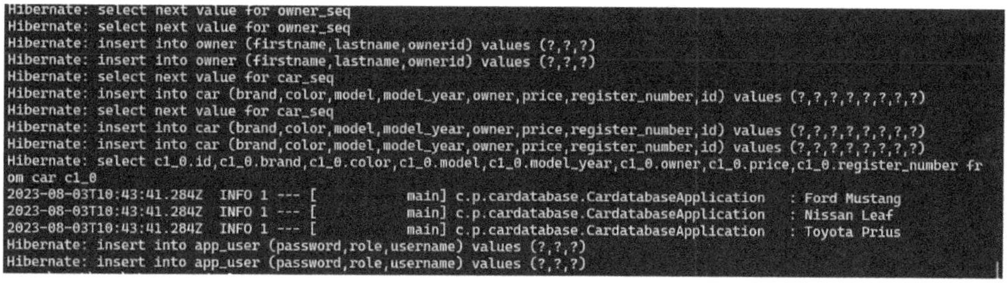

```
Hibernate: select next value for owner_seq
Hibernate: select next value for owner_seq
Hibernate: insert into owner (firstname,lastname,ownerid) values (?,?,?)
Hibernate: insert into owner (firstname,lastname,ownerid) values (?,?,?)
Hibernate: select next value for car_seq
Hibernate: insert into car (brand,color,model,model_year,owner,price,register_number,id) values (?,?,?,?,?,?,?,?)
Hibernate: select next value for car_seq
Hibernate: insert into car (brand,color,model,model_year,owner,price,register_number,id) values (?,?,?,?,?,?,?,?)
Hibernate: insert into car (brand,color,model,model_year,owner,price,register_number,id) values (?,?,?,?,?,?,?,?)
Hibernate: select c1_0.id,c1_0.brand,c1_0.color,c1_0.model,c1_0.model_year,c1_0.owner,c1_0.price,c1_0.register_number fr
om car c1_0
2023-08-03T10:43:41.284Z  INFO 1 --- [          main] c.p.cardatabase.CardatabaseApplication   : Ford Mustang
2023-08-03T10:43:41.284Z  INFO 1 --- [          main] c.p.cardatabase.CardatabaseApplication   : Nissan Leaf
2023-08-03T10:43:41.284Z  INFO 1 --- [          main] c.p.cardatabase.CardatabaseApplication   : Toyota Prius
Hibernate: insert into app_user (password,role,username) values (?,?,?)
Hibernate: insert into app_user (password,role,username) values (?,?,?)
```

Figure 17.36: Application log

Our application has started successfully, and the demonstration data has been inserted into the database that exists in the MariaDB container. Now, you can use your backend, as seen in the following screenshot:

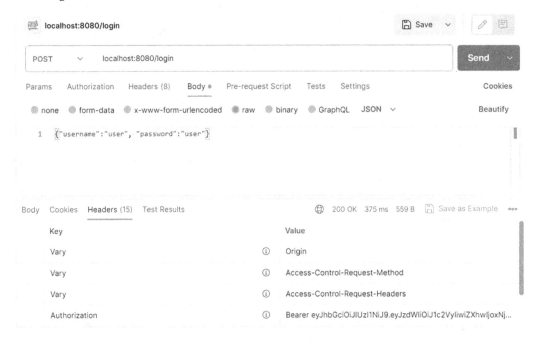

Figure 17.37: Application login

We have learned a few different ways to deploy your full-stack application and how to containerize your Spring Boot application. As a next step, you could study how to deploy Docker containers. For example, AWS has a guide to deploying containers on Amazon ECS: `https://aws.amazon.com/getting-started/hands-on/deploy-docker-containers/`.

Summary

In this chapter, you learned how to deploy our application. We deployed the Spring Boot application to AWS Elastic Beanstalk. Next, we deployed our React frontend using Netlify. Finally, we used Docker to create containers for our Spring Boot application and the MariaDB database.

As we reach the final pages of this book, I hope you've had an exciting journey through the world of full-stack development with Spring Boot and React. As you continue your full-stack development journey, remember that technologies are evolving all the time. For a developer, life is constant learning and innovation – so stay curious and keep building.

Questions

1. How should you create a Spring Boot executable JAR file?

2. What AWS services you can use to deploy a database and Spring Boot application to AWS?

3. What command can you use to build your Vite React project?

4. What is Docker?

5. How should you create a Spring Boot application container?

6. How should you create a MariaDB container?

Further reading

Packt Publishing has other resources available for learning about React, Spring Boot, and Docker. A few of them are listed here:

- *Docker Fundamentals for Beginners [Video]*, by Coding Gears | Train Your Brain (`https://www.packtpub.com/product/docker-fundamentals-for-beginners-video/9781803237428`)

- *Docker for Developers*, by Richard Bullington-McGuire, Andrew K. Dennis, and Michael Schwartz (`https://www.packtpub.com/product/docker-for-developers/9781789536058`)

- *AWS, JavaScript, React - Deploy Web Apps on the Cloud [Video]*, by YouAccel Training (`https://www.packtpub.com/product/aws-javascript-react-deploy-web-apps-on-the-cloud-video/9781837635801`)

Learn more on Discord

To join the Discord community for this book – where you can share feedback, ask the author questions, and learn about new releases – follow the QR code below:

`https://packt.link/FullStackSpringBootReact4e`

`packt.com`

Subscribe to our online digital library for full access to over 7,000 books and videos, as well as industry leading tools to help you plan your personal development and advance your career. For more information, please visit our website.

Why subscribe?

- Spend less time learning and more time coding with practical eBooks and Videos from over 4,000 industry professionals

- Improve your learning with Skill Plans built especially for you

- Get a free eBook or video every month

- Fully searchable for easy access to vital information

- Copy and paste, print, and bookmark content

At www.packt.com, you can also read a collection of free technical articles, sign up for a range of free newsletters, and receive exclusive discounts and offers on Packt books and eBooks.

Other Books You May Enjoy

If you enjoyed this book, you may be interested in these other books by Packt:

Microservices with Spring Boot 3 and Spring Cloud - Third Edition

Magnus Larsson

ISBN: 9781805128694

- Build reactive microservices using Spring Boot
- Develop resilient and scalable microservices using Spring Cloud
- Use OAuth 2.1/OIDC and Spring Security to protect public APIs
- Implement Docker to bridge the gap between development, testing, and production
- Deploy and manage microservices with Kubernetes
- Apply Istio for improved security, observability, and traffic management
- Write and run automated microservice tests with JUnit, test containers, Gradle, and bash
- Use Spring AOT and GraalVM to native compile the microservices
- Use Micrometer Tracing for distributed tracing

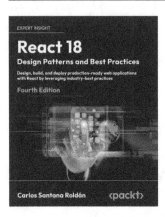

React 18 Design Patterns and Best Practices, 4e

Carlos Santana Roldán

ISBN: 9781803233109

- Get familiar with the new React 18 and Node 19 features
- Explore TypeScript's basic and advanced capabilities
- Make components communicate with each other by applying various patterns and techniques
- Dive into MonoRepo architecture
- Use server-side rendering to make applications load faster
- Write a comprehensive set of tests to create robust and maintainable code
- Build high-performing applications by styling and optimizing React components

Packt is searching for authors like you

If you're interested in becoming an author for Packt, please visit authors.packtpub.com and apply today. We have worked with thousands of developers and tech professionals, just like you, to help them share their insight with the global tech community. You can make a general application, apply for a specific hot topic that we are recruiting an author for, or submit your own idea.

Share your thoughts

Now you've finished *Full Stack Development with Spring Boot 3 and React, Fourth Edition*, we'd love to hear your thoughts! Scan the QR code below to go straight to the Amazon review page for this book and share your feedback or leave a review on the site that you purchased it from.

https://packt.link/r/1805122460

Your review is important to us and the tech community and will help us make sure we're delivering excellent quality content.

Index

Download a free PDF copy of this book

Thanks for purchasing this book!

Do you like to read on the go but are unable to carry your print books everywhere?

Is your eBook purchase not compatible with the device of your choice?

Don't worry, now with every Packt book you get a DRM-free PDF version of that book at no cost.

Read anywhere, any place, on any device. Search, copy, and paste code from your favorite technical books directly into your application.

The perks don't stop there, you can get exclusive access to discounts, newsletters, and great free content in your inbox daily

Follow these simple steps to get the benefits:

1. Scan the QR code or visit the link below

https://packt.link/free-ebook/9781805122463

2. Submit your proof of purchase
3. That's it! We'll send your free PDF and other benefits to your email directly